Travel & Tourism

Book 2

Gillian Dale

Heinemann

Inspiring generations

Heinemann Educational Publishers
Halley Court, Jordan Hill, Oxford OX2 8EJ
Part of Harcourt Education

Heinemann is the registered trademark of
Harcourt Education Limited

Text © Gillian Dale
First published 2005

10 09 08 07 06 05
10 9 8 7 6 5 4 3 2 1

British Library Cataloguing in Publication Data is available
from the British Library on request.

10-digit ISBN 0 435 44645 2
13-digit ISBN 978 0 435446 45 1

Designed by Lorraine Inglis
Typeset and illustrated by ⊼ Tek-Art, Croydon, Surrey
Original illustrations © Harcourt Education Limited, 2005
Cover design by Wooden Ark Studio
Printed by Bath Colourbooks
Cover photo © Alamy

Websites
Please note that the examples of websites suggested in this book were up to date at the time of
writing. It is essential for tutors to preview each site before using it to ensure that the URL is still
accurate and the content is appropriate. We suggest that tutors bookmark useful sites and consider
enabling students to access them through the school or college intranet.

Contents

Acknowledgements

Gillian Dale gives grateful thanks to:

Michele Bretenoux at Canvas Holidays for providing information about procedures and documentation

Sarah Jones at the Cambridge Moat House for being so informative and helpful

And Ann Lertora for sharing her missing luggage story

Every effort has been made to contact copyright holders of material produced in this book. Any omissions or errors will be rectified in subsequent printings if notice is given to the publishers.

The author and publisher would like to thank all those who have granted permission to reproduce copyright material.

Accor – page 204
Alton Towers – page 163
Associated British Ports – page 15
BAA Heathrow – page 220
BAA Stansted – page 222–3
Bales Worldwide Holidays – page 14
BCT Travel Group Ltd – page 21
Best Western Hotels – page 187
British Air Transport Association – page 239
British Airways – page 232
British Hospitality Association – page 185, 188
British Travel Trade Fair – page 121
Canvas Holidays – page 65–66
Caterer & Hotelkeeper magazine – page 187
Central Statistics Office of St Lucia – page 55
Chatsworth House Trust – page 175
Compass Group – page 193
Cosmos – page 49
Costa Cruises – page 10–11
Countryside Agency – page 155
cruiseplacement.com – page 26
DFDS Seaways – page 20
Direct Travel Insurance – page 215
Discover Coral Reefs School Programme – page 48
easyJet – page 212–213
The Eden Project, © The Eden Project. Reproduced by kind permission – page 160, 171
European Tour Operators Association – page 103
ExCel – page 128
Excel Airways – page 234, 236–7
expresstravelandtourism.com – page 37

First Choice – page 52, 61
Gretna Green Story Exhibition (gretnagreen.com) – page 158
Haworth Village Trust (haworth-village.org.uk) – page 40
The Hotel Show – page 141
IRN (www.irn-research.com) – page 9, 21
Kuoni – page 53
Lithuania State Department of Tourism – page 58
Manchester Airport – page 219
Metropolitan Police Service – page 94
The Michelin Guide – page 206
Micros.com – page 195
Moat House Hotels – page 130, 135, 196, 203
The National Trust, Registered Charity No. 205846 – page 157
The Original Tour – page 80
P&O Cruises – page 7, 12, 23
PKF Regional Trends Survey – page 183
Pleasurewood Hills – page 159
Princess Cruises – page 11, 13, 19
Reed Exhibitions – page 127, 136, 143
Sandstone Ltd – page 122
Science Museum, London – page 170
SHG (shgjobs.co.uk) – page 63
Sovereign Holidays – page 62
SustainBiz, East Hampshire District Council – page 144
The Tate Gallery. First published at Tate Online (www.tate.org.uk) Updated 2004 – page 165
Tourism Concern – page 40, 50–51
Tourism South East – page 106
TravelMole Ltd (travelmole.com) – page 24, 142
Travelwire News – page 35
TTG – page 4, 15
TUI UK Ltd – page 68, 83
Virgin Atlantic – page 233
VisitBritain – page 96, 99, 101, 105, 152
VisitCambridge – page 109
VisitLondon – page 106
Wales Tourist Board (VisitWales) – page 39, 106
Woburn Safari Park (woburnsafari.co.uk) – page 168, 174
The World Factbook, CIA – page 54, 57
World Heritage Centre – page 117
World Tourism Organization – page 32, 35, 50

Crown copyright material is reproduced under Class Licence No. C01W0000141 with the permission of the Controller of HMSO and the Queen's Printer for Scotland – page 38, 91, 92, 97, 98, 99, 100, 151, 167, 169, 172, 180, 181

The author and publisher would like to thank the following for permission to reproduce photographs:

Alamy Images – page 189
Alamy Images/Aflo Foto Agency – page 63
Alamy Images/Alex Segre – page 186
Alamy Images/Cassida Images – page 3
Alamy Images/Colinspics – page 224
Alamy Images/Comstock Images – page 191
Alamy Images/CuboImages srl – page 47
Alamy Images/Design Pics Inc. – page 198
Alamy Images/David Hoffman Photo Library – page 224
Alamy Images/Image State/Pictor International – page 142
Alamy Images/Jon Arnold Images/Walter Bibikow – page 54
Alamy Images/Justin Kase – page 162
Alamy Images/Jeff Morgan – page 123
Alamy Images/Photofusion Picture Library – page 44
Alamy Images/Photofusion Picture Library/Steve Morgan – page 154
Alamy Images/Robert Harding Picture Library Ltd – page 35
Alamy Images/Robert Harding Picture Library Ltd/Rob Cousins – page 155
Alamy Images/Howard Sayer – page 157
Alamy Images/The Flight Collection – page 227
Art Directors and Trip – page 70, 74, 121

Corbis/Yann Arthus-Bertrand – page 13
Corbis/Bettman – page 2
Corbis/Johnathan Blair – page 34
Corbis/Stephane Cardinale/People Avenue – page 61
Corbis/Jason Hawkes – page 117
Corbis/Jeremy Horner – page 165
Corbis/Bob Krist – page 197
Corbis/Jacques Langevin – page 167
Corbis/NRF – page 64
Corbis/SABA/David Butow – page 194
Corbis/John Slater – page 175
Corbis/Johnathan Smith; Cordaiy Photo Library Ltd – page 17, 22
Corbis/Bill Varie – page 152
Corbis/Patrick Ward – page 40
Gillian Dale – page 81
Digital Vision – page 128
Empics – page 205
Getty Images – page 77, 210
Getty Images/Digital Vision – page 45, 48
Getty Images/Lonely Planet Images – page 57
Getty Images/News – page 5
Getty Images/Photodisc – page 113
Getty Images/Robert Harding World Imagery – page 12
Getty Images/Stone – page 34, 223
Harcourt Education/Debbie Rowe – page 42, 78, 91, 93, 95, 100, 101, 108, 115, 132, 171
Harcourt Education/Renato Turchetta – page 156
Robert Harding – page 65, 131, 145
IRM Holiday Homes – page 134
Mirrorpix – page 186
Ginny Stroud-Lewis – page 108

Introduction

This BTEC Travel and Tourism course book accompanies Book 1 and covers many of the option units you will be taking if you are studying for a BTEC National Certificate in Travel and Tourism or a BTEC National Diploma in Travel and Tourism.

Like Book 1, this book follows the BTEC specification closely so that you can easily find relevant information and see where you are in your studies.

There are lots of new case studies and activities to help you understand the different units and make your study enjoyable. You will find many opportunities for research and you will be able to extend your research sources as you study different areas of the travel and tourism industry.

Some of the units are specialised so I hope you will find information that helps you decide in which sector of the industry you would like to work or study further.

Features of the book

This book has a number of features to help you relate theory to practice and reinforce your learning. It also aims to help you gather evidence for assessment. You will find the following features in each unit.

Consider this...

These are points for individual reflection or group discussion. They will widen your knowledge and help you reflect on issues that impact on travel and tourism.

Key concepts and terms

Issues and terms that you need to be aware of are summarised under these headings. They will help you check your knowledge as you learn, and will prove to be a useful quick-reference tool.

Theory into practice

These practical activities allow you to apply theoretical knowledge to travel and tourism tasks or research. Make sure you complete these activities as you work through each unit, to reinforce your learning.

Case studies

Interesting examples of real situations or companies are described in case studies that link theory to practice. They will show you how the topics you are studying affect real people and businesses.

Knowledge checks

At the end of each unit is a set of quick questions to test your knowledge of the information you have been studying. Use these to check your progress, and as a revision tool.

Assessment assignments

Each unit concludes with a full unit assessment, which taken as a whole fulfils all the unit requirements from Pass to Distinction. Each task is matched to the relevant criteria in the specification. If you are aiming for a Merit, make sure you complete all the Pass (P) and Merit (M) tasks. If you are aiming for a Distinction, you will also need to complete all the Distinction (D) tasks.

Assessment activities

Assessment activities are also provided throughout each unit. These smaller assessments are linked to real situations and case studies and they can be used for practice before tackling the final assessment assignment. Alternatively, they can contribute to your unit assessment if you choose to do these instead of the final assessment at the end of each unit.

As in the assessment assignments, each task is followed by an indication of which grading criteria may be achieved by good work – P1 means the first of the Pass criteria listed in the specification, M1 the first of the Merit criteria, D1 the first of the Distinction criteria, and so on. Your tutor should check that you have completed enough activities to meet all the assessment criteria for the unit, whether from this book or from other tasks.

Tutors and students should refer to the BTEC standards for the qualification for the full BTEC Grading criteria for each unit.

About this book

This book covers eight specialist units:

* ✱ The cruise sector
* ✱ Tourism development
* ✱ Holiday representatives
* ✱ Incoming and domestic tourism
* ✱ Conferences, exhibitions and events
* ✱ Visitor attractions
* ✱ Hospitality operations in travel and tourism
* ✱ Handling air passengers

As always I am grateful to the many travel and tourism industry colleagues and organisations who have lent their support to this book in the form of company information and material for case studies.

Travel and tourism is a challenging and dynamic industry and provides wonderful opportunities. I hope you discover them and that you enjoy your studies.

Gillian Dale

UNIT 9

The cruise sector

Introduction

This is a fascinating sector of travel and tourism to study as the market for cruises is growing as cruise operators respond to demand for different types of cruising across all market segments. In addition, there are lots of opportunities to work in the cruise sector and it is a popular choice for young people with no family commitments as you can travel the world as you work.

In this chapter you will find out about the cruise sector, how it developed and how it relates to other sectors of travel and tourism. You will investigate the cruise areas of the world, including gateway ports and ports of call. Different types of cruises will be explained and you will find out how they appeal to different markets. You will find out about the types of work available in the cruise sector and what skills and qualities are needed to apply for jobs. You will explore the work environment on board ship and the roles and responsibilities of the staff.

It would be a good idea for you to collect a selection of cruise brochures to help you work through this chapter. You will also be introduced to a number of websites which you should bookmark for future reference.

How you will be assessed

This unit is internally assessed by your tutor. A variety of exercises and activities is included in this unit to help you develop your knowledge and understanding of the cruise sector and prepare for the assessment. You will also have the opportunity to work on some case studies.

After completing this unit you should be able to achieve the following outcomes:

→ examine the development of the cruise sector of the travel and tourism industry
→ investigate cruise areas of the world
→ explore the types of cruises and how they appeal to different markets
→ investigate employment opportunities within the cruise sector.

The cruise sector

History and development of the cruise sector

Steamships and ocean liners

Transport by a fast regular steamship service was the key to a successful trade empire in Victorian Britain. The government sponsored routes and the building of ships, and the Royal Navy was responsible for protecting the routes and their supply bases.

In the nineteenth century, steamships regularly crossed the Atlantic. The first company to operate on the transatlantic shipping routes was the British and North American Royal Mail Steam Packet Company. This later became Cunard Steamships Limited, a famous cruise ship name. The company's first steamship was the Britannia and sailed from Liverpool to Boston with a passenger and cargo service in 1840.

The famous engineer Brunel was responsible for the design of the *Great Britain*, a ship built to provide transatlantic services. This ship set the standard for ocean liners for many years to come.

It was a 3,270 ton ship and was equipped with cabins and staterooms for 360 passengers. It was the first large ship to be screw driven. By 1853 the *Great Britain* had been refitted to accommodate up to 630 passengers. It operated a London to Australia service and continued to do so for nearly twenty years.

Brunel was responsible for another ship, the *Great Eastern*. This could carry 4,000 passengers and enough coal to get to Australia without refuelling on the way. This was the largest ship in the world until it was taken out of service and broken up in 1888.

Some ships were requisitioned for the Crimean War in 1855 and 1866 as troopships. This is a pattern that continued throughout the world wars and to the more recent Gulf War.

Many passengers on ships in those days were migrants going to new lands and new lives. There were few passengers going for pleasure, as the journey would take such a long time.

In 1881 electricity was introduced onto a passenger ship for the first time. By 1911 a ship, the *Franconia*, had a gym and health centre on board.

CASE STUDY

The Titanic *before departure*

I am sure you have seen the film *Titanic* but do you remember where the ship was going and what type of people it was carrying? The ship began her maiden voyage from Southampton to New York on 10 April 1912. On the night of 14 April the ship struck an iceberg. The RMS *Titanic* was the largest passenger steamship in the world at the time of her launching and it was hoped that she would dominate the transatlantic ocean liner business. The owners were the White Star Line. The ship could hold up to 3,300 passengers and had 899 crew. RMS stands for Royal Mail Steamer and meant that the ship carried mail. The ship was supposed to be at the forefront of technology and unsinkable. It was also extremely luxurious as we see clearly in the film.

On this maiden voyage there were 2,208 passengers; 1,496 of them died. There were not enough lifeboats on board to save all the passengers – the number of lifeboats needed was calculated on the ship's tonnage not on passenger numbers. After the sinking of the *Titanic*, changes were made in ship construction and in wireless telegraphy. There was also the first International Convention on the Safety of Life at Sea held in London. This conference led to the formation of the International Ice Patrol, which is an organisation that monitors and reports on the location of icebergs in the North Atlantic which might threaten ships. Following the sinking, other important safety measures were introduced, including lifeboats for everyone on board, drills and radio communications operated 24 hours a day along with a secondary power supply, so as not to miss distress calls.

1. **Summarise the impact of the sinking of the Titanic on the cruise-ship industry at the time.**
2. **Find out about the International Ice Patrol today. Write a few sentences on its mission. You can find information at www.uscg.mil/lantarea/iip.**
3. **Choose a cruise ship that is currently operating. Find out what safety measures it has on board. Cruise brochures will help you with this.**

Golden age

The period from the 1930s to the 1950s was known as the 'golden age' of cruising. Liners such as the *Queen Elizabeth* and the *Queen Mary* used to compete on transatlantic crossings for the famed 'Blue Ribbon', recognition of the fastest crossing. Cruising was a means of luxury travel and could only be afforded by the more affluent classes.

The *Queen Mary* was to make 1,001 journeys across the Atlantic in her time of service. Queen Mary launched this liner in 1934 and it was the largest liner ever built at that time. The ship was in service until 1967.

The *Queen Elizabeth* was launched in 1938 by Queen Elizabeth (Queen Elizabeth, the Queen Mother). This liner did not enter commercial service until 1946 due to the war.

1960s

In 1961 the 44,807-ton *Canberra* was launched. She was the largest post-war British passenger ship. Other ships at this time were about 20,000 tons. The ship was to serve as a long-distance liner on the route from Southampton to Australia. The name was in honour of the Australian capital. The ship was built by Harland and Wolff at a cost of £17 million and became known as the Great White Whale. Her maiden voyage was on 2 June 1961.

The *Canberra* carried out many trips to Australia. Many of these trips were to take emigrants from the UK to Australia. These passengers were able to buy a one-way ticket for only £10 under the government's

The Canberra

assisted passage scheme. By the end of the decade there were not so many emigrants and so the *Canberra* became a full-time holiday cruise ship.

1970s, 1980s and fly-cruises

Once it was easy to cross the Atlantic by air the lucrative cruise transatlantic route went into decline. Cruise operators had to find new, alternative routes, such as Caribbean destinations. Also tour operators began to appreciate the demand for cruising, and began to create cruise packages. Some operators bought their own ships and introduced cruises at competitive prices. Cruise ships at this time were smaller than today, carrying about 600–800 passengers, and cruising was very much a luxury activity.

In the 1980s 'straight-to-the-sun' fly-cruising took off, enabling people to take Caribbean and other far away cruises without the long ship journey to reach the destination. This meant a cruise could be taken in a week or two-week holiday.

Consider this...

The *QE2* allows dogs on her transatlantic runs; she has a kennel on board and even a lamp post to make dogs feel at home!

The cruise sector today

Currently the cruise sector is popular with travel agents as it is one of the few sectors where high commissions are to be earned. Passengers are more likely to book with a travel agent than over the Internet as they are spending a lot of money and are likely to need advice about the type of ship, cabins and facilities.

The market is growing with an increase of 17.4 per cent from 2002 to 2003 in the number of UK passenger departures for ocean-going cruises. Indeed the total number of cruises sold annually in the UK passed the one million mark for the first time in 2003. The Passenger Shipping Association predicts further growth to 1.3 million passengers by 2007.

The chart below shows the increases in ocean cruising.

The rise of UK ocean cruising

	Annual growth	Passengers
1992	+19%	229,000
1995	+26%	340,000
1998	+27%	662,000
2001	+2.4%	776,000
2002	+5.7%	820,500
2003	+17.4%	963,500
2004	estimate	1 million+
2007	estimate	1.3 million

Source: TTG Expert Cruises 2004

CASE STUDY

The *QE2* undertook her maiden voyage on 2 May 1969 from Southampton to New York. It had cost her owners, Cunard, £2.5 million to build the ship. The ship undertook her first world cruise in 1974. The trip generated over £1 million in profit. In 1982 the *QE2* was called into war service. The ship was requisitioned by the Government for service as troop transport. In Southampton, the ship had to be converted and had a communication system installed and helicopter flight decks added. The 5th infantry brigade, comprising of the Scots and Welsh Guards and the Gurkhas, then boarded the ship and it set off for South Georgia on 12 May. It arrived on 27 May and disembarked the troops and then took on board the survivors of the HMS *Ardent*. It was later converted back to commercial service.

1. **Where is the QE2 now? Visit the website www.queenelizabeth2.fsnet.co.uk to find out where the ship is.**
2. **Find out how long the cruise is and what the ports of call are.**

To cater for this demand and to encourage growth in the market, the cruise lines are building new ships and providing a greater variety of types of cruises. Ten new ships were delivered in 2004.

Another factor leading to growth in the market is that for the last three years prices of cruising have been heavily discounted as more competition enters the market. Lower prices have encouraged first-time cruisers and changed the profile of the market.

Cruise ships are getting longer, wider and taller to accommodate more people and generate more revenue for cruise lines by achieving economies of scale. The average number of passengers aboard a modern cruise ship is approximately 1,500, with some ships carrying as many as 3,000 passengers. The average width of new ships is 90 feet, which is almost the maximum allowed for going through the Panama Canal. If they were much wider they would not fit.

New and better ships are being built to provide more cruise capacity. One example is the launch of the *Queen Mary 2* by Cunard in 2004. The *Queen Mary 2* is the world's largest, longest, tallest and most expensive passenger liner. The *Queen Mary 2* can take 2,620 passengers and has 14 decks with 10 different restaurants.

Larger ships impact on ports, which have to be able to accommodate them and the large numbers of passengers and baggage. Berths have to be wider, and gangways and terminals have to be higher to meet the passenger disembarkation point.

Structure of the cruise sector
Horizontal and vertical integration

As in the rest of the travel and tourism industry, a few companies dominate the market. The cruise industry is a highly competitive industry, and is becoming more so each year. Carnival Cruise Lines has acquired many cruise lines to form a company that controls 33 per cent of the cruise market. Royal Caribbean is also growing; it recently purchased the Celebrity cruise line and has invested $1,500 in three 3–4,000 passenger ships.

> **Key concept**
>
> **Horizontal integration** – two companies offering competing products merge or one takes over the other.
>
> **Vertical integration** – companies merge or one takes over the other at different levels in the chain of distribution, for example, Carnival also has an airline.

The Queen Mary 2

There are benefits of integration for cruise operators:

* economies of scale
* control over the supply of berths on ships
* control over distribution
* larger market share
* less competition
* established reputation.

You can see from the mergers and acquisitions described below that horizontal integration is very common in the industry. However, there are examples of vertical integration such as Carnival acquiring an airline.

There may be many new ships and destinations but they are controlled by a few major companies.

Carnival Cruises

Carnival Cruise Lines is the giant of the sector and comprises 12 different brands:

* Carnival Cruises
* Princess Cruises
* Holland America
* Windstar
* Seabourn
* P&O Cruises
* P&O Cruises (Australia)
* Cunard
* Ocean Village
* Swan Hellenic
* AIDA/A'ROSA
* Costa Cruises.

Some of these brands arrived in 2003 when the company merged with P&O Princess.

The Carnival Corporation began as an independent company in 1972. It carries more than 2 million passengers a year and has its headquarters in Miami. The brands operate 77 ships totalling more than 128,000 lower berths with nine new ships scheduled for delivery between November 2004 and December 2006.

Royal Caribbean

Royal Caribbean Cruises Ltd. is a global cruise company that operates Royal Caribbean International and Celebrity Cruises, with a combined total of 29 ships in service and a passenger capacity of approximately 60,500.

The company will introduce one more ship, the *Ultra Voyager*, by the end of 2006, when it will have a total passenger capacity of approximately 64,000. The ships operate worldwide with a selection of itineraries that call on approximately 160 destinations.

NCL/Star

Norwegian Cruise Line is owned by Star Cruises plc of Malaysia. This is the third-largest parent group, operating a combined fleet of 20 ships. Carnival has, however, acquired a 40 per cent stake in this group.

Tour operators

Tour operators have made forays into cruising over the last few years, wishing to take advantage of a growing market. The UK's major operators have cruising divisions. My Travel incurred losses of £8 million on three of its four ships in the year to September 2003 and decided to get rid of them to reduce fixed costs. One of them, *Sunbird*, was bought by Thomson and was renamed *Thomson Destiny*. With this addition Thomson now has a fleet of four ships.

Island Cruises, a First Choice subsidiary, is a joint venture with Royal Caribbean Cruise Lines.

Links with transporters

Many cruises are fly-cruises. This means the passengers are flown to the departure port to start the cruise. As the new ships are so large the cruise operators are able to charter planes, as any tour operator would to transport their passengers from their home country to the port. The cruise lines have flights departments whose role is to organise the flights and liaise with suppliers and passengers.

Princess Cruises, for example, have a charter arrangement with Virgin Atlantic with dedicated charters hired to serve their 'Golden Princess' cruises. In addition, cruise lines work with 'preferred partners'. Princess works with British Airways as a preferred partner – so when there isn't a dedicated charter for a cruise, flights are provided with British Airways.

The cruise lines have links with other transporters, for example, coach operators, to bring passengers to the ship when they are joining at a home port.

A lucrative source of revenue for cruise lines is the provision of shore excursions. The liner makes advance arrangements with local coach or taxi operators to give tours. A full-day shore excursion will cost about £45 to £75 per person. It would usually be much cheaper for passengers to make their own plans but many prefer to have everything done for them. These tours can be booked before departure or in the tour office on board the ship.

Links with travel agents and other distributors

There are many dedicated websites and travel agents for selling cruises. This is not surprising as it is the sector of travel and tourism that pays the highest commission.

Some established travel agents have their own cruise division, for example, 1st4cruising is operated by one of the UK's leading independent travel agents Page & Moy. Agents who sell a large volume of cruise holidays earn cruise line membership of their prestigious agents 'clubs', with higher commissions. An example of a large independent agency is Cruise Control (UK) Ltd. who claim to book 15 per cent of UK cruises. They are based in Romford and have a call centre with 300 staff. They aim to make margins of 15 per cent on sales.

Consider this...

Cruise Control want cruise lines to give them preferential commission rates as they sell so many cruises. Do you think they should?

CASE STUDY

Cruiselink

Eavesway Travel Ltd operates coach services direct to the cruise terminal on 9th and 7th January for *Aurora*'s and *Oriana*'s departures and on 22nd April and 29th March for their return.

All coaches are equipped with reclining seats, are non-smoking and normally have WC and washroom. In addition, comfort stops are made en route.

Joining your fly-cruise

So that you can get your holiday off to a relaxing start, we offer an overnight hotel stay at the airport of your departure the night before your flight.

There are car parking facilities available at the airports, details of which will be sent to you 2–3 weeks before you travel.

All fly-cruises

For *Aurora*'s and *Oriana*'s fly-cruise holidays featured in this brochure, we will arrange either economy class flights on scheduled services of international airlines or, for passengers travelling to and from Buenos Aires or Santiago, dedicated charter flights using reputable carriers, chosen by P&O Cruises.

Source: P&O Worldwide Winter Holidays Jan–April 2005

1. This extract explains links with transporters and hotels. Can you identify them?
2. Why don't P&O prefer the passengers to make their own arrangements to join the cruise?

Trade and Regulatory Bodies

Passenger Shipping Association

This body is the main trade association serving the cruise sector. In fact, it represents all passenger shipping interests within the UK. The PSA Membership is divided into two sections, cruise and ferry. There are regular meetings to discuss matters of interest to the members.

The main objectives are:

* the promotion of travel by sea by the public

* to encourage expansion in the volume of passenger travel, by sea and river

* to work towards the removal or prevention of the imposition of restrictions or taxes on passenger travel by sea

* to advise Member Lines to ensure that passengers travel in a safe, healthy and secure environment.

The Association is also an important corporate contact for the media, seeking information on both cruising and ferry markets.

In 1987, the PSA formed a subsidiary company, The Passenger Shipping Association Retail Agents Scheme (PSARA). This organisation has the role of educating travel agents about the cruise and ferry sector.

International Council of Cruise Lines

This is a US-based organisation but it is worth noting as all the large passenger cruise lines are members. The mission of the International Council of Cruise Lines (ICCL) is

> 'to participate in the regulatory and policy development process and promote all measures that foster a safe, secure and healthy cruise ship environment.'

The ICCL actively monitors international shipping policy and develops recommendations to its membership on a wide variety of issues including:

* public health

* environmental responsibility

* security

* medical facilities

* passenger protection

* legislative activities.

Cruise areas

Geographical areas

In this section we will investigate the different cruise areas available to UK cruise passengers.

The following chart shows the breakdown of destinations chosen by cruise passengers. It also shows the growth in passengers to each area.

We will look at some examples of cruises in these popular areas to see what they have to offer to travellers and what kind of people they appeal to.

We will investigate:

* the Mediterranean
* the Caribbean
* the Baltic
* South America
* Alaska
* the Nile (a river cruise).

Mediterranean

The Mediterranean is the most popular destination for British travellers whether sailing from home ports or by fly-cruise. Some of the increase in fly-cruises to the Mediterranean was accounted for by a new brand, Ocean Village. This is a P&O subsidiary and targets younger, first-time cruisers in the UK. The advantage of a fly-cruise to the Mediterranean is that the flight is very short and the passengers are quickly into the sunshine. Another reason for the increase in trips to the Mediterranean is the greater range of UK departure ports for cruises, especially in the south of England. Using these ports allows passengers to take a western European cruise for a week or two without having to fly.

Cyprus used to be a popular departure port for cruises but it has slumped in popularity as it is so close to the Iraq conflict zone.

More than 20 cruise companies operate in the Mediterranean. It is split into four seas, the Adriatic, the Aegean, the Ionian and the Tyrrhenian, and cruises take varied routes around these seas.

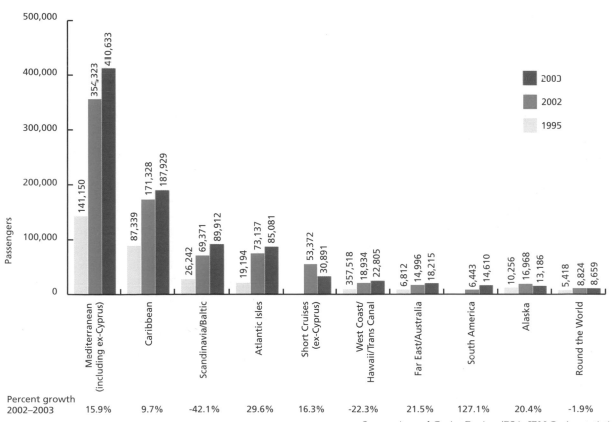

Source: Annual Cruise Review/PSA–IRN Cruise statistics

Fly-cruise from Civitavecchia

Our case study example is from Costa Cruising and is a Mediterranean fly-cruise starting in Civitavecchia in Italy.

Note that the ship returns to Civitavecchia in the middle of the cruise to collect more passengers, thus it would be possible to do a seven-night cruise on this ship. The route includes possibilities for sightseeing and for visiting shopping areas or beaches, for example, Palma in Majorca.

1. **What type of people do you think would take this cruise and why? Make notes.**
2. **Try to use your knowledge of market segmentation to draw up a description of the type of people.**

Grand Mediterranean 1
14-night fly-cruise from Civitavecchia

		PORT	ARR	DEP
MON	1	Fly UK/Rome Transfer to Costa Tropicale Civitavecchia (Italy)		17.00
TUE	2	Catania (Italy)	13.00	20.00
WED	3	Valletta (Malta)	08.00	18.00
THU	4	cruising		
FRI	5	Ibiza (Balearic Islands)	08.00	–
SAT	6	Ibiza	–	03.00
		Palma (Majorca)	09.00	18.00
SUN	7	Ajaccio (Corsica)	14.00	19.00
MON	8	Civitavecchia (Italy)	10.00	17.00
TUE	9	Catania (Italy)	13.00	20.00
WED	10	cruising		
THU	11	Patmos (Greece)	08.00 •	13.00
		Bodrum (Turkey)	17.00 •	–
FRI	12	Bodrum	–	02.00
		Marmaris (Turkey)	08.00	19.00
SAT	13	Santorini (Greek Islands)	07.00 •	13.00
SUN	14	cruising		
MON	15	Civitavecchia Transfer to airport Fly Rome/UK •ship is at anchor – disembark by tender	10.00	

Source: Costa Cruising Summer 2004 brochure

The Caribbean

This is the second most popular cruise area for UK cruisers. Almost all of these cruises are fly-cruises. The appeal lies in being able to take a one- or two-week cruise in the hot sun of the Caribbean without having to sail there first. It enables passengers to fit a cruise into their annual holiday period. The Caribbean is a popular area for cruising for North American passengers because of the proximity of the islands to home. The Caribbean is also suitable for all year round cruising whereas the Mediterranean has far fewer cruises in winter. This means that there are a lot of ships operating in the Caribbean and therefore a lot of capacity available.

The advantage of going on a cruise to the Caribbean is that the passengers get to see many of the islands, visiting a different one each day. The disadvantage is that they don't get to know any of the islands very well and don't have an opportunity to meet local people. There are many islands to visit all with different characters. French islands are Guadeloupe, Martinique, St Barthelemy and St Martin. There are the Dutch Antilles islands, the US Virgin Islands and Spanish-speaking islands of Cuba, Dominican Republic and Puerto Rico. Former British islands are Barbados, Jamaica and St Lucia.

CASE STUDY

Our example this time shows the itinerary for a cruise offered by Princess Cruises in the Caribbean.

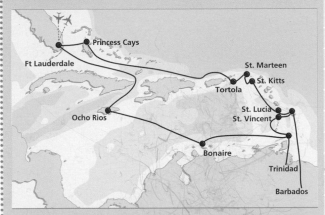

1. Using a blank map of the Caribbean, dowloaded from www.geoexplorer.com or from your atlas, plot the route of this itinerary around the Caribbean.
2. Choose two of the islands to be visited and describe what there is for cruise passengers to do in a day's visit.

Make notes on your findings.

Sea Princess
Fort Lauderdale to Fort Lauderdale

DAY	PORT	ARRIVE	DEPART
1	Fly UK/Fort Lauderdale (USA) Transfer and embark Sea Princess		7.00pm
2	Princess Cays (Bahamas)	10.00am	4.00pm
3	At sea		
4	Tortola (British Virgin Islands)	8.00am	6.00pm
5	St. Maarten	7.00am	6.00pm
6	St. Kitts	8.00am	6.00pm
7	St. Lucia	8.00am	6.00pm
8	Barbados	7.00am	midnight
9	St. Vincent	8.00am	5.00pm
10	Trinidad	7.00am	2.00pm
11	Bonaire	12 noon	7.00pm
12	At sea		
13	Ocho Rios (Jamaica)	8.00am	4.00pm
14	At sea		
15	Fort Lauderdale Disembark Sea Princess. Transfers and use of hospitality facilities are provided before your overnight flight to the UK.	7.00am	
16	Arrive UK		

Source: Princess Cruises brochure Caribbean 2005/2006

The Baltic

The Baltic region has been growing in popularity for a decade. The region includes the countries of Scandinavia and Russia and Estonia. People who choose Baltic cruises are more likely to be interested in seeing the culture of historic cities like St Petersburg and beautiful scenery rather than beaches. Good weather is not guaranteed although the summer months can be good and it is possible to see the midnight sun in Norway.

This extract from Costa Cruises brochure gives a flavour of what is on offer in the Baltic.

Set sail for Northern Europe and prepare to be spellbound by a land of mesmerising scenery and natural splendour – waterfalls, islands, lakes, streams and rivers, not to mention green or snow-topped mountains! Quaint little villages, some dating back to mediaeval times and lively modern cities which all add up to create a place where beauty and wonder combine in perfect harmony, where the magnificence of the midnight sun will inspire you and the culture and traditions of the northern capitals will captivate you...

Source: Costa Cruising Summer 2004 brochure

The fjords of
Norway

Theory into practice

Use brochures to find an example of a week's Baltic cruise that would be suitable for two friends of about 40 years old to take together. They are both art teachers and very interested in culture and history. Describe the cruise and say why it would appeal to them. Include maps and itineraries. Present the cruise to your colleagues who will take the role of the two friends.

South America

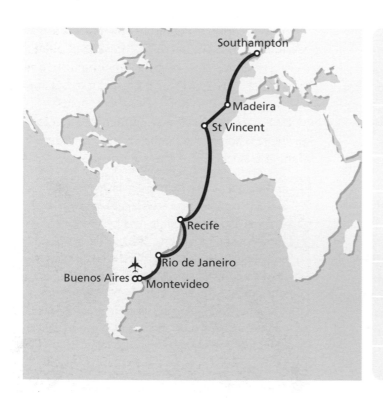

Aurora Holiday ROE

Southampton
Sun 9 Jan cruise check-in
2.30pm – 4.30pm. Sail late afternoon

Madeira
Wed 12 Jan arr 1.00pm dep midnight
* Evening in port

St Vincent – *Cape Verde Islands*
Sat 15 Jan arr 8.00am dep 12.30pm

Recife – *Brazil*
Tue 18 Jan arr 1.00pm dep 6.00pm

Rio de Janeiro – *Brazil*
Fri 21 Jan arr 8.00am dep 6.00pm

Montevideo – *Uruguay*
Mon 24 Jan arr 8.00am dep 5.00pm

Buenos Aires – *Argentina*
Tue 25 Jan arr 8.00am.
Disembark and fly to UK

London
Wed 26 Jan arr am

Source: P&O Cruises Worldwide Holidays 2005

The example shown on the previous page illustrates the upper end of the cruise market for the following reasons:

* the trip takes 17 days so it is for people with more time to spare than a two-week holiday
* it has several days at sea so it is not for those who want to be in a new place every day
* it is very expensive
* it is to far-flung places unlikely to be chosen by 'new' cruisers.

This is typical of South American and Far Eastern cruises. Passengers opt to join the cruise at a stage of its journey around the world. In the case of our example, the passengers start out at the beginning with the ship from Southampton and then when they disembark in Buenos Aires they fly back to the UK. Other passengers meanwhile fly to join the ship in Buenos Aires for the next leg.

Alaska

Cruise ships only visit this area in the summer months as some parts become unnavigable in the winter. UK passengers fly from home to join their ships in North America, often in Vancouver or Seattle. Visitors experience wonderful scenery at close hand on these voyages. They can see fjords, waterfalls and mountains.

Many trips include the cities and towns of Ketchikan and Juneau. Some of the ships pass along 'The Inside Passage'. This is a narrow pass, shaped by the force of massive glaciers, through a chain of islands surrounded by mountains and forests. The islands separate the Inside Passage from the Pacific Ocean.

It is possible to take a route that goes from Vancouver to Anchorage and includes glaciers such as Hubbard Glacier in Yakutat Bay and Columbia Glacier in College Fjord.

Assessment activity 9.2

Choose three of the cruise areas described in this section. Describe the appeal of each area to
a) a honeymoon couple
b) a group of ten third-age travellers
This task could provide evidence for P3.

Make a comparison of the appeal of two of the areas to
a) a honeymoon couple
b) a group of ten third-age travellers
You could present this information as a chart and include factors such as scenery, excursions, climate, accessibility from the UK and cost.
This task could provide evidence for M2.

Nile

Some cruises take place on rivers and this type of cruising is also growing.

We will look particularly at the Nile as a destination. It is traditionally the most popular river cruise area but has fallen in popularity due to terrorist activity in Egypt against tourists and problems with food hygiene on river boats.

Holidays on the Nile are primarily intended for those who want to sightsee. This includes highlights such as visits to the temples of Karnak

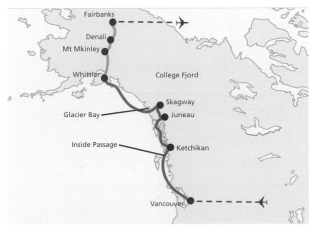

Source: Princess Cruises Alaska brochure 2005

A cruise ship on the Nile

and Luxor, and the magnificent Valley of the Kings. At certain times of the year, particularly in the winter months, there can be low water levels on the Nile and the itinerary then has to change. The river is very busy with cruise ships – some might find it overcrowded – and when boats are moored for the night all the passengers can see is the next boat. However, as we noted, numbers are now declining.

Here is an example of a typical Nile itinerary.

DAY 1
In the afternoon visit the well-preserved XVIIIth Dynasty Temple of Luxor and the enormous Temple of Karnak, whose construction took more than 1,000 years.

DAY 2
Early in the morning cross to the West Bank of the Nile to explore the tombs of the Pharaohs in the Valley of the Kings. We also see the Valley of the Queens, the elegant mortuary temple of Queen Hatshesput at Deir el-Bahri and the Colossi of Memnon. Sail in the afternoon to Esna.

DAY 3
Sail to Edfu where a visit is made to the monumental Temple of Horus. Continue sailing to Kom Ombo.

DAY 4
At Kom Ombo visit the Ptolemaic temple dedicated to the two gods Sobek and Haroeris, from where there is also a fine view over the Nile. Sail to Aswan, where afternoon sightseeing includes the High Dam, the ancient Granite Quarries and the beautiful Temple of Isis at Philae.

DAY 5
Optional excursion to Abu Simbel.

Source: Extracted from 'Treasures of the Nile' cruise from Bales Worldwide

---

Ports

Types of ports

Ports can be:

* ports of call
* home ports
* ports of embarkation
* hybrid ports.

In this part of the chapter we will be looking at examples of these types of port all over the world and we will examine the impact of thousands of visitors on these ports. Let us first ensure we understand the different types.

Key concept

Ports of embarkation are places where the passenger can choose to either begin or end their cruise.

A home port is a port where the ship has its base. It is also a port of embarkation where the ship picks up and discharges all its passengers at once when it has been on a round trip.

Ports of call are ports that the ship visits and the passengers can take a shore excursion if they wish. They have to get back on before the ship sails again! Hybrid ports are a mixture of all the others. When ports provide a major link to other countries or access to destinations within a country for trade or passengers, they are described as gateway ports.

Port of embarkation

Miami is the busiest port of embarkation. A port of embarkation must provide facilities for ships and their passengers. These will include:

* berths with enough space around them for cruise ship and tug manoeuvres
* access for service vehicles
* terminal building with check-in and lounge areas for passengers
* immigration area
* baggage checks and security
* restaurants, toilets etc.
* car parks
* foreign exchange.

Home ports

Southampton is the UK's premier cruise port, handling almost half a million passengers. In 2003, Southampton handled in excess of 200 cruise calls. It is the home port to all of P&O's and Cunard's UK cruise vessels, and is regularly chosen by cruise lines for the promotion of their new vessels and for the hosting of naming ceremonies.

Established operator P&O made further investments in its Southampton-based fleet, with the addition of *Oceana* and *Adonia* cruise liners in 2003. Long-established customer Cunard has chosen Southampton as the home port for *QM2* (the world's largest-ever cruise liner).

Southampton offers:

- three dedicated cruise terminals, each with first-class reception and baggage-handling facilities

- excellent road and rail links with the UK's major cities, including convenient access to Southampton International Airport and to Heathrow and Gatwick airports

- direct rail link to the *QE2* terminal, which accommodates passenger trains including VSOE's Orient Express

- Southampton has seen a doubling of cruise calls and passengers handled in the past five years. To accommodate this growth and improve passenger facilities, ABP has recently invested in excess of £10m in Southampton's cruise business, including the construction of a further dedicated facility.

Source: Extracted from www.abports.co.uk

If you were embarking on a cruise, what would be the appeal of embarking at Southampton? Draw up a publicity flyer with all the advantages.

TOP HOME PORTS

The busiest ports, for passengers embarking on a cruise holiday.

1. Miami, US
2. Port Everglades, Florida, US
3. Port Canaveral, Florida, US
4. San Juan, Puerto Rico
5. Vancouver, Canada
6. Barcelona, Spain
7. New York, US
8. Los Angeles, US
9. Palma, Majorca, Spain
10. Tampa, US

Source: TTG Expert Cruises 2004

Consider this...

Note that most of these ports are in the US. Why do you think that is?

Ports of call

TOP DESTINATIONS

The most popular ports for visits by cruise passengers.

1. Cozumel, Mexico
2. Grand Cayman, Caribbean
3. Nassau, Bahamas
4. St. Thomas, US Virgin Islands
5. St. Maarten, Caribbean
6. Key West, Florida, US
7. Juneau, Alaska, US
8. Skagway, Alaska, US
9. Aruba, Caribbean
10. Bridgetown, Barbados
11. Naples, Italy
12. Civitavecchia, Rome, Italy

Source: TTG Expert Cruises 2004

The majority of ports in the Caribbean and Alaska are ports of call. Many of them are isolated and have little infrastructure and few facilities. When ships call at ports without terminal facilities, they anchor out to sea and take passengers in by tender. Local people are aware of cruise ship arrival times and will flock to the port to sell their local produce or offer taxi services to the passengers.

Impacts of port development

Economic impact

The economic benefits of port activity and development are as follows:

* jobs in servicing the port
* jobs in construction
* increased spending by visitors boosts the economy
* increased prosperity for residents.

The UK is benefiting from the growth in ocean cruising. From 2000–2003 there was an increase of 55 per cent to 227,000 in the number of cruise passengers visiting UK ports of call as more cruise lines included the UK on their itineraries. It is estimated that 150,000 of these passengers were from overseas. The rest were UK residents on UK port-to-port cruises. There was also a 46 per cent increase in the same period of passengers embarking at UK ports.

The economic value of the cruise sector has been recognised by VisitBritain which has set up a new initiative named Cruise UK to develop cruise business in the UK. Cruise UK encompasses all cruise-related organisations in Britain. It aims to increase the number of visitors taking a cruise to the UK and acts as the first point of contact for developing the cruise industry to Britain's ports. Its first task was to get representatives from different parts of the cruise sector to participate. It set up an advisory board with members from tourist boards, ports, tour operators, airlines and airports. The next step was to set up regional partnerships combining the interests of the different groups.

According to Cruise UK, the economic value of cruise ships to Britain is worth about £17.5 million to ports of call. Add to this the value of ships using UK ports for embarkation, and the value soars to about £35 million.

Raising funds

It is very expensive to build a cruise terminal and the primary use of the terminal, that is, accommodating ships, may not generate enough revenue to cover the costs. For this reason terminal developments often include shopping centres, hotels and conference rooms to increase revenue. Funds have to be found to construct the terminal and the public sector may have to join with private investors to raise the finance.

Depending on its location, the terminal may not be used all year round, and this causes problems of lack of revenue in the off-peak season and seasonal employment. One way of alleviating this problem is to provide recreational and entertainment activities around the port that will attract local people to the area. This can have a positive social impact on the region.

You should remember that ports are not only used for passengers. In fact for most ports, the primary source of revenue is cargo, although cargo and passenger facilities are kept apart.

In some cases cargo operations have been moved to secondary ports to make way for passenger ships. Examples are banana loading in the Caribbean where stevedores have lost jobs as their trade has moved to a different port.

Environmental impact

New development inevitably takes up land or sea and may result in the loss of a historic landscape. All nature groups in and around Southampton are protesting about the proposed port development at Dibden Bay which impinges on the New Forest National Park. This is to be a container port not a passenger port but will destroy salt meadows and the habitat of rare birds and plants. Residents will experience an increase in heavy traffic to the port. The regional authorities argue that developing sea trade is vital to the region's economy.

Social/cultural impact

Where new facilities are provided, such as shops and restaurants, they can provide a social benefit to local people – if they can afford to use them. However, many cruise shopping centres are closed to local residents and built purely for the use of cruise passengers. With some types of tourism, local residents benefit from interaction with different cultures and from the provision of goods and services. Although we have noted that cruise passengers do increase spending in the ports of call, this type of tourism has severe drawbacks for locals. Passengers get all their meals on board so they do not need to eat in port. They do not stay in hotels so they spend less than those tourists who spend one or two weeks. They are unlikely to interact with local people on a fleeting day visit.

Consider this...

What could passengers do to try to bring positive impacts to a destination port?

Assessment activity 9.3

The Maltese government is backing the addition of a new cruise terminal in order to boost tourism business from cruising. Currently Valletta is a port of call but the government believes that cruise operators might adopt Valletta as a home port for embarkation of passengers if the right facilities were provided.

The development will cost $27 million but will enable 2,000 passengers an hour to be accommodated through the terminal. The knock on benefits are that passengers would fly in and out of Malta to join cruises and may require overnight hotels.

In addition to the terminal there will be entertainment provision, a shopping centre and a ferry terminal.

1 Outline the advantages to Malta of building this terminal?

2 What are the drawbacks?
   This task could provide evidence for P2.

3 Find out more about the new terminal at Valletta. Evaluate the economic, environmental, social and cultural impacts of the development.
   This task could provide evidence for D2.

Valletta in Malta

The cruise industry in San Francisco is seasonal, lasting from May to October. This is because many cruises to Alaska start from San Francisco and these only take place in the summer. San Francisco is a port of embarkation for Alaskan cruises and also a home port as many Americans drive to the port to embark on their cruise and disembark at the end.

'Repositioning' also occurs in San Francisco. This means that ships which have been cruising in the Caribbean, for example, come to San Francisco at the end of the season in order to begin the Alaskan season. This happens in reverse at the end of the summer. San Francisco is also a port of call for round the world cruises.

As a port of embarkation it is vital that the city has access to a major international airport so that passengers can be flown in to join their cruise.

1. **How can San Francisco alleviate the problems of seasonal activity at their ports?**

Repositioning – cruise lines have to move ships at the end of a season to get them to the right place to start the next season. If they can they will sell these cruises to passengers. The cruise is a different itinerary to those advertised with less time in ports but represents good value for money.

Exploring the types of cruises

In this section we are going to examine the different types of cruises and see how they differ in terms of facilities and target markets. We will also look at some examples of new products in cruising.

The following types of cruises are currently available:

* fly cruise
* round the world
* mini cruise
* river cruise
* luxury cruise e.g. ultra voyager and luxury cruises
* niche cruises e.g. soft adventure and sail ships
* cruise and stay
* special interest e.g. chess
* all inclusive.

Fly-cruise

Look back at the example itineraries given in the earlier part of this chapter. They are all fly-cruises, even the cruise which starts in Southampton has passengers flying back from Buenos Aires. All the major cruise lines offer fly-cruises and that means that the prices quoted usually include the flight and all the arrangements are made for the passenger. Flights may be charter, where the ship is large enough to warrant charters arriving from various departure airports, or they may be scheduled. The more expensive cruises often use scheduled flights because of the extra flexibility and the perception of luxury. Also included in the prices are the accommodation in cabins, all meals and usually room service, activities and entertainment on board. Advantages of fly-cruises are:

* passengers can be speedily delivered to the destination region

* baggage can be checked at the departure airport and taken straight to the cabin

* regional departures are possible

* there is a wide range of destinations and categories of ship available to choose from

* cruises can be from a few days to a few weeks.

Fly-cruises take the biggest market share for UK travellers with 72 per cent of all cruises fly drive (Annual Cruise Review 2004).

The nature of fly-cruises varies according to cost and the cruise line chosen. Some have extremely good service and are very luxurious, like Cunard cruises. Others are less formal and appeal to package holiday makers, like Thomson cruises or Carnival.

Round the world

This has to be the ultimate cruise experience. World cruises appeal to lots of people but they can't usually afford the time or the money to do them! Prices start at around £11,000 per person and can be two or three times that depending on the choice of accommodation. Also it obviously takes some time to sail around the world so work commitments might get in the way. The customer profile tends to be older retired people – with plenty of money. Here are a couple of examples of world cruises extracted from the website www.discover-cruises.co.uk. Have a look at the website if you would like to know more – or to plan your own world cruise.

CASE STUDY

The *Star Princess* and *Grand Princess* are two of the luxury superliners operated by Princess Cruises. The extract below outlines the facilities on both ships.

Star Princess and *Grand Princess*
2,600 passengers 109,000 tons

These innovative sister ships provide you with unparalleled onboard choice whether you're sailing on *Grand Princess* around the Mediterranean or *Star Princess* through the Baltic Sea, you'll be onboard a ship that is guaranteed to turn heads.

- 710 staterooms with private balconies

- 3 main dining rooms, 2 with 'anytime dining', 24-hour restaurant, Sabatini's Italian Trattoria, Sterling Steakhouse, pizzeria, patisserie and hamburger grill

- 4 glistening swimming pools, one with retractable magradome, 9 revitalising whirlpool spas and a children's splash pool

- 'Movies Under The Stars' (*Grand Princess* only)

- Wrap-around promenade deck

- 3 state-of-the art show lounges

- Lotus Spa health and beauty salon and ocean view gymnasium

- Wide variety of bars and lounges, including a wine and caviar bar

- 'Skywalkers' nightclub suspended 150 feet above the ocean

- Wedding chapel

- Writing room and Library

- Sport bar with live TV sports coverage

- 9-hole golf putting course, golf simulator and sports court

- 24-hour AOL, Internet Café and virtual reality centre

- Youth and teen centres

- Grand casino

- Shopping gallery

- Free 24-hour room service.

Source: Princess Cruises brochure

1. **Find details of another fly-cruise ship in a brochure or on the Internet. Choose one of the less formal cruises like Carnival or Thomson. Compare the range of facilities on board and draw up a comparative chart. Decide which cruise ship you would prefer and say why. Share your findings with your group.**

Cunard Line

The world cruises of Cunard's flagship, *Queen Elizabeth 2*, continue a Cunard tradition that dates back to 1922 when the *Laconia* undertook the first ever world cruise. From New York to Southampton, *QE2's* 'Voyage of Great Discoveries' circles the world in 99 nights and calls at 27 ports; including cities such as Los Angeles, Auckland, Sydney, Hong Kong, Singapore and Bombay. A maiden call will be made at Phuket. Prices start at £15,548 per person and include taxes and port and handling charges. Gratuities, normally added to the shipboard account, will also be included for those undertaking the complete world cruise.

P&O Cruises

P&O Cruises programme includes the chance for passengers to circumnavigate the globe 'Jules Verne' style in an 80-day voyage on board the *Aurora*. The new worldwide programme also includes a 100-day Grand Voyage, the longest journey ever taken by P&O Cruises. This takes place aboard the luxurious new ship *Adonia*, which joined the fleet in May 2003.

An epic 100-day cruise aboard *Adonia* departed from Southampton on 4 January. She headed eastward, visiting the Mediterranean, Suez Canal, Red Sea, Indian Ocean, Far East, Australia and Africa, and returned on 13 April.

Harwich–Cuxhaven

Departing from Harwich onboard M.S. *Duchess of Scandinavia* you will have time to check in to your comfortable cabin before relaxing in the bar to enjoy a pre-dinner drink and live entertainment which is available throughout the outward and return journeys.

You'll also have time to enjoy the onboard facilities – perhaps visit the cinema, the shops, bars and later in the evening dancing to the live band.

On reaching the port of Cuxhaven the following day, you'll have time to browse a little and enjoy the scenery before lunch.

Once back onboard ship, it's time to get into the festive spirit with your fellow revellers, starting with a pre-dinner drink followed by the Gala buffet dinner inclusive of wine, coffee and liqueur!

At midnight we will charge your glass with champagne to celebrate the coming of the New Year – it's magical to be at sea as you toast in the New Year!

Source: DFDS Seaways brochure
September 2004 – March 2005

Mini cruise

Mini cruises have been developed as a means of bringing more business to passenger ferries. These ships have improved in the last few years and offer a good range of facilities to passengers, including cabins, restaurants, shops and cinemas. The cruise may be for one or two nights and is sometimes combined with a city stay in the middle. They depart from many UK ports including Hull, Harwich and Newcastle. Cruises to Amsterdam from Newcastle are very popular with students especially as the cost can be as low as £34.50!

The following mini break is a 2-night New Year's Eve cruise from Harwich to Cuxhaven. Note that very little time is spent in port.

River cruise

You have already looked at an example of a river cruise – on the Nile. Many other destinations are popular for river cruising. The chart opposite shows the relative popularity of river cruise areas.

River cruising and ocean cruising are quite different experiences. On a river, passengers are close to shore and can see sights very clearly. Often shore excursions are included in the price. This is important because passengers are unlikely to want to spend all their time on the ship as the facilities are not as varied as on an ocean-going liner due to restrictions on space. A river vessel may carry 100 or 200 passengers rather than thousands.

Passengers from the UK Destination	2000 Pax	2003 Pax	% share 2003
RIVER CRUISE HOLIDAYS, 2000 AND 2003			
– Rhine/Moselle/tributaries	31,564	26,131	29.0
– Danube	11,696	10,129	11.2
– Russian	7,982	6,004	6.7
– French (Rhône/Seine)	7,876	8,840	9.8
– Italian (Po)	3,560	1,445	1.6
– Elbe	2,091	3,203	3.6
– Other European	7,839	5,533	6.2
Total European	**72,608**	**61,285**	**68.0**
– Nile	40,998	15,818	17.5
– Far East/China	3,030	11,043	12.2
– Other non-European	1,183	2,001	2.2
Total non-European	**45,211**	**28,862**	**32.0**
Total	**117,819**	**90,147**	**100.0**

Source: IRN Research

The number of river cruise holidays taken decreased by 23% in 2003 to 90,147 passengers. European rivers represented 68% share and non-European rivers 32%. The uncertainty in the Middle East continued to undermine demand for Nile cruises, which declined 38%.

CASE STUDY

Look at the extract from Bridge River Cruise Collection below.

M.S. *Viking Fontane*

This vessel is a member of the famous Viking River Cruises Fleet. It is comfortable and tastefully furnished throughout with a welcoming lounge with panoramic windows, bar, delightful dining room, gift shop and large sundeck.

M.S. *Viking Fontane* accommodates 124 passengers in comfortable twin cabins. All cabins have a private shower, toilet, radio and television and are 11 sq metres.

M.S. *VIKING FONTANE*

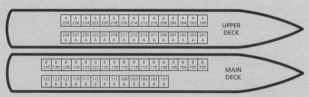

This ship provides full board accommodation. Enjoy an embarkation buffet, buffet breakfast, three course lunch/buffet lunch, afternoon tea or coffee and pastries and a four course dinner.

Source: Bridge River Cruise Collection
March 2004 to December 2004

Who do you think would go on this type of ship? What clues are there in the extract from the brochure?

Luxury cruise

Ultra-luxury cruise lines are defined by the Passenger Shipping Association as ships with fewer than 1,000 passengers, a staff/customer ratio of at least one to two and a space to passenger ratio of more than 40 square metres. The cost will be at least £350 per day.

There is an alliance called the Exclusive Collection for ultra-luxury cruise lines. Members include Crystal Cruises, Hebridean Island Cruises, Seabourn and Windstar.

Consider this...

Royal Caribbean Cruises has developed a design for an Ultra-Voyager ship in conjunction with Finland's Kvaener Masa-Yards. It will be large enough to carry 3,600 passengers and will be 160,000 gross tons.

Niche cruises

Most of the cruises we are studying are on the huge ocean-going liners. However, customers are always looking for something different and this sector of travel and tourism is no different. Niche cruise operators offer a more unusual product, focusing on unusual destinations like Christmas shopping in Rio offered by Discovery World cruises or the Indian Ocean offered by African Safari Club. Ships used by niche operators are often smaller and can access ports which are inaccessible to larger ships. These specialist cruises are likely to be more expensive than mainstream cruises.

Many of these specialist cruises cater for a younger clientele who are looking for more activity on their cruise and a little bit of adventure. Some Alaskan cruises offer excursions like dog sledding, whale watching and rock climbing.

Celebrity Cruises offer a trip to the Galapagos islands with lots of exploration for adventurous types, going ashore in inflatable landing crafts.

An exciting way to cruise the Caribbean is to take a tall sail ship cruise. This very informal type of cruising on a 'Windjammer' ship is described here:

Lazy days at sea – I spend hours reading the latest bestsellers and watching the sails in the breeze. Luckily no seasickness for me, though some of my friends are not so lucky. It's great to get away from city life – we don't have to dress up – in fact I only packed shorts, sandals and swimsuits. Some days I haven't even bothered to put shoes on. I'm slapping moisturiser on every five minutes but haven't used make-up.

The food on board is simple but tasty and we all sit round one huge table sipping rum punch along with our meal. You can have wine if you want it – but it costs extra. Coke flows freely for the kids and iced water is always available.

When we reach the shore life is equally laid back. We transfer to a launch boat and go to the beach. There we can swim, sunbathe or snorkel to our heart's content.

A tall sail ship

Cruise and stay

There is a wide range of cruise and stay holidays available. The idea is to combine a cruise with a week or two in a hotel but it is all arranged in one package. This is an ideal way for first-time cruisers to see if they like cruising.

Special interest cruises

These are cruises which are planned around a particular theme, for example playing bridge, dance or health and fitness. Those who are not interested in the theme can still go on the cruise and carry on with the usual activities.

New products

Ocean village

This brand of cruising was introduced in 2003 by P&O. The brand firmly targets British first-time cruisers, specifically in the 30 to 50-something age group. Now you might think that's old! However, cruises have a reputation for attracting much older people and for being very 'fuddy duddy'. Ocean Village tried to get right away from this image and appeal to someone like this:

'You like doing your own thing and you'd rather dress down than up when you go away. You're adventurous, a bit of a thrill seeker – not the usual cruise holiday type. Relax. Ocean Village is no ordinary cruise. Informal and easy-going, it's for thirty to fifty-somethings who want to explore new places without the formality of traditional cruises.'

Source: Ocean Village website

This is clever marketing as who doesn't want to be adventurous and a thrill seeker?

The cruises are based in the Mediterranean and in the Caribbean and offer lots of ports of call with action activities on shore, for example, river rafting and mountain biking.

Thomson from home ports

About a quarter of a million people chose to start their cruise from the UK in Summer 2003. Thomson is backing this trend and has put the Thomson Spirit on cruises from UK ports of Newcastle, Harwich and Southampton to the Mediterranean, the Norwegian fjords and to northern European cities over a five-month summer season. Thomson increased its fleet by buying one of My Travel's ships.

CASE STUDY

I am sure you are familiar with easyJet. Now there's easyCruise, and this will be the cheapest cruise ever. EasyCruise follows the trend set by Ocean Village in ditching formality on cruises. This product is aimed at 20, 30 and 40 year olds.

As you might expect there are no frills but prices are cheap with cabins from £29 per night. The first ship launched in May 2005. It is not a new ship but has been refitted and can carry 180 people. The ship will cruise in the Mediterranean and then in the Caribbean. Passengers will make their own arrangements to reach the ship and will book nights on board as you would a hotel. Passengers will be encouraged to book over the Internet with early bookings attaining cheaper prices. Food and drinks will be available but passengers will have to pay for them – just like on an easyJet flight.

1. **Draw up a profile of the type of passenger that this type of cruising would appeal to. You already know the age group.**

You can take a virtual tour of an easyCruise at www.easycruise.com

Target markets

In the examples of cruises we have looked at you have seen that there are cruises to suit all tastes and budgets. Some cruise lines aim their product squarely at a traditional market whilst others aim at younger and more adventurous customers.

Factors influencing choice of cruise

General factors include:

* discounted prices
* longer holidays
* more affluence in society
* more choice of cruises
* press coverage.

Some of these factors have led to a growth in cruise taking but what influences a customer to take one cruise rather than another?

* Destination – the cruise has to be travelling to an area that the passenger would like to visit.

* Ports of call – some cruises pack as many ports as possible into the itinerary, others are more leisurely.

* Cost – some ships are more expensive than others and more luxurious. Cost is also affected by cabin choice.

* Formality – we have noted that some cruises have dispensed with formality and do not have a dress code and have a freer atmosphere – this is used in marketing to first-time cruisers.

* Children's activities – families will not be attracted to a cruise unless there are facilities and activities for the children.

* Food – the standard and quantity of food served may be a factor.

* Facilities on board – the longer the cruise the more important these might be. Keeping in touch by email or having lots of things to keep you occupied on board are more important if you are on the ship for months.

* Passenger crew ratio – the more crew the better the service.

Assessment activity 9.5

Study the customer profiles given here and then find a suitable cruise for them. Describe the cruise chosen for each customer and say why it would appeal to them.

This task could provide evidence for P4.

Explain the factors that would affect the choice of cruise for each customer profile.

This task could provide evidence for M3.

Profiles

1. Graham Cutter is 75 years old and he is an experienced cruiser. He has been on 16 cruises. He always travels with his partner, Gordon. All the cruises they have been on have been luxury cruises and now they would like a world cruise – money is no object.

2. Sanjit is a first time cruiser and is choosing a cruise for his honeymoon. He wants to try scuba diving so he thinks the Caribbean is a

good idea. He wants a romantic cruise and he doesn't want to be on a ship with hundreds or even thousands of people. He thinks a sail ship might be a good plan. He wants a personal ambience.

3. Rodney Burrows is taking 11 friends with him on holiday. Some of them have a limited budget so they don't want a very expensive cruise and they don't want a long flight either. They only want to go for a week and they want to have lots of things to do. They are all keen on adventure. They want entertainment in the evening too.

4. James and Jessie Stavros want a family cruise with their four-year-old son. They have never been on a cruise before. They don't want a long flight with a child. They hope that there will be other children so that their child makes friends and that there are children's clubs and activities.

Employment in the cruise sector

When we talk about working in the cruise sector remember that not all jobs are on board ship. There are many opportunities at corporate headquarters and at terminals. However, it is likely that if you are attracted to this sector then you are thinking about travelling the world as you work!

Consider this...

Do you get seasick? It's worth thinking about this because you won't be able to work on a ship if you do!

Negative aspects

We'll start with the negative aspects of working on board.

You will work long hours – it isn't a nine-to-five type of job. You might have to work seven days a week as well. You don't really get to be off duty because when you are not working you are still on the ship and you have to be pleasant to the passengers. You can't escape from the work environment or your colleagues and that can be a cause of stress.

As a worker you will not get the 'royal suite' kind of accommodation! You will get the most basic cabin on the lowest deck and you will have to share. However, as ships become more and more luxurious it is true to say that the staff accommodation also improves. Also, the more senior your position the better your accommodation.

Your contract will be for a few months and you won't be paid in the off-contract time. If you leave during the contract you will have to pay your fare home.

It will be your responsibility to make sure that passport, visas and vaccinations are up to date, although you will be told what is required.

Positive aspects

You will have the chance to see the world. There are opportunities to visit ports of call and the ship will revisit the same places regularly so you will get to know them quite well.

As you work so closely with colleagues, you will hopefully make friends that you will keep for many years. The staff will be multinational and you can learn about different cultures and improve your language skills.

There is no journey to work, no commuting and even if you don't get paid much you will have food and accommodation provided. You will be able to save most of your earnings.

There are lots of different kinds of jobs on ships, some of which require specialist skills like engineering or catering. Once you have got a job and completed the contract successfully then you can be sure of getting another contract and getting more choice about the type of work and ship.

You won't need too many clothes as you will be wearing a uniform most of the time and this will be provided.

Crew members can buy duty free goods on board ships, they also get discount on goods purchased in the on-board shops.

If you are very interested in working for a cruise line take a look at www.cruiseplacement.com. It gives brief profiles of cruise lines and what to expect from working for them. There are also details of current vacancies.

Job opportunities on board

Theory into practice

Spend a few minutes with your group discussing what types of jobs are available on cruise ships. Make a list.

There are probably more than 150 different jobs available on a ship so we will not attempt to cover them all. You should have thought about these different departments:

* retail
* entertainment
* engineering
* bars and restaurants
* fitness
* shore excursions
* reception
* beauty and hairdressing
* decks
* housekeeping
* tours
* medical
* casino.

There may also be openings for photographers, lecturers and florists.

Sometimes departments are contracted out and that means if you want to apply for a position you have to apply to the contracted company not to the ship. Beauty salon positions are often assigned in this way. Steiner is a salon that has many cruise ship contracts.

You need to match your qualifications and jobs to specific skills. It is likely that, as you are reading this book, you are a travel and tourism student and therefore interested in the types of positions that such a course could lead to. Of course, if you have a fitness training qualification, have done bar work before or worked in a shop, you have more areas open to you. Our examples will be those most closely related to travel and tourism.

Whatever job you are interested in, you will have to speak English fluently, and many jobs require one or two further languages so sign up for those language classes now!

Here are two examples of cruise ship jobs for which travel and tourism students could apply. The second one requires a degree so we are thinking ahead in this case.

Job descriptions

Job title: Tour Assistant

Department: Tours

Responsibilities:
* gives passengers information about excursions
* takes bookings for shore excursions
* arranges disembarkation
* accompanies tours.

Person specification:

Must have customer service experience. Must have travel related or cruise ship experience – one year minimum. Good social and communication skills needed. Must be fluent English speaker. Second language preferred.

Location: Alaska cruises

Salary: 2,300 US$ per month plus percentage of sales revenue.

Job title: Customer Service Director

Department: Administration

Responsibilities:

- achieves service goals through co-ordinating hospitality activities
- ensures that all guest requests, enquiries and complaints are responded to promptly
- arranges necessary maintenance and repairs

Person specification:

- good team-working skills
- professional appearance and excellent social skills
- degree in Hospitality Management or Tourism Management
- cruise ship experience desirable
- fluent English, additional languages preferred
- computer knowledge: Word and Excel.

CASE STUDY

1. **Considering what you have read about the working environment on board ship and the examples of jobs available, study the three profiles of travel and tourism students and say which ones are suitable for employment on a cruise ship. Explain why and say what kind of job they could do.**
2. **Now draw up a similar profile about yourself. Swap with a colleague and consider who is suitable for work on cruise ships. Decide what steps you might have to take to prepare for work on a cruise ship and produce a plan of action.**

Job profile 1
Malika has completed a BTEC National Certificate in Travel and Tourism. She is 27 and wants to see the world. Before she returned to college to take her BTEC she worked in a bank for 6 years so she has lots of customer service experience. She also has several bookkeeping and banking qualifications which she achieved at the bank. Malika was born in Morocco although she does have a British passport now. She speaks fluent French, Arabic and English. Whilst studying for her BTEC qualification she worked at the airport on check-in. She is sociable, charming and of smart appearance.

Job profile 2
Greg has completed a BTEC National Certificate and wants to see the world. He has found all the details of cruise lines and recruitment on websites already as he is very good at using the Internet. Greg is a fairly quiet person. He doesn't contribute much in class as he is never sure that he has the right answers. His written work is poorly produced and without depth although he did do enough to pass the course. The other students never wanted to work with him as he has little to contribute to group work. His hobby is train spotting and he has a part time job in a cafe. He went to Majorca on holiday with two friends last year and enjoyed it. There was a residential study trip to Barcelona on his course but he didn't go as he didn't want to take the time off work.

Job profile 3
Charlotte is 19 and has also completed a BTEC qualification, the Diploma in Travel and Tourism. She has travelled quite a lot on holidays with her family and twice with friends. She is a very loyal person and conscientious and has a lot of respect from others in her group. She is very well presented and works in a hairdressing salon in her spare time. She wants to work on a cruise ship but doesn't know how easy it will be to get a job at 19. She hasn't worked in travel and tourism apart from work placements as she has had the job in the salon for 3 years. The manager of the salon wants her to work full-time and complete the NVQ in hairdressing.

Job opportunities on land

The opportunities with cruise lines on land are similar to those of any tour operator. Some of the cruise lines are based in America and therefore, it would be unlikely that British students would be able to get jobs with them. Some cruise lines have offices in Europe, for example, Royal Caribbean has an office in Weybridge.

The jobs you would expect to find would be in:

* marketing
* finance
* human resources
* customer service
* reservations.

Here is an example of a position in telesales.

TELESALES – CRUISE COMPANY
OTE 25K BASIC TO 16K

Responsibilities:

- to make outbound and receive inbound sales calls to sell cruises
- to maximise revenue by offering alternative dates, routes, classes, upgrades and other services to customers
- to participate in promotional campaigns.

The applicant must have at least 18-months' sales experience, preferably within a call centre. Must be a team player and must be able to meet performance targets.

Key concept

OTE or on target earnings – often seen in advertisements for jobs, this means that you can expect to earn the stated figure if you meet the set targets. The basic salary may be only half this amount.

Some homeworkers in travel sales prefer to specialise in selling cruises. They can earn higher commissions than from other sales and it is a growing market so there are many customers to target. Homeworkers are sometimes called 'travel counsellors' and may be affiliated to a large network. You can't set up as a homeworker without a lot of experience in a travel agency.

Job opportunities in port

The jobs available in a port are very similar to those in an airport.

Customers have to be checked in, their baggage has to be transferred to the ship and in addition staff are needed to run all the facilities at the terminal, such as restaurants and shops. These jobs do not require many qualifications or experience unless you are applying for supervisory or management level positions. As many of the jobs are customer facing, experience of customer service is useful.

Knowledge check

1 Describe the 'Golden Age' of cruising.

2 What is a fly-cruise?

3 What is the difference between horizontal and vertical integration?

4 What are the benefits of integration?

5 What does the Passenger Shipping Association do?

6 What is the appeal of the Mediterranean as a cruise area?

7 Describe the different kinds of ports.

8 What is the environmental impact of port development?

9 What is a repositioning cruise?

10 What is new about the 'Ocean Village' cruising concept?

11 What is new about 'easyCruise'?

12 Why is there an increase in cruising amongst UK tourists?

13 What are the pluses and minuses of working on a cruise ship?

14 Why are languages useful to work on a ship?

15 What kind of jobs are available on shore?

UNIT 9 ASSESSMENT ASSIGNMENT

You have managed to get a work placement on a travel and tourism trade magazine. This is a very prestigious placement and you are delighted. You are spending four weeks at the magazine. The first week was an introduction to the work and meeting all the staff. Now, your line manager wants you to take on your own project. The magazine produces a specialist supplement every three months and one of them is to be about cruising. The content has already been decided and your job is to do the research and put all the information together. You can include suggested text, illustrations, photos, maps and charts but the printing and publication will be done professionally later.

When you are doing your research and putting your information together remember that the supplement is not aimed at the general public but at the travel and tourism trade.

Tasks

1 The development of the cruise sector and the cruise sector today

Describe the development of the cruise sector.

Consider:

- key milestones
- new technology
- patterns of demand
- changes in cruise areas.

This task provides evidence for P1.

Discuss the impact of the developments described on the cruise sector.

This task provides evidence for M1.

Give a critical analysis of the cruise market today including examples of integration, interrelationships with other sectors and how these impact on the sector. Illustrate your findings with relevant statistics.

Make predictions for the future of cruising, giving reasons for your thoughts.

These tasks provide evidence for D1.

2 The impact of the cruise sector on ports

Describe, in general terms, the impact of cruising on ports of call and gateway ports. Give specific examples to illustrate your work.

This task provides evidence for P2.

Choose a specific port and evaluate the impact of cruising on that port. You should discuss developments that have taken place, economic, environmental and social impacts and use statistics to support your findings if available.

This task provides evidence for D2.

3 Types of cruises

Choose three cruise areas with different types of cruises and describe why they appeal to different types of passengers.

Example:

Caribbean – upmarket cruise with Holland America appeals to older couples

– Ocean Village cruise appeals to groups of friends ages 30 to 50

Your work would describe:

- why the Caribbean appeals to these passengers
- why a Holland America cruise appeals to older couples
- why Ocean Village appeals to groups of friends.

This task provides evidence for P3 and P4.

Compare the appeal of two of your areas to different markets. You could do this as a chart with comments.

Explain in general terms the factors which affect the appeal of different cruises to customers.

Here are some examples to start you off:

- cost
- dress code
- ports visited
- children's facilities
- size of cabins.

These tasks provide evidence for M2 and M3.

4 Employment opportunites

Describe employment opportunities available on a cruise ship. Choose two jobs and describe them in detail.

This task provides evidence for P5.

UNIT 10

Tourism development

Introduction

In this unit you will find out why tourism development occurs and why it is important at local, national and international levels. We will look at the objectives of tourism development in destinations with some specific case studies as examples.

You will examine agents involved in tourism development and their roles in the process of development.

We will investigate the impact of tourism development and find out the ways that the positive impact can be maximised whilst minimising the negative impact.

We will also study the principles of sustainable tourism and how these ideas and measures can be used to benefit destinations and their host communities.

How you will be assessed

This unit is internally assessed by your tutor. A variety of exercises and activities is included in this chapter to help you develop your knowledge and understanding of tourism development and prepare for the assessment. You will also have the opportunity to work on some case studies.

After completing this unit you should be able to achieve the following outcomes:

→ examine the objectives of tourism development in tourist destinations
→ examine the agents involved in tourism development
→ investigate the impact of tourism development on the destination
→ explore how the principles of sustainable tourism can be used to benefit destinations and their communities.

Objectives of tourism development

Tourism development can be defined as the process of providing facilities and services for visitors to a destination in order to gain economic and other benefits. Although it occurs throughout the world, it does not occur at the same rate. Some countries and destinations are just beginning tourism development whilst others are highly established. Tourism development is complex as it may mean a local area opening up to visitors, the development of a specific resort or hotel, or a country setting up policies and tourist board structures to promote tourism. On a national level tourism development is driven by governments setting a policy for tourism and creating a structure that promotes tourism. In this first section of the unit we will consider why tourism development occurs.

Economic objectives

In most cases economic objectives are the aim of tourism development. This is not surprising as worldwide tourist arrivals and receipts are increasing, and all countries would like a piece of the action. World Tourism Organization estimates for 2004 suggest an all-time record of 760 million international tourist arrivals. This means an increase of 69 million arrivals from 2003. The chart below shows which areas received the new arrivals in 2004.

New arrivals 2004 by region (worldwide 69 million)

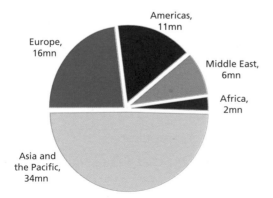

Source: World Tourism Organization

In the UK inbound and domestic tourism provided over £74 billion in 2003. This represented 4 per cent of gross domestic product (GDP).

The economic objectives of tourism development include:

* employment creation
* the multiplier effect
* increasing foreign currency earnings
* economic regeneration.

Employment creation

In 2003 2.1 million people worked in tourism in the UK. This represented over 7 per cent of the working population and more jobs than in construction or transport.

	Total (millions)	Tourism-related (millions)
Total employment	28.1	2.17
Employee jobs	24.4	2.01
Self-employment	3.6	0.16

Source: Labour Market Statistics 2003

Employment in tourism is growing at a faster rate than in other industries. Tourism is a service sector and therefore jobs can be created with low start-up costs unlike manufacturing where plant and equipment are needed.

Direct employment occurs in hotels, airports, airlines, tour operators, travel agents and tourist offices.

Indirect employment occurs in industries and businesses that service the travel and tourism industry. For example, construction workers are needed to build the infrastructure that supports tourism such as roads and rail networks, hotels and gas and electricity services. Also, local shops and services benefit from tourist business and need more employees.

The multiplier effect

Direct tourism expenditure has a wider impact on the economy. If a tourist visits a destination and stays in a hotel, the hotel then spends money on local services and provisions to run the business and provide food and facilities for guests. Staff working at the hotel receive wages which are then used to buy further goods and services. Thus, the impact of the initial spend is 'multiplied' throughout the economy. The multiplier is expressed as a ratio. It can also be applied to jobs, as the building of the hotel leads to direct employment in the hotel but also to extra employment in the construction and service industries. The World Travel and Tourism Council estimates that tourism generates an indirect spend equal to 100 per cent of direct tourism spend.

Increasing foreign currency earnings

Tourism generates foreign exchange earnings. Tourism is an invisible export. It equates to exporting manufactured goods abroad as it earns foreign currency. Inbound tourists spend money whilst in the UK and some also spend money on travel with UK carriers. The more tourists who come into the UK the more the spend increases and the more revenue the economy gains. You can find out more about this in Unit 15 on incoming and domestic tourism.

Economic regeneration

Tourism development is often used as a tool for regeneration both in cites and in coastal resorts in the UK. Areas which are in decline, perhaps because traditional industries like mining have closed down, are in need of employment and investment. Tourism can be a means of injecting new life into an area. Grants from Regional Development Agencies and the European Union can help and local authorities will invest funds.

Political objectives

Tourism is related to politics in that it is the government of a country that determines tourism policy. The policy is often to use a national network of tourism organisations to attract greater numbers of tourists to generate revenue or to manage tourism in a sustainable way. There may be other political objectives too.

Creating a national identity

Our national identity comes from images and experiences within our country but also from how others perceive our country. How a country is perceived is often related to tourism and the perceptions of visitors.

Raising the profile of a country internationally

Where a country has suffered conflict and is in the stage of recovery, tourism can be a means of proving to the international community that the country is stable and safe. Croatia provides a good example. As part of the former Yugoslavia the area was a very popular tourist destination. The civil war in the 90s meant that the tourism industry was devastated. Although a lot of Croatia was unaffected by conflict, tourists naturally stayed away. Now, tourism is an essential part of the country's regeneration.

Croatia is building on its tourism industry

National Parks are protected from overdevelopment

Changes in legislation

Sometimes a country introduces or abolishes a law which impacts on its inbound tourism. Stringent visa requirements can deter tourists. Until recently many tourists to India had to take indirect flights to certain destinations. However, India has liberalised its aviation policy and has granted rights for 21 new services to UK airlines. This move will open up direct routes and provide competition for British Airways who dominated the routes. This should also mean a reduction in prices.

Environmental objectives

Environmental improvements

Investment in tourism can bring about improvements to areas which benefit local people as well as visitors. This might include cleaning buildings, providing riverside and canal walkways and getting rid of litter.

Habitat and heritage preservation

Revenue from tourism can be used to preserve heritage sites. Ironically, the preservation is sometimes necessary because of increased tourism. National parks and other protected countryside areas are common in most countries to enhance the environment for the benefit of visitors and to protect the areas from over-development.

Environmental education

Visitor centres are usually a source of information for tourists and school groups. Such education helps the tourists understand the reasons for conservation and encourages them to respect the environment. It also allows children and students to learn about the environment in a practical way. Some national parks provide information and fact sheets for schoolchildren that they can download from the Internet.

Tourism has often, rightly, been blamed for environmental problems. We will explore these later in the unit and look at how sustainable tourism aims to preserve the environment.

Socio-cultural objectives

Development of community facilities and improving quality of life

Sometimes planning permission is only given to developers as long as they provide facilities for the host community alongside or as part of their development. Examples include leisure facilities or even schools. In addition the host community has a better standard of living because of the increased revenues from tourism.

Promoting cultural understanding

Welcoming visitors to our country or community can promote mutual understanding, it can inspire people to learn new languages and to try new foods and experiences. On a global level such interaction can help promote peaceful societies.

Maintaining cultural traditions

Traditions may be lost as younger generations lose interest in them. The objective of tourism may be to preserve such traditions and in fact cultural and heritage tourism are rising in popularity.

Assessment activity 10.1

Read the following article about a World Tourism Organization Executive Council Plan to revitalise tourism in areas which were devastated by the December 2004 tsunami.

> 'Tourism experts from across the world and from different sectors met together in Phuket, Thailand to draw up the 'Phuket Action Plan' to restart the region's tourism industry. The devastating impact of the tsunami has clearly indicated the dependence of the region on tourism. Tourists have abandoned the area although there are some areas which suffered little impact and are able to operate normally. It is estimated that about 75 per cent of Phuket resorts are open and in the Maldives some 80 per cent. Sri Lanka's beach areas are mainly closed. The plan is to save jobs, to restart small businesses and to reassure people that it is in order to travel to the region once again.
>
> 'Resources are needed – money, materials and expert staff and skilled workers – to help people survive the recovery period and to start a programme of restoration and building as appropriate. It is also an opportunity to put sustainable principles of tourism into practice.
>
> 'The prime minister of Thailand, Thaksin Shinawatra, approved the plan saying, "The livelihood of thousands of people living in the affected area depends on tourism and their livelihood cannot return to normal if they cannot earn their living from tourism. Our task is to return trust and confidence to the international community of tourism".'
>
> Source: World Tourism Organization

1 Describe the objectives of tourism development for the region in terms of economic, political and socio-cultural objectives.

Read the following article which outlines the objectives of increased tourism in Albania.

> 'In 2004 World Day of Tourism was celebrated in Albania by a special event to highlight the country's potential as a tourist destination. The event was hosted by travel and tourism organisations and organised by Albania's Tourism Industry cluster. Foreign journalists were invited to report on the event and on the types of holiday available in Albania. These included spa packages, city breaks, historical attractions and outdoor activities. The country also boasts beaches, mountains, and archaeological sites.
>
> 'The Tourism Minister reported a 15 per cent increase in visitors to Albania in 2004 to 355,000. The tourists are mainly from Kosovo and from Europe.
>
> 'Albania is just beginning to develop tourism as for years development was prevented by the prevailing communist regime.

Tourism is on the increase in Albania

> A digital postcard campaign, supported by US Peace Corps volunteers, with cards offering "Greetings from Albania" promoted the country. Education in tourism has begun with a programme at the University of Tirana. It is hoped that tourism will become a major source of revenue for Albania.'
>
> Source: Adapted from an article in Travelwirenews (www.travelwirenews.com) 12/12/04

2 Describe the objectives of tourism in Albania.

  Produce a chart detailing your findings from 1 and 2.

  These tasks may provide evidence for P1.

Agents of tourism development

Partnership is important in tourism development. All the agents we examine in this section ideally work together towards the same objectives. This is not always straightforward as they may have conflicting objectives as shown in the table below.

SECTOR	PRIVATE SECTOR	PUBLIC SECTOR	VOLUNTARY SECTOR
Objectives	To make a profit	To generate revenue to improve the economy and to create jobs	To conserve heritage and the environment, to educate
Example	Tour Operator	Department of Culture, Media and Sport	Tourism Concern

In the UK, most organisations recognise that the sectors need to work together and that they all have a responsibility to the environment. In developing countries there may be greater conflict.

Private sector agents

Landowners

Landowners and owners of stately homes are not always cash rich and seek to develop their properties and land to benefit from tourism. Most British stately homes are open to visitors for some part of the year. Many welcome film crews to their parks and houses and then benefit from increased tourism as the films gain publicity.

In developing countries, land owned by local people is often bought up cheaply by developers. If local authorities are powerful enough they can prevent this happening and ensure that local people are involved in development. Where locals own the land they can make money from tourism and stop the advent of large hotel chains. In Tobago there are very few large hotels as local people own the land – and want to keep it. They welcome tourists and cater for them with local produce. Some of the hotels are all inclusive and these are not so beneficial to the economy as tourists have all their needs catered for in the hotel.

CASE STUDY

In Barbados, all beaches are public. Everyone is entitled to access. However, access to beaches has become an issue of contention in recent years because:

- there is a lack of vacant coastal land
- when land is available it is very expensive
- landowners want properties which reach to the sea to have boundaries and want to prevent access to their properties
- new beach land with disputed ownership has appeared through coastal works.

The declared policy is that all citizens and visitors alike must have access to all beaches, including, where possible, windows to the sea.

1. **Do you think the policy should be changed? What would be the benefits/disadvantages to tourists, landowners and local people of changing the policy?**
2. **Draw up a chart illustrating your findings.**

Consultants

These are companies and individuals who provide specialist advice. They may be advising governments on policies, advising on new products or helping tour operators restructure their business. Consultants work in all industries but examples in tourism are Equinus, a technology consultant, and PA Consulting Group who provide services to private tourism companies, international tourism development organisations and government agencies. Their stated aim is to maximise the economic benefits of businesses and destinations without jeopardising long-term environmental, cultural or social integrity.

Here is an example of a tender being placed for consultancy services:

'In a bid to enhance the tourism potential of the country, the Department of Tourism (DoT) has recently issued a tender proposing to utilise the services of competent and experienced consultants/agencies to undertake a research study. The tender was put forth by the joint director general-market research division, department of tourism, government of India. The research study would be conducted in countries like Japan, Malaysia, Singapore, Australia and China, in order to assess the interest and perception of prospective tourists in these countries.

'The findings of the proposed study will then be used in developing an innovative market strategy, launching new products and for other policy measures. Interested consultants and agencies have been called upon to submit a technical proposal citing experience in undertaking large scale surveys related to tourism in India and abroad, annual turnover, particulars of the research team (including qualifications) in statistics and economics for supervising the survey.'

Source: www.expresstravelandtourism.com

Developers

Developers may be individuals who decide to open a hotel or major international companies responsible for developing whole resorts. Developers are in business to make money out of their development and are often in conflict with host communities who do not want to lose their land or see overdevelopment. The public sector has to take responsibility for overseeing development and ensuring that community needs are met and that development is sustainable.

Leisure and entertainment organisations

These companies usually enter into a development in the later stages and choose a location where they will benefit from the advent of tourism. Examples include cinemas, casinos and leisure centres.

Theory into practice

Think about the last holiday you went on. What were the leisure and entertainment centres in your resort? Did they contribute or detract from your holiday experience? Why? Discuss your ideas with your colleagues.

Travel and tourism industry members

Travel and tourism organisations have a part to play in tourism development. Airlines and tour operators often instigate development by introducing services and package holidays to a destination. They are also represented by their industry bodies allowing them to have a voice in government policy decisions.

Consider this...

India has decided to open up the airport in Srinagar, Kashmir, to international flights. The aim is to attract more tourists to the Himalayan region, giving a much needed boost to the economy. Tourists may not be aware that this is an area of conflict as militants fight against Indian rule in the region.

Public sector agents

The public sector role is of utmost importance as it is responsible for setting policy on tourism and for putting in place the legislation needed to implement policy. In a developed country like the UK the public sector structure is well established and works in harmony with the private sector to develop and monitor tourism. In countries where the tourism industry is in its infancy, the government may have less control over development than private enterprises and has to begin the process of establishing national tourism organisation networks.

National, regional and local organisations

The structure of public sector tourism in the UK is shown in the following flow diagram:

> Department for Culture, Media & Sport
>
> ↓
>
> National Tourist Boards
> (VisitScotland, VisitBritain, Wales Tourist Board, Northern Ireland Tourist Board)
>
> ↓
>
> Regional Tourist Boards
>
> ↓
>
> Tourist Information Centres

You can find out more information about the structure and the responsibilities of the various organisations in Unit 15. Here we will look at how policy is determined and implemented through the public sector.

The Department for Culture, Media and Sport (DCMS) set down its strategies for tourism in the UK in 1999 in 'Tomorrow's Tourism'. Fifteen action points were at the core of this document:

- a blueprint for the sustainable development of tourism

- initiatives to widen access to tourism

- more money for a more focused and aggressive overseas promotion programme

- new Internet systems to deliver more worldwide tourist bookings for Britain

- new computerised booking and information services

- a major careers festival and image campaign

- a hospitality industry programme to sign up 500 employees to work towards Investors in People standard

- a new strategic national body for England

- a new grading scheme for all hotels and guest houses

- new targets for hotel development in London and a further £4.5 million for marketing

- more integrated promotion of our wonderful cultural, heritage and countryside attractions

- the development of innovative niche markets, such as film tourism and sports tourism

- encouraging the regeneration of traditional resorts

- more central government support for the regions

- a high profile Tourism Summit bringing together industry and government.

Source: Extracted from 'Tomorrow's Tourism' 1999

These targets are still valid but in July 2004 an update 'Tomorrow's Tourism Today' was published reporting on progress and establishing further targets under categories of marketing and e-tourism, product quality, workforce skills, improved data and advocacy across government.

Theory into practice

Divide up the action points from Tomorrow's Tourism equally between your group. Work in pairs if you prefer. Find out whether the targets have been implemented. Gather information on progress and make a presentation to your group.

Use the websites for DCMS and VisitBritain to help you.

Tourist boards

VisitBritain and the other national boards are responsible for implementing government policy nationally and the regional tourist boards are responsible for implementing it in their regions alongside the regional development agencies. The regional development agencies have a remit that extends beyond tourism. The tourist boards have to promote their areas as destinations and work to influence government policies. They also advise businesses in their area about government policy.

Regional development agencies (RDA)

These agencies were set up by the government to promote sustainable economic development in England. Since 2003 they have had strategic responsibility for tourism in their regions. They work in conjunction with the tourist boards. Whilst the development agency determines policy, the tourist board is responsible for delivering it. The tourist board develops its business plans with the development agency and has them approved by the development agency board members.

Key concept

QUANGO – this is an acronym which stands for quasi autonomous non governmental organisation, otherwise known as non-departmental public bodies. They are set up by government with government funding but they work independently of government. Examples include the regional development agencies. Can you think of others?

Assessment activity 10.2

This extract from VisitWales.com explains the structure and roles of public sector organisations involved in Welsh tourism.

Tourism in Wales is a devolved function, coming under the direct responsibility of the National Assembly for Wales. As a key economic driver in many parts of Wales, tourism is part of the Economic Development & Transport Minister Andrew Davies' portfolio in the Welsh Assembly government. He – along with the twelve Economic Development Committee members – sets our budgets and targets and regularly monitors our progress in achieving these goals.

The Wales Tourist Board is responsible for the strategic development and marketing of tourism in Wales. We receive our funding from the Welsh Assembly government and are answerable to the Minister for Economic Development & Transport. Our mission is to improve the economic and social prosperity of Wales through the effective marketing and development of tourism. All our activity concentrates on improving the quality of the visitor's experience in Wales – through strategic investment in raising the quality of the product on offer and through investment in the promotion of the Wales brand.

Four Regional Tourism Partnerships (RTPs) were set up in 2002 to cover north, mid,

south-west and south-east Wales. Their principal role is to lead the implementation of four regional tourism strategies which seek to improve the competitive performance of tourism so that it makes a better contribution to the economic and social prosperity of Wales. The RTPs will work in partnership with the Wales Tourist Board, local authorities, tourism businesses and with other organisations to undertake a range of marketing, product investment and business support activities on behalf of the tourism industry. Most of these activities will be delivered under contract by third parties. Tourism associations are groups of local tourism business people who have come together to form Tourism Associations to promote tourism in their local community.

Source: www.visitwales.com

1 Describe the agents of tourism development in Wales and explain their role. You will need to do some further research to find out about private and voluntary sector agents. Start with the Regional Tourism Partnerships.

This task may provide evidence for P2.

2 Discuss the conflicting objectives and positions of agents of tourism in Wales.

3 Discuss the impact of these conflicting positions on tourism development in Wales.

Tasks 2 and 3 may provide evidence for M1.

Voluntary sector agents

Community groups

Community groups may be formed specifically to deal with proposed tourism (or other) developments or may have been formed for a different purpose but become involved in tourism development. Local people wish to be consulted on possible developments to protect their personal and community interests. Community groups can also act as pressure groups.

The Haworth Village Trust is an example of a community group which has interests in tourism. Haworth is a major tourist attraction as it was home to the famous Brontë literary family and houses a museum about them in the old parsonage. The tourists outnumber local people and have brought traffic congestion to the village as well as increased revenue to the economy. This extract from www.haworth-village.org.uk explains how the group is funded and its current projects.

Haworth Village

'The Haworth Village Trust was formed in 2000 by a group of local people committed to the unique nature and circumstances of Haworth.

'The Trust is a company limited by guarantee and gained charitable status in 2003. Its membership is drawn from local villagers.

'The Trust has several projects in hand at any one time. To date these are the promotion of a cycle path from Oxenhope to Keighley, to reinstate the Bandstand in the park, the preservation of the old school building at Butt Lane, the redevelopment of the Community Centre, Weavers Hill car park.

'The Trust relies on its membership for support, and grant giving bodies for funding.'

Source: www.haworth-village.org.uk

In the assessment at the end of this unit you will learn how community groups in St Lucia got involved in tourism.

Pressure groups

These organisations work to lobby government and change policies. Many of them are concerned with protecting the environment and wildlife. Examples include the Wildlife Trust which is a conservation charity dedicated to wildlife and Tourism Concern whose role is described in our case study.

CASE STUDY

Tourism Concern has been working since 1989 to raise awareness of the negative impacts of tourism, economic, cultural, environment and social. Advocacy is a major part of our work and time and again, the message from our Southern (Third World) partners is the same: 'We want tourists, but at the moment we don't benefit from them.' Communities often find they have tourism imposed on them by governments and foreign developers and tourism businesses; that there is little linkage between tourism especially at a mass scale – and local industry, such as agriculture; that land and natural resources are frequently co-opted, often illegally; and that their cultural traditions are appropriated and commercialised.

Our links with communities and agencies working in developing countries show that there is great concern that the trend in tourism is towards greater control by multinationals, more all-inclusive tourism which excludes local people and businesses, and greater numbers. The consequence of such a trend proving true could prove disastrous for local people.

Source: www.tourismconcern.org.uk

Visit the Tourism Concern website and choose one current campaign. What is the role of Tourism Concern in this campaign? How do the objectives of Tourism Concern in your chosen campaign conflict with those of government or developers?

Other examples of pressure groups in tourism are the Responsible Tourism Partnership and Pro-Poor Tourism. The Responsible Tourism Partnership is a not-for-profit organisation that aims to improve destinations for local people and their visitors. The organisation works with private tourism businesses, governments and with local communities. Pro-Poor, as the name suggests, works to help poorer people in local communities benefit from tourism activities.

> ### Consider this...
>
> The websites of Pro-Poor and Responsible Tourism will help you with your research for this unit. They are full of examples of good practice in minimising the negative impacts of tourism and in helping local communities.

Membership organisations

The National Trust is a membership organisation with over 3 million members. It looks after over 200 properties and 248,000 hectares of land. The Trust is a registered charity and is funded by membership fees, revenue from entrance to properties and donations. It is not funded by the government. The National Trust for Scotland is a similar organisation and cares for over 100 properties.

English Heritage is also a membership organisation but is responsible to the government and receives government funding. However, it does not receive sufficient funding to finance all its activities and raises extra funds in the same way as the National Trust.

The Scottish equivalent is Historic Scotland and in Wales, CADW (a Welsh word meaning to keep).

The Historic Houses Association represents a group of privately owned stately homes and its aim is to help with the preservation of privately owned historic houses, their contents and their gardens. Its mission is to

> *'work for a fiscal, political and economic climate in which private owners can maintain Britain's historic houses and gardens for the benefit of the nation and for future generations.'* (Source: www.hha.org.uk)

The HHA has emphasised the contribution of the private sector historic house owners to our economy:

* annual contribution to rural economy: £1.2 billion
* employment in all tourism and commercial operations: over 10,000.

The Landmark Trust acquires historic properties and renovates them so that they are suitable for holiday lets.

The Churches Conservation Trust cares for 300 churches which might otherwise have fallen into disrepair. Some of these are open to visitors.

> ### Assessment activity 10.3
>
> #### Health tourism in India
>
> It is becoming more common for people unable to get timely operations on the NHS to seek care abroad. This development has been termed health tourism. Sometimes the NHS pays for the operations if they are within three hours flying time but often patients opt to pay themselves. India is a destination that aims to benefit from this type of tourism. It has state of the art private hospitals with English-speaking staff. Doctors are highly trained and medical centres are built with all modern facilities. A heart bypass costs about £5,000 including flights whereas in the UK it would cost £19,000. Operations in India can be combined in a package with sight seeing or yoga experiences. In 2004, 150,000 foreigners visited India for treatment, and it is estimated that this is rising by 15 per cent per year.
>
> 1 Find out more about health tourism to India.
> 2 Explain who the agents of development would be in this type of tourism. Discuss their role.
>   These tasks may provide evidence for P3.
> 3 Discuss the conflicting objectives and positions of the agents of tourism development involved in health tourism to India.
>   This task may provide evidence for M1.

Impact of tourism development

Economic impact

Positive economic impacts

Improved infrastructure

Development may bring about improved infrastructure which can be used by tourists and local people alike. For example, improvements in roads allow people to travel more easily or improvements in plumbing may provide clean water supplies.

Increased income

We have already noted that tourism development brings economic benefits in terms of increased expenditure in an economy. This may come from domestic or inbound tourism. Inbound tourism brings with it increased earnings from foreign currency exchange. In developing nations, investment from foreign companies helps build the infrastructure and the facilities needed for tourism.

The government also benefits from increased revenue as it receives taxes from businesses earning revenue from tourism and in VAT from goods and services bought by tourists.

Increased employment

Tourism is not a statutory duty for local authorities, that is, they don't have to spend money on it – but they do, an estimated £90 million per year. In Birmingham, they claim that their tourism business has provided 31,000 jobs and a return to the local economy of £1.13 for every 87p of council tax spent on generating tourism (*Sunday Times* 21 Nov 2004). Greenwich also used tourism to regenerate the area. It had very high unemployment in the 1990s as it lost traditional jobs. Now, after the programme of regeneration, 25 per cent of jobs are provided by tourism and £327 million is generated for the local economy.

Consider this...

Persuading tourists to visit urban areas doesn't always work – in 2005 a Valentine's break in Rotherham was on sale for only £39 in a Thomson's agency. Attractions of the town included pedestrianised areas and cheap parking. Unfortunately, no bookings were taken and the offer was withdrawn.

Negative economic impacts
Leakage

Economic benefits can be lost if there are high imports of goods and services used in tourism, for example, if food and drink for hotels are imported rather than bought locally. Similarly, if materials and workers for construction projects are imported then the local economy does not benefit. These are examples of leakage.

Type of employment

Jobs provided by tourism are often less than ideal. They may be seasonal, part-time and low paid. In addition, international hotels often bring in management from developed countries rather than train local staff. This leaves only low paid, less skilled jobs for local people. Traditional industry can be penalised by tourism if workers choose to leave their employment in search of jobs in the tourist industry. This often occurs in developing economies where the jobs in tourism may initially provide more pay.

Dependence on tourism

Economic distortion can occur when one region of a country is highly developed for tourism and other areas have none. This occurs to an extent in the UK where the south east and London receive far more tourists than other regions. It is a greater problem in countries where there is little other industry. Overdependence on tourism is a potential problem. Tourists are fickle and fashions change quickly. An economy dependent on tourism will suffer if tourists leave or if a natural disaster occurs, like the hurricane that devastated Grenada in 2004.

Environmental impact

Positive environmental impacts

Conservation and preservation

Sites and properties are protected and preserved for the enjoyment of visitors and to conserve our heritage. Tourism contributes enormously to this conservation in several ways:

* the fact that a site is a tourist attraction means it is recognised as warranting preservation

* National parks and other conservation bodies provide information and education for tourists helping tourists' environmental awareness

* revenue from entrance fees to attractions pays for conservation activities

* conservation holidays are a growing market sector as offered by BTCV and the National Trust.

Regeneration

Both the built and natural environment benefit from upgrading and regeneration when a tourist opportunity is uncovered by local and national government. Examples include the Liverpool and Salford dock areas. Salford has a theatre and museum besides new residential and shopping developments.

Education

Through tourism people can be made more aware of environmental issues. They may become more

in touch with nature and schoolchildren may benefit from visits to attractions such as the Eden Project in Cornwall where environmental projects are undertaken.

Negative environmental impacts
Traffic congestion
Within the UK, most day visitors and domestic holidaymakers travel by car causing traffic congestion and pollution at destinations and attractions. Some villages in Yorkshire and in the Lake District are now closed to traffic whilst large car parks have been built on the outskirts to accommodate coaches and cars bringing visitors.

Pollution
Pollution arises from noise, for example, jet skis and motor boats in coastal resorts. It also arises from petrol fumes. Pollution may cause distress to wildlife through noise affecting their normal activities or by destroying marine life.

The disposal of sewage is a problem, particularly in developing destinations where sewage plants either do not exist or are not able to cope with the extra waste. The cruise sector is booming but cruise ships produce tonnes of waste. Sewage pollutes seas and rivers, damages wildlife and encourages the growth of algae which in turn damages coral reefs.

Coral suffers damage in many ways including trampling by snorkellers and divers, anchors from boats chipping it away and even mining for building materials.

Erosion of resources
A problem in many destinations is that the influx of tourists puts pressure on scarce resources. Water is a scarce resource in many places and tourists tend to use up more than local people. Where there are golf courses and gardens even more water is used.

Land is taken for development of hotels, airports and roads causing loss of natural habitats. Soil is eroded for development changing landscapes. Forests are cleared for ski resort development.

Trampling occurs on well-trodden trails spoiling the countryside that people have come to see. Walkers are encouraged to stay on paths in order to reduce the erosion.

Ramblers are encouraged to stay on paths to reduce erosion

The presence of tourists can be detrimental to wildlife which can be frightened away from its natural habitat by noise and disturbance. The Greek island, Zakynthos, is the home of the loggerhead turtle. Turtles come back each year to the beaches to nest and lay eggs. It is only the female who returns, males do not leave the sea. The females return to the same place where they themselves hatched to lay their eggs. The species is under threat because Zakynthos is also a

vibrant tourist destination. The turtles are prevented from coming onto the beach by the noise from nightclubs and from beach parties. The eggs that do get laid may be inadvertently smashed by tourists on the beach. Those babies who do mange to hatch get confused by the bright lights and instead of heading for the sea and moonlight, go the wrong way. In spite of a European Court judgement condemning

Greece for not protecting the turtles' breeding grounds, action has not been taken. The World Wildlife Fund has launched a campaign to help protect the turtles.

What do you think the Greek government could do to protect the turtles without losing their tourism business? Discuss your ideas with your group.

Social impact

Positive social impacts

Community facilities and services

Roads and rail networks may be introduced to cater for tourists but are also of benefit to locals. Sport and leisure facilities may be introduced and the standard of living for the host community may generally improve.

Education and training

Jobs in tourism are generally desirable in developing destinations. Employees may be able to undertake professional training and improve their job prospects. The quantity and quality of training naturally varies across countries and companies. In areas of good practice, line staff may receive weekly training and support for higher education programmes.

Improved social status

The status of local people can be improved by the recognition of the local culture by tourists where they hold it in respect. Also gaining a job in tourism can lead to enhanced status in the community.

Negative social impacts

Conflict with host community and changes in living patterns

Western tourists visiting developing countries represent an entirely different and sometimes unknown society. Members of the host community may try to copy western behaviour or dress resulting in changes to their traditional way of life or causing conflict between the hosts and the visitors. Tourists sometimes fail to respect the customs and traditions of the host country causing irritation. The host population may feel resentful about the wealth of the incoming tourists. Even though the tourists may not be wealthy in western terms they have a lot more disposable income than the people in the developing destination. This resentment can lead to crime.

Crime

Increases in tourism numbers are often accompanied by a rise in levels of crime. Tourists may carry expensive cameras and wear expensive clothes and jewellery so they become targets for criminals. Resorts may be built in enclaves next to poor areas. The problem perpetuates as tourists become afraid to leave the resort for fear of crime and the host population becomes more resentful about people who do not mix with their society and spend their money in resorts and not in the community.

Prostitution

Tourism has encouraged the growth of prostitution in destinations as young women are willing or persuaded to sell their bodies to get an income. There is even an industry defined as 'sex tourism'. There are several organisations that are fighting against sex tourism. One is ECPAT (End Child Prostitution, Child Pornography and Trafficking of Children for Sexual Purposes) which is a network of organisations and individuals working together to eliminate the commercial sexual exploitation of children. In 1998 they produced a code of practice for endorsement by tour operators and other travel organisations. The code aims to prevent sexual exploitation of children in tourism destinations. The code is implemented by 45 countries across the world.

Displacement

When tourism is regionalised in a country, people may leave their homes and communities to take up jobs in tourism. More serious displacement occurs when whole communities are moved on to make room for tourism development. Recently, there was contention as hundreds of people were displaced from Chattisgarh in India to make room for a national park aimed at bringing tourism to the area.

Cultural impact

Positive cultural impacts

Cultural identity

Travelling to new places can bring about a better understanding of different cultures. In the best case scenario, tourists learn about the food and traditions of their destination and the hosts learn about their visitors. Having visitors interested in the host culture can reinforce the cultural identity of the nation as they proudly show it to visitors.

Preservation of traditional customs and crafts

Sometimes festivals and events are kept going because of tourist interest. Traditional dances and ceremonies may be staged for the benefit of tourists. Sometimes crafts are revived because the tourist trade makes them viable again, such as lace making in Malta. Lace making is a traditional craft in Malta and has undergone a revival in popularity as tourists are keen on buying the tablecloths and napkins produced by local women.

Negative cultural impact

Changes in cultural tradition

Critics sometimes believe that traditional events and dances are degraded by being put on specifically for the entertainment of tourists.

Dilution of cultural identity

As it becomes easier, faster and cheaper to travel the world, so each destination begins to look something like another. For example, McDonalds can be found almost anywhere including eastern Europe and Africa. Some tourists want to carry on exactly as they do at home – but with sunshine; in many resorts in Spain you see English pubs and English food advertised for sale. This kind of development results in a loss of the destination's cultural identity. In the southern resorts of Tenerife, there are beautiful hotels with excellent facilities and good food but there isn't anything remotely Canarian, even the hotel workers are from mainland Spain. You have to hire a car and travel away from the purpose-built resorts to find the Canarian culture.

An example of an agro-tourism restaurant in Sardinia

local producers to help them meet the needs of large hotels. Hotels or local government may supply seeds and agrochemicals on credit to producers to help them set up. In some cases hotels have participated in 'adopt a farmer' projects.

Where tourism takes place in particular geographic regions, tours should be set up to other areas to allow other communities to benefit from tourism. A good example of this is 'Agro-tourism' where local people turn their farmhouses into tourist accommodation or restaurants. The restaurants provide meals serving traditional local delicacies. The aim of these projects is to help local people benefit from tourism, especially when they are no longer able to make their living from agriculture.

Reinvestment of tourism income

Income from tourism should be reinvested in social and public projects. Tourism taxes are often in place for such purposes. In The Gambia, tourists are subjected to a £5 tax on arrival. This money is earmarked for improving the infrastructure of the country and for training local people to enable them to work in tourism.

Education and training of local people

Hotels should employ local people wherever possible. Where local people lack the necessary skills, training programmes should be implemented. Some large hotel groups have a good record of doing this. An example is Sandals in the

Maximising positive impacts

Leakage avoidance strategies

Where tourist facilities are owned by local people, more of the income from tourism is retained in the community. This can be achieved in various ways:

* regulation on ownership of hotels so that they cannot be entirely foreign owned

* encouraging the development of small businesses

* encouraging partnerships between local people.

Hotels should be encouraged to buy produce locally wherever possible rather than importing. This may mean that support has to be given to

Caribbean which claims to have obligatory training for 120 hours per year for line staff in their hotels.

Minimising negative impacts

Planning controls

Restrictions on the quantity and type of building help prevent a destination becoming overdeveloped. In Majorca, tourism has become the most important source of revenue to the economy. Parts of the island have become over-developed due to mass tourism. Eventually action had to be taken to try to reverse the decline in the island's image as a cheap destination for low-spending, heavy-drinking tourists. Building restrictions were imposed on hotels throughout the island and the capital, Palma was restored.

Visitor and traffic management

It should not always be assumed that the objective of tourism is to maximise visitors. Where resources and space are limited then the aim is to manage visitors and prevent negative impacts which occur through erosion of paths, buildings and overdevelopment. Examples of such visitor management occur in many historic towns and at historic sites such as Stonehenge.

Another means of attempting to control the flow of visitors is through ecotourism. Eco-tourism represents the ideal of minimising negative impacts and practising sustainable tourism as tourists and service providers actively strive to minimise the negative impacts. The idea is to bring small numbers of people to enjoy the natural resources and culture of a destination without changing the basic culture or ecology.

Key concept

Ecotourism – The Ecotourism Society defines it as 'responsible travel to natural areas which conserves the environment and improves the welfare of the local people'.

Environmental auditing

Key concept

Green building uses energy efficient and non-polluting materials for construction.

Environmental auditing should begin with analysis of the environmental resources in the area. Careful planning, a long time in advance, can help ensure that environmental resources are protected and conserved during development. Green building helps decrease the negative impact of tourism on the environment.

Examples of environmental auditing include several programmes which aim to protect coral reefs throughout the world. These include monitoring the state of the reefs and education programmes to help conserve them. Here is an example from Florida.

CASE STUDY

Discover Coral Reefs School Programme: Our award-winning program provides every 4th grade student in the Florida Keys with an introduction to the coral reef. Educator Joel Biddle begins with a video/talk at the Reef Relief Environmental Centre (for Lower Keys students) or the John Pennekamp Coral Reef State Park Visitor Centre (for Upper Keys students), an excursion to the reef aboard a Glassbottom Boat, a follow-up slide show entitled 'We All Live Downstream' and use of printed materials including the 'Coral Reef Guide for Kids of All Ages' and 'South Florida's Water Wonderland'. The Reef Relief Teacher Kit enables educators around the world to introduce their students to coral reefs.

Source: www.reefrelief.org

Do some research and find out your own example of a coral reef audit or conservation programme. Produce a poster with an explanation of the programme.

Have you heard of Earthwatch? The organisation arranges expeditions worldwide to enable ordinary people to take part in scientific field research and education to promote the understanding and action necessary for a sustainable environment.

It is common practice in most hotels to try and conserve water by cutting down on laundry and by asking guests to use less water. This is done by placing explanatory notices in bathrooms as shown in the example below:

As early as 1994, Scandic took a step towards a better environment by discontinuing the use of disposable soap and shampoo packages at all hotels. Instead, you can now enjoy enviromenmentally friendly shampoo and soap, smartly packaged and as good for your skin as it is for the environment.

If you use your towels more than once you can contribute to lower water and energy consumption. When you want a new one, leave the towel in the shower or bath.

Many thanks for your help!

Assessment activity 10.4

The following Gambian resorts are advertised in Cosmos Winter Sun brochure 2004/5:

Kotu/Kololi

South of Banjul lie the resorts of Kotu and Kololi. Whilst tourism is taking off in these areas, it remains fairly low-key with plenty of opportunities to experience typical Gambian culture. Kotu is more a selection of hotels strung along the beach (often considered one of Gambia's finest) with a sprinkling of shops and market stalls offering handicrafts such as batiks and woodcarvings. An 18-hole golf course overlooking the Atlantic Ocean is also available at a small fee – clubs, balls and caddies are available for hire. Kololi is more developed offering a hotel-based holiday resort, with a casino and several, reasonably priced international restaurants including Chinese, Lebanese, Asian and European cuisine.

1 Describe the positive and negative impacts of tourism at the Gambian resorts featured above.
   This task may provide evidence for P4.

2 Explain how the negative impacts of tourism in The Gambia can be minimised and how the positive aspects can be maximised.
   This task may provide evidence for M2.

   NB: You may need to find out more about The Gambia to help you give a detailed answer.

Principles of sustainable tourism

We have looked at some examples of maximising the positive impacts of tourism and minimising the negative impacts. When such practices are integrated into the planning of tourism development and all parties adhere to them, rather than just being isolated incidences, then the basis of sustainable tourism exists.

Key concept

Sustainable tourism means developing and managing tourism in such a way that the positive economic and socio-cultural benefits to the environment, the host community and the visitor are maximised without using up or abusing precious natural or cultural resources.

In 1992 an Earth Summit on Environment and Development took place in Rio. It produced a programme of action to sustain the future of our planet. This programme is known as Agenda 21 and was endorsed by 182 governments.

In 1996, the World Travel and Tourism Council (WTTC), the World Tourism Organization and the Earth Council worked together to develop an action plan entitled Agenda 21 for the Travel and Tourism Industry: Towards Sustainable Development. From these beginnings the principles of sustainable tourism have grown and been adopted by our own government and by many private sector organisations.

The World Tourism Organization says that sustainable tourism should:

- **make optimal use of environmental resources** that constitute a key element in tourism development, maintaining essential ecological processes and helping to conserve natural heritage and biodiversity
- **respect the socio-cultural authenticity of host communities**, conserve their built and living cultural heritage and traditional values, and contribute to inter-cultural understanding and tolerance

- ensure viable, long-term economic operations, **providing socio-economic benefits to all stakeholders** that are fairly distributed, including stable employment and income-earning opportunities and social services to host communities, and contributing to poverty alleviation.

Source: World Tourism Organization

Key concept

Tourism Concern is a registered charity which encourages sustainable tourism in destination countries by working with communities and trying to find ways of reducing the social and environmental problems connected to tourism and increasing local benefits.

Tourism Concern's 10 Principles for Sustainable Tourism were produced to coincide with the Rio Earth Summit and aim to influence the policies and programmes adopted by the travel and tourism industry worldwide.

- Using resources sustainably – the conservation and sustainable use of resources – natural, social and cultural – is crucial and makes long-term business sense.
- Reducing over-consumption and waste – reduction of over-consumption and waste avoids the costs of restoring long-term damage and contributes to the quality of tourism.
- Maintaining diversity – maintaining and promoting natural, social and cultural diversity is essential for long-term sustainable tourism, and creates a resilient base for the industry.
- Integrating tourism into planning – tourism development which is integrated into a national and local strategic planning framework undertakes environmental impact assessments, increases the long-term viability of tourism.
- Supporting local economies – tourism that supports a wide range of local economic activities and which takes environmental costs and values into account, both protects those economies and avoids environmental damage.
- Involving local communities – the full involvement of local communities in the tourism sector not only benefits them and the environment in general but also improves the quality of the tourism experience.

- Consulting stakeholders and the public – consultation between the tourism industry and local communities, organisations and institutions is essential if they are to work alongside each other and resolve potential conflicts of interest.

- Training staff – staff training which integrates sustainable tourism into work practices, along with recruitment of local personnel at all levels, improves the quality of the tourism product.

- Marketing tourism responsibly – marketing that provides tourists with full and responsible information increases respect for the natural, social and cultural environments of destination areas and enhances customer satisfaction.

- Undertaking research – ongoing research and monitoring by the industry using effective data collection and analysis is essential to help solve problems and to bring benefits to destinations, the industry and consumers.

Source: www.tourismconcern.org.uk

Planning for sustainable tourism

In recent years the importance of sustainable tourism has been increasingly recognised and, in developed destinations especially, an integrated approach to development is either in place or being put into place. This means that partnerships are essential in planning so that all parties are aware of sustainability and its issues. For sustainable tourism to occur it has to be an issue at all planning levels from international to local and across sectors so that planners, transport departments, marketing agencies and economic development units are all party to it.

Following Agenda 21, the Department of Culture, Media and Sport (DCMS) is committed to sustainable tourism and seeks to promote it by working closely with other government departments such as the Department for Transport, the Office of the Deputy Prime Minister on planning issues and the Department for Environment, Food and Rural Affairs (DEFRA) on countryside and wildlife issues.

Sustainable tourism was established as a priority for the UK in the government publication 'Tomorrow's Tourism' in 1999. The policy followed a consultation exercise with a wide range of organisations. The policy suggested action was needed in six areas. These were to:

* establish an effective policy framework

* maximise tourism's potential to benefit local communities

* manage visitor flows

* address the transport issues associated with tourism

* address the planning issues associated with tourism

* build partnerships between the public, private and public sectors.

These action areas were then developed into a strategy, 'Time for Action' by the English Tourism Council (now VisitBritain). The strategy had three objectives for sustainable tourism:

* to benefit the economy of tourism destinations

* to support local communities and culture

* to protect and enhance the built and natural environment.

These were then expanded into objectives and targets for the national tourist boards. Regional tourist boards and local authorities must also be aware of these objectives and incorporate them into planning.

Theory into practice

Go to the VisitBritain website www.visitbritain.com/corporate and find the report entitled 'The Sustainable Growth of Tourism to Britain'. Read the report and think about its implications for planning. Find the national sustainable indicators for your country (England, Scotland, Ireland or Wales). See if you can think of any local examples which show that the objectives are being met or worked towards.

You can see that the basis for planning exists internationally and in the UK throughout our public sector but it is essential that foreign governments also adopt the principles of sustainable tourism in their planning and also that private organisations are committed to it.

Developing sustainable tourism

Sustainable tourism initiative – the sustainable tourism initiative was a multi-stakeholder partnership seeking to introduce sustainable tourism practice in the UK outbound tourism industry.

The sustainable tourism initiative was developed in 2003 in preparation for the World Summit on Sustainable Development. The aim was to encourage sustainable tourism practice in the UK outbound tourism industry, that is acknowledging that there is a responsibility to sustainability, not just in our own country but to the destinations we visit. The organisations subscribing to the Initiative included government, tour operators and other industry members.

Its aims were to:

✱ raise awareness amongst the industry and the public about the issues of tourism and sustainable development via clear communications and training programmes

✱ research, develop and demonstrate best practice initiatives for companies to adopt.

You can find out more at www.fco.gov.uk.

Private organisations, such as tour operators, working in destinations abroad are in a position to influence sustainable tourism and there are many examples of good practice. In the UK, in line with the Sustainable Tourism Initiative, 25 different tour operators have banded together to develop 'The Tour Operator's Initiative'. The Initiative is a commitment to sustainable tourism by these tour operators and is open to any others to join. They have produced a report which gives examples of different actions that tour operators can take to contribute to sustainable tourism.

One example is 'Supply Chain Management for Tour Operators – Three Steps Toward Sustainability'. This is a guide which gives a three-step approach for integrating sustainability criteria into choice of suppliers.

Some tour operators, for example Thomson, support 'The Travel Foundation', a UK charity that claims to help protect the natural environment, traditions and culture. You can find out more at their website www.thetravelfoundation.org.uk.

First Choice is one of the tour operators keen to develop a sustainable tourism strategy. Their vision and policy is shown here.

First Choice UK & Ireland Sustainable Tourism Vision & Policy

Vision

Enable people to explore and enjoy the world without harming it.

Policy

We recognise that the environment, the communities and cultures within which we operate and our relationships with key groups and individuals are vital to the success of our business. We therefore commit in the long term to:

- minimising the direct environmental impact of our operations and being proactively involved in activities and projects that work to protect and restore the natural environment

- working with customers, employees, shareholders, suppliers, industry partners, local communities and other relevant interested parties, to understand and respect their needs and also supporting them in delivering our commitments

- using the collective influence of the First Choice Group responsibly to create momentum to make tourism more sustainable

- being open, honest and realistic about our environmental and social impacts, targets and achievements in the context of our business objectives.

In support of the above we will work to:

- engage First Choice employees and gain their commitment to action, by raising awareness and understanding of sustainable tourism and the benefits of addressing it

- promote fair working conditions throughout our own business and our supply chain

- comply with all relevant legislation, act in advance of it where possible and keep pace with best practice

- review current business practices and ensure plans are in place to embed the company's sustainable tourism vision

- deliver long-term strategic benefits and shareholder value by maximising the synergies that sustainable development provides.

Source: Sustainable Tourism: The Tour Operators' Contribution

Theory into practice

There are other tour operators who support sustainable tourism. One such is Discovery Initiatives. Have a look at their website at www.discoveryinitiatives.co.uk and find at least 5 examples of how they contribute to sustainable tourism in destinations. Draw up an information sheet of your findings. These examples of good practice may help you with your assessment.

Theory into practice

Is it enough? Have a look at some brochures and find out how many tour operators give information about sustainable tourism. Do you think the principles are put into practice? Discuss your own experiences on holiday.

Benefits to the destination

One of the major benefits to the destination is the improved management of resources resulting in:

* less pollution
* better management of waste and sewage
* better management of water consumption.

In addition, sustainable tourism results in the protection and conservation of:

* scenery
* heritage
* natural habitat
* countryside
* coast
* marine life.

There may be fewer tourists where sustainable tourism is practised, as the aim is quality not quantity thus the mass market, low-spending tourists are avoided.

Benefits to the host community

Companies practising sustainable tourism try to employ and train local people, buy local produce and use local transport.

Tourists are more likely to learn about the local culture and respect it. They may be encouraged to learn at least a few words of the host language.

Benefits to the tourist

The quality of the tourism experience should be improved where sustainable tourism is implemented. The tourist should experience more of the host culture and local traditions. The holidaymaker will be aware of the benefits to the destination and to their host community and feel satisfaction that they are contributing rather than taking from the community.

The tourist needs to be aware of and understand sustainable principles before they travel. Many tour operators now give advice to travellers on responsible tourism. An example is shown here from the Kuoni Worldwide brochure 2005.

Featured in this brochure are some of the most beautiful countries in the world. We believe tourism should work positively towards protecting the natural beauty, culture and wildlife of the destinations we visit so that future generations of visitors and residents alike can continue to enjoy them.

Can we ask you to join us to

- support the local economy wherever possible by buying local produce and services
- respect the traditions and culture of the local people particularly when taking photographs
- support the efforts of many countries to protect their heritage and environment, by visiting museums, historic houses and local wildlife conservation projects
- never buy products made from ivory, cat furs or sea turtle shell
- respect the habitat and natural behaviour of wildlife when in their environment
- not stand on coral reefs – they are fragile living environments and can be easily damaged
- not collect coral (or shells) as in many countries this is illegal, and they are also the beaches of our future
- 'take only photographs, leave only footprints.'

1 Give examples of political objectives of tourism development.

2 Outline the economic objectives of tourism development.

3 Can a host community benefit culturally from tourism?

4 Describe private sector agents of development and their role.

5 Draw a chart illustrating the public sector organisation of tourism in the UK.

6 What is the government role in policy formulation?

7 Explain the role of Tourism Concern.

8 How does tourism development create jobs?

9 Explain leakage and how it occurs.

10 What is meant by enclave tourism?

11 Give examples of negative social impact of tourism development.

12 How can leakage be avoided?

13 Give examples of how the positive impact of tourism development can be maximised.

14 What is meant by sustainable tourism?

15 Give some examples of good practice in sustainable tourism in specific destinations.

UNIT 10 ASSESSMENT ASSIGNMENT

You have been invited to contribute to a seminar on sustainable tourism. Sustainable tourism has been designated a priority for your local authority and members of the tourism department at the council will be presenting their ideas for a forthcoming strategy. To add interest to the debate they want to look at examples of tourism development in other countries. This will give them more depth of knowledge and possibly give them some examples of good practice. You have been asked to research a developed and a developing destination in terms of their tourism development and to report on your findings. You will prepare materials for a presentation including handouts and visual aids.

The destinations you are to research are St Lucia and Lithuania. Background on both destinations is given here but you should be prepared to do further research. Remember that you must research both destinations.

St Lucia

St Lucia is an island in the Windward Islands of the Eastern Caribbean. It is volcanic with high rainfall and dense forests. It also has beautiful beaches, natural harbours and coral reef. The population is over 150,000 inhabitants.

Its industries are made up of:

Agriculture	21.7%
Industry, commerce and manufacturing	24.7%
Services including tourism	53.6%

Source: *The World Factbook*, CIA, figures for 2002

St Lucia

St Lucia's traditional export crops were coffee, sugar cane and bananas. Bananas are still the main crop but exports are threatened by the loss of preferential trading agreements with the UK due to changes in EU policy. The government wants to revitalise the banana industry but must also look to other industries for income. The island is becoming increasingly dependent on tourism but has also attracted foreign investment into offshore banking.

Tourism has transformed St Lucia in the last 20 years. Beach resorts and marinas have been built on the west coast. Cruise ships visit almost daily to purpose-built facilities in Castries. Tourism is the main source of foreign exchange and the main contributor to gross domestic product. Over 10,000 people are employed in tourism.

The formulation of policy for tourism is the responsibility of the Ministry of Tourism. The St Lucia Tourist Board is responsible for marketing. The St Lucia Hotel and Tourism Association and the Chamber of Commerce and Industry represent the private sector. A more recently formed organisation is HERITAS which represents ten tourist sites and attractions.

Two major hotel developments, the Hyatt Regency and the Rosewood were completed in 2000. These two hotels cost more than $US 34 million. The St Lucia Sandals was also expanded in that year. Land and sea transport and restaurants also benefited from greater investment in 2000.

Identified positives

In 2004 plans for establishing, upgrading and implementing quality standards for the island's tourism product were made. Tourism officials have developed five draft standards for the tourism sector in the areas of accommodation, food and beverage, vending, water-based tourism, and ground transportation. Workshops are being held to develop the plans further.

St Lucia is able to welcome large numbers of cruise passengers, over 400,000 per annum, berthing has been created at Port Castries for large cruise ships.

The table gives an overview of tourism statistics.

	2001	2002	2003
Tourists stayover	250,132	253,463	276,948
Excursionists	6,422	7,712	12,817
Visitor arrivals	256,554	261,175	289,765
Cruise ship passengers	489,912	387,180	393,240
Cruise ship calls	327	245	262
Yacht passenger arrivals	...	...	...
Average hotel occupancy	57.0	56.1	62.7

Source:www.stats.gov/lc

NB. Excursionists are day visitors whereas tourists stay at least one night.

A successful campaign has already been mounted to encourage hotels to buy more of their produce from local farmers.

Identified problems

Land and habitat has been lost to hotel and infrastructure development.

Coral reef has been destroyed through increased sedimentation from land clearing and beach maintenance. Anchoring of boats has also caused damage.

Waste management is not sufficient for the needs of hotels, causing pollution to areas of coastline and land pollution from waste sites.

The government is concerned that the number of all-inclusive hotels is too high and that local people are not benefiting from the tourism they attract. The government needs to find ways of reducing the estimated 60 per cent of leakage from these hotels and encourage tourists to leave the hotels and visit the island spending their money more widely.

Local people have a poor perception of enclave resorts.

Tourism is dominated by large operators and it is very difficult for small businesses to enter the market.

New developments

There is a proposal to redevelop the area of Soufriere following the inscription of the Pitons Management Area as a World Heritage Site in 2005. The area includes the Piton twin peaks, the Sulphur Springs and the Diamond Falls, all of which attract thousands of tourists.

The government has developed national policies on waste management using funds from a tourism tax.

The government decided to introduce a Heritage Tourism Programme. The aim was to achieve more equitable and sustainable tourism development and to enhance the impact of tourism.

The programme is funded by the government of St Lucia and the European Union. Ten sites and attractions were identified to be marketed as heritage attractions. Jobs have been created with tour guides and craft producers needed as well as employees at the attractions. The owners of the attractions are members of HERITAS.

Useful websites

www.globaleye.org.uk   www.stlucia.org
www.intracen.org   www.heritagetoursstlucia.com
www.infoplease.com   www.stats.gov.lc
www.geographia.com

1 Describe the objectives of tourism in St Lucia.

2 Describe the agents of tourism in St Lucia and explain their role.

   These tasks may provide evidence for P2 and P3.

3 Discuss the conflicting objectives and positions of the agents of tourism development in St Lucia and explain how these might impact on tourism development.

   This task may provide evidence for M1.

4 Describe the positive and negative impacts of tourism in St Lucia.

   This task may provide evidence for P4.

5 Explain how the positive impacts of tourism can be maximised and the negative impacts minimised in St Lucia.

   This task may provide evidence for M2.

6 Evaluate the effectiveness of measures taken to maximise the positive impacts of tourism and minimise the negative aspects in St Lucia.

   This task may provide evidence for D2.

Lithuania

Lithuania is one of the Baltic states, formerly part of the USSR. It shares borders with Belarus, Latvia, Poland and Russia. The population is 3.4 million. The capital city is Vilnius.

Lithuania

In 1990 Lithuania declared its independence from Russia. However, independence was not finally achieved until 1991 as the Moscow administration turned troops on Lithuanian demonstrators.

English is widely spoken and Lithuanian is the mother tongue, although Russian and Polish are also spoken.

The country has a good transport network so it is relatively easy to get about. It has 90 kilometres of coast. There are no mountains or forests but there are hills and pleasant countryside. Art festivals are an attraction. The food tends to be heavy with meat and potatoes, pancakes, dark bread and cakes and fried cheese. The local beer is good. The currency is the Litas.

Its industries are made up of:

Agriculture	20%
Industry, commerce and manufacturing	30%
Services including tourism	50%

Source: *The World Factbook*, CIA, figures for 2002

Since independence, more than 80 per cent of businesses, previously state owned, have been privatised. Foreign investment is helping to boost the economy and Lithuania is forging trade links with the west. Unemployment is high at over 10 per cent.

Tourism is seen as a means of growth to the economy and a major tourism offensive was launched in 2003 by the State Department of Tourism. Lithuania has joined the World Tourism Organization and was the first Baltic state to do so. The country became a member state of the European Union in 2004. Many steps have already been taken to develop tourism:

- a law on tourism has been approved
- a National Tourism Development Programme up to 2006 has been prepared
- an information system on tourism in Lithuania was prepared
- a marketing plan was developed, funded by state and local authorities and representatives of the tourism industry. Part of the plan concerned presenting a positive image of Lithuania. Various publications were marketed in languages such as Latvian, German, English, Polish and even Esperanto. Lithuania was represented at 19 International Fairs on Tourism.
- Tourist Information Centres have been opened in Helsinki and in Warsaw
- sightseeing tours have been arranged for journalists and travel organisers from Finland, Germany and the US

- three hotels have been awarded the 'Green Key Award' for meeting over 70 environmental criteria in three categories including decreased power and water consumption, economic use of heating energy, waste separation and the possession of an environmental policy.

The chart shows the numbers of tourist arrivals between 1997 and 2003. Figures are in thousands.

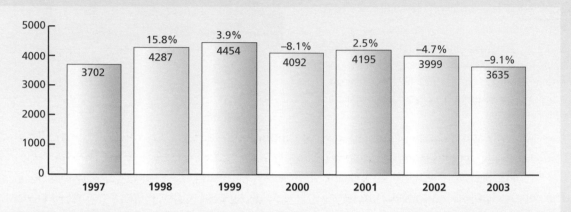

Source: www.tourism.lt

Most visitors are from neighbouring countries and they travel by car. However, numbers of visitors from western Europe are increasing.

Websites

Useful websites for further research:

www.tourism.lt   www.neris.mii.lt
www.travel.lt   www.lonelyplanet.com
www.cia.gov

7 Describe the objectives of tourism development in Lithuania.

   This task may provide evidence for P1.

8 Describe the agents of tourism development who are and who could be involved in Lithuania. Explain their role.

   This task may provide evidence for P2.

9 Discuss the conflicting objectives and positions of agents of tourism development in Lithuania. Discuss their impact on development.

   This task may provide evidence for M1.

10 Describe the principles of sustainable tourism and how they can be used to benefit destinations and their host communities.

   This task may provide evidence for P5.

11 Explain how the principles of sustainable tourism can be used to benefit Lithuania and its communities.

   This task may provide evidence for M3.

12 Use examples of good practice from other destinations to suggest and justify possible improvements within Lithuania.

   This task may provide evidence for D1.

Holiday representatives

Introduction

Most students look forward to finding out about the role of the holiday representative. You have probably seen representatives at work when you have been on holiday and thought that it looked like an exciting life. It can be a very interesting and fulfilling job but you should realise that it is often very hard work too. It is a job that gives you great experience of customer care and organisational skills and allows you to live abroad if you choose. It can be a fun temporary job in a gap year or after leaving education, or it can be a serious career path leading to other positions within a tour-operating company. Many of the people at the very top level of tour operation started out as holiday representatives.

The role of holiday representatives is to look after holidaymakers whilst they are on holiday either in the UK or abroad. In this unit you will find out about the different categories of holiday representative and their roles and responsibilities.

You will examine the legal responsibilities of the holiday representative and the role they play in relation to health and safety in the holiday environment. We will look at the key legislation and you will see how holiday representatives have to identify and minimise hazards in different situations.

We will use some practical activities to allow you to develop your communication skills in dealing with customers in a range of situations. You will also practise your social and customer service skills.

How you will be assessed

This unit is internally assessed by your tutor. A variety of exercises and activities is included in this chapter to help you develop your knowledge and understanding of the roles and responsibilities of holiday representatives and prepare for the assessment. You will also have the opportunity to work on some practical exercises as well as case studies.

After completing this unit you should be able to achieve the following outcomes:

→ investigate the roles and responsibilities of different categories of holiday representatives

→ examine the legal responsibilities of the holiday representative and the role they play in relation to health and safety in the holiday environment

→ use a range of communication techniques to meet customer needs

→ apply social and customer service skills in different situations.

Different categories of holiday representatives

There are many different types of holiday representative. The most common example that springs to mind is the overseas resort representative, in uniform and working for one of the big four tour operators.

There are many others. Camping and holiday home operators employ a lot of seasonal representatives who spend their summers under canvas. Some overseas representatives look after customers from several tour operators at once and are employed by local companies and then, of course, there are holiday representatives working in holiday parks and hotels in the UK looking after domestic and inbound tourists.

In this first section of the unit we will find out about the roles and responsibilities of the different types of representative and consider where they might be located.

Property representatives

A property representative is responsible for customers in a number of different hotels, apartments or villas in a resort. This role typifies that of a holiday representative and most people employed by the major tour operators have this role. They live in the resort, usually in separate accommodation from the guests but with other representatives. Firstly, we are going to examine the general role and responsibilities of a property representative.

What do property representatives do?

Role

✳ Represent the tour operator – the property representative may be the only person from the tour-operating company that the holidaymaker meets. Therefore, the impression presented by the rep is of vital importance. A poor rep can lose many customers and do great harm to the company's image.

✳ Give customer service – the rep is there to make sure that the customer has an enjoyable holiday and any problems are swiftly solved.

Responsibilities

✳ conducting welcome meetings for new arrivals

✳ preparing an information file about the resort for guests' use

✳ keeping the notice board in the hotel or apartment block updated

✳ visiting properties every day to answer guests' queries

✳ selling and booking excursions

✳ handling payments

✳ keeping paperwork up-to-date

✳ booking hire cars etc. for guests

✳ guiding tours

✳ doing airport transfers according to a rota

✳ participating in entertainment for guests

✳ checking properties for health and safety

* liaising with hotel management
* dealing with problems and emergencies.

The representative will receive training and be given a uniform. They are also provided with accommodation and a basic salary. Commission is earned on the excursions sold.

You can see that there is a lot to the job and of course the representative has to be on call in case of emergency, although when there are several reps in a resort they have a rota for this. Problems may range from over-bookings to serious illness or even death. You will have an opportunity later in this chapter to consider some of the problems that you might face as a rep and see how you would deal with them.

CASE STUDY

First Choice

This extract from www.firstchoice.co.uk summarises the role of the rep. If you look at the website you can see all the different types of representative jobs available and even apply on line. Take a look and make some brief notes as an introduction to the next section.

'You'll make sure every customer enjoys a great holiday. You're always around to offer practical advice, or simply to recommend great places to go or fun things to do.

'Of course, you'll also deal with unexpected situations coolly and professionally. Every day will be different! You're able to think on your feet, have fantastic problem solving and communication skills, and be full of initiative.

'You'll need to be flexible, over 21 and passionate about delivering excellent customer service. Also important are sales skills and an energetic approach.'

The role and responsibility vary according to the type of property and holiday brand the representative is working with. We are going to look at some of the variations on the property representative role.

Holidays for young people

Representative work for companies such as 18–30s, 2wentys and Escapades is often very appealing to young people, as there is a great deal of partying! These representatives have to party almost every night even when they don't feel like it. In addition to the usual duties of a representative, they are expected to take their guests on pub crawls and to clubs and to arrange games and drinking competitions so that they go home having had a wonderful time. Reps need to have lots of energy and stamina as there isn't much time for sleep and they need to be able to keep sober and sensible when all around are not. They must have initiative because with the kind of nightlife that is going on there may be many problems of sickness, injury or theft to sort out. They also have to be young so that they fit in with the age group of the client. These positions are seasonal and the representatives can expect to be employed from May to September or October. There is a lot more demand for 18–30 type holidays in the peak summer season so there are more jobs for reps in that period which means this job can fit in with studying. These representatives work in major summer holiday resorts all over western Europe.

Villa representatives

These employees need to be drivers and are usually provided with a company car. Unlucky ones might only get a moped. Villas are likely to be located at considerable distances from each other so it may be time consuming reaching them and ensuring that all clients are welcomed. The nature of the job is different in that the customers' needs are different. Villa holiday customers are less likely to join excursions and are usually more independent and happy to organise their own activities. Thus the representative may only be called on when there is a problem. The advantage for the representative is that they should have more free time than other kinds of representatives if all is running smoothly.

There may be another dimension to this job – villas have owners – and the representative may have to mediate between an owner and a customer if there is a problem. As the owners cannot all be expected to speak English, the representative should speak the local language. Some tour operators choose to employ local people as villa representatives. They like the fact that their local knowledge is excellent so they can advise customers and there is no language problem. Villa representatives are employed all over Europe and indeed in further flung destinations but are likely to be in the less busy resorts.

'Prestige' or 'select' representatives

Most tour operators have brands that are aimed at older or more discerning customers.

You can imagine that these customers are expecting a different kind of holiday to the 18–30 customer and so a different personality of rep is needed. Sovereign, the tour operator, looks for representatives with more maturity, good communication skills and a second language as shown in this extract from their website. Although they ask for an age of over 21, it is likely that suitable candidates are much older. Some tour operators deliberately target older people (50 plus) in their recruitment as they think their older clients will be more comfortable with a more mature representative. Note how Sovereign gives these representatives a special title to give them enhanced status.

Sovereign Service Executives

Sovereign is renowned for delivering outstanding levels of service. Through acting as a source of information on the local area, offering excursions or simply advising customers on how they can get the most out of their holidays, you'll exceed our customers' high expectations.

Over 21 with a very mature approach, you have excellent interpersonal and communication skills and ideally a second European language. You can manage your own time easily because of your outstanding organisational ability and will also need a current driving licence.

You'll be independent, interested in culture and history, flexible, over 21 with common sense and ideally a second language.

Source: www.sovereign.co.uk

Campsite couriers

These reps are often students who want to work abroad for the summer. Besides all the usual tasks that we described above, couriers are responsible for cleaning the tents and holiday homes in between clients. This can be quite a task – depending on how customers leave their accommodation. The couriers are provided with tents in a staff area of the campsite. The downside of this kind of work is that the guests know where you live and will find you!

Ski-resort representatives

Ski resorts offer lots of seasonal jobs and of course if you work successfully as a ski-resort representative, you shouldn't have any problem getting a transfer to warmer climes in the summer. Tour operators prefer to keep trained and proven staff. Ski-resort representatives do the same job as other property representatives. They are allocated a number of hotels or chalets and visit their guests, solve problems and sell excursions in the same way. They are likely to be keen skiers or snowboarders as that is all there is to do in free time.

In addition to the property representative you will find chalet hosts and assistants in the ski resort. A chalet for 12 people will typically be run by two chalet hosts. They are expected to clean daily, order food and cook it for the guests. If they become very efficient they can get their morning

breakfast and cleaning routine finished by late morning. Then they are free until it is time to cook the dinner at about 5pm. This gives a good few hours skiing a day and is definitely the perk of the job. The chalet hosts are expected to give excellent customer service but don't book excursions or do airport duty. They can call on the property representative if they have any problems.

Assessment activity 13.1

The following table outlines a ski-resort representative job for Crystal Holidays and Jetsave.

RESORT REPRESENTATIVES CRYSTAL HOLIDAYS AND JETSAVE
Resort representatives are responsible for the smooth running of the resort and have a great deal of client contact.
Ideally possessing a customer service background and sales skills, applicants need to be friendly, outgoing, self-motivated, show initiative and have good communication skills.
In many resorts the resort representatives provide a ski and snowboard escorting service (N.B. we do not employ ski guides).
A minimum of 12 weeks skiing or snowboarding experience is required, with confidence on all types of terrain.
Resort representatives based in Europe are required to speak a second language (French, German, Italian or Spanish) to a good conversational standard and this will be tested at interview.

www.shgjobs.co.uk

Produce a flyer for recruitment purposes that describes in detail the role and responsibilities of the ski-resort representative job illustrated above. Present the information in a way which is appealing for potential applicants.

This task could provide evidence towards P1.

Resort managers

It is important that you realise that there is a career structure within holiday representation, especially in busy resorts. There is likely to be a resort office supported by administration and financial staff and a management structure. Experienced reps may be promoted to supervisory roles and eventually to resort manager.

The responsibilities of the resort manager are to:

* manage sales, operations and customer service
* represent the company to customers
* monitor, train and develop the team of reps
* to deliver excellent customer service.

Key concept

Finding out about holiday representative jobs – there are careers sections and links to jobs on all the major tour operator websites. Just search for the name of the tour operator that interests you. Tui (Thomson) has a dedicated jobs website for all its brands at www.shgjobs.co.uk

Transfer representatives

Role

Transfer representatives meet and greet holidaymakers at the airport and take them by coach to their hotel. If passengers are travelling by taxi or hire car they are welcomed and sent on their way. The job of the transfer representative is possibly the least appealing of the rep jobs as the hours are long and there is little variation in the work. You might be interested in this work if you really like a challenge because transfer representatives face all the problems and angry customers caused by delayed aircraft. Property representatives often take turns to do airport duty to share the load.

Responsibilities

The responsibilities of a transfer representative include:

* meeting and greeting guests arriving at the airport
* checking arrivals against manifest
* directing guests to coaches or taxis
* accompanying guests on the coach
* giving welcome speech and commentary
* checking guests into hotel
* collecting guests from hotel at the end of their stay
* accompanying guests to the airport
* directing guests to check-in
* staying at check-in until all guests are checked in.

Some ski operators such as Crystal and Thomson offer a more unusual form of transfer representative job. This is the job of ski-train representative. The job involves working weekends and accompanying customers on the ski train from the UK to France. The reps have to welcome customers as they check in for the train and show them to their seats or beds. If necessary they issue tickets and deal with paperwork. They sort out any problems and maintain a high level of customer service. They also have to speak French.

Children's representatives

A children's representative usually needs to hold an NNEB or NVQ Level 3 in Childcare and have some experience of working with children and a First Aid certificate. This is important to note as for most holiday representative jobs there are no specific qualifications required, although a good standard of education equivalent to 5 GCSEs is likely to be asked for. The age criterion for children's reps is generally lower at 19 years old.

Duties involve looking after groups of children for several hours a day and organising activities for them. There is usually different provision made for different age groups. The extract from Canvas Holidays website shows that they have four different levels of free club activity, a good selling point for families. At Canvas the children's couriers are expected to help with other duties if needed. Also Canvas do not ask for a specific childcare qualification but do require formal experience of working with children.

Free clubs for all

Keeping your children happy is part of the Canvas recipe for a successful and relaxing holiday.

Our children's clubs are a great way for them to have fun and make new friends. We provide a range of activities to satisfy even the most creative minds and energetic bodies. Admission to all the clubs is free and exclusive to Canvas holidaymakers.

Toddler Club – A play centre with activity sessions for the under 4s.

Hoopi's Club – A fun-filled and imaginative programme for 4 to 11 year olds.

Buzz Club – An all-action social club for 12 to 17 year olds.

Wild & Active Club – Especially for nature lovers. A mixture of environmental games for children plus activities for the whole family.

Time for you to relax.

Source: www.canvasholidays.co.uk

Assessment activity 13.2

The following extract has been taken from Canvas Holidays children's courier job description:

Job title: Children's courier
Reports to: Area Manager, Site Manager, Site Supervisor, Senior Courier
Liaises with: Camp Proprietors, Operations Department, Warehouse Personnel

General function:

To ensure that every aspect of our customers' holiday is of as high a standard as possible by participating in montage & demontage and, in the role of Children's Courier, by being fully committed to providing excellent Customer Service through the regular organisation and supervision of safe and fun children's activities on site. This will be measured through feedback from Customer Questionnaires and Area Managers.

Duties and responsibilities

- Participate in montage and demontage as and when required, ensuring compliance with Health and Safety guidelines and in accordance with laid down procedures and standards.

- Assist the Campsite Courier, as per duties and responsibilities laid out in Campsite Courier job description as and when required.

- Organise and supervise a regular programme of events for children, aged 4–ll years, 5 hours per day, 6 days per week, ensuring that the programme is advertised in a way so that Canvas customers are kept aware of the programme of events and timings.

- Ensure the safety of all children whilst attending Hoopi Club.

- Encourage participation of all Canvas Holidays' customers' children, regardless of nationality, to be achieved by the use of all available resources such as noticeboards, flyers, Welcome Sheets and daily customer visits.

- Maintain staff accommodation unit and the unit/equipment supplied specifically for the children's Hoopi Club, ensuring hygienic and safe living and play conditions for themselves and their clients.

Source: www.canvasholidays.co.uk

Produce a flyer for Canvas Holidays for recruitment purposes which describes in detail the roles and responsibilities of children's couriers. Present the information in a way that is appealing to potential applicants.

This task could provide evidence towards P1.

Compare and contrast the role and responsibilities of the Canvas children's courier with those of the ski-resort representative you studied earlier. You can produce this comparison as a separate flyer.

This task could provide evidence for M1.

Analyse the contribution that the children's representative can make to enhance the customer's holiday experience and the potential effects of failure to provide an appropriate level of service. Present this as an information sheet to give to Canvas's recruitment manager.

This task could provide evidence for D1.

Tourist guides

Tourist guides may be employed by the tour operator or may be self-employed and contracted as needed.

Role

Their role is to accompany tourists on excursions and provide information and interpretation about monuments, sites of interest and landmarks in the destination. They should be able to deliver their tour in the tourist's own language. They may accompany large parties or small groups or individuals. Professional tourist guides will hold a qualification. This differs according to the country of residence but in the UK tourist guides hold the 'Blue Badge' qualification which takes about 18 months to study for.

Key concept

Blue Badge – the Blue Badge is the British national standard guiding qualification and internationally recognised bench mark of excellence.

Responsibilities

A tourist guide's responsibilities include the following:

* meeting guests and welcoming to the tour
* accompanying guests on tour either on foot or with agreed transport
* carrying out guided tours according to an agreed itinerary
* giving a commentary on the points of interest
* answering questions
* working to a professional standard
* representing the tour operator.

Resort representatives are often expected to accompany tours as part of their duties. In this case, they have to learn all the history and information relating to the tour. They may hand over to a qualified guide when reaching a destination such as a visitor attraction. Some tour operators prefer to employ qualified guides who can give detailed information on the tour and are easily able to respond to questions.

On some trips it may be necessary for health and safety reasons to employ a fully qualified tourist guide, for example if you were trekking through a rain forest you would probably prefer to have a local guide rather than the British rep!

Legal responsibilities and health and safety

Legal responsibilities

Early in 2004, holiday firms were told by the Office of Fair Trading (OFT) to offer consumers a fairer deal. New guidance was issued on unfair terms in package holiday contracts.

Denying liability after a short period of time or unfairly limiting compensation when a holiday goes wrong are amongst the acts deemed unfair. The guidance came about because of numerous tour operators having contravened the Unfair Terms in Consumer Contracts Regulations and the Package Travel Regulations.

UK Package Travel Regulations 1992

As far as the holiday representative is concerned their most important legal responsibilities are covered by the UK Package Travel Regulations of 1992.

Regulation 15 covers unsatisfactory holiday arrangements.

Regulation 15 imposes a strict fault-based liability on the tour operator for the proper performance of the obligations under the contract by their third-party suppliers. This means that the tour operator is responsible for anything that goes wrong in the hotel or other accommodation and during transfer and has to compensate the customer for any faults. The holiday representative has responsibility for carrying out health and safety checks in properties and reporting any faults.

Regulation 14 covers alternative accommodation arrangements.

Regulation 14 states that if after departure a significant proportion of services contracted for is not provided, the organiser will make suitable alternative arrangements, at no extra cost to the consumer, for the continuation of the package and will, where appropriate, compensate the consumer.

For the holiday representative this means that in the case of overbooking or accommodation being unavailable, they must offer the customer alternative accommodation of at least the same standard.

There are requirements under the Package Travel regulations for the customer also. If a customer has a complaint they should report it in resort so that the rep has an opportunity to resolve it. If they need to write to the tour operator to complain, this should be done within a reasonable period (usually 28 days).

Supply of Goods and Services Act 1982

The Supply of Goods and Services Act 1982 (amended 1994) says that the tour operator must ensure that the contract for the holiday should be carried out using 'reasonable skill and care'. Also the holiday should comply with any descriptions and be of a satisfactory standard. Some holidaymakers take their holiday brochure with them. This means they can easily check whether the holiday has been described accurately. The operator may also have committed a criminal offence under the Trade Descriptions Act of 1968 if there is a misdescription.

Trade Descriptions Act 1968 and 1972

The purpose of this Act is to control the accuracy of statements made by business about goods and services. It is an offence to apply a false trade description to goods, or to supply goods to which a false trade description is applied. The Act also applies to services like holidays but is difficult to prove as the false statement must have been made 'knowingly' or 'recklessly'.

Booking conditions

Booking conditions are laid out in the brochure or provided to the customer before departure. They are based on the requirements of the Package Travel Regulations but written in plain English so that they are easily understood.

The booking conditions are fairly lengthy and will run to two or more pages. The extracts here, from the Thomson Al Fresco brochure, illustrate the refund and compensation arrangements if booked accommodation is unavailable.

> ### Changes to your holiday arrangements on arrival
>
> On rare occasions the accommodation we have reserved for you may not be available on your arrival due to circumstances beyond our control, and we may not have been notified in time to advise you before your departure. If this occurs we will endeavour to provide accommodation of equivalent standard in the same location or region. If we are unable to do so and the only available accommodation is of a lower standard we will refund the difference in price together with a compensation payment per booking as described in paragraph 3 above. If during your holiday it is necessary for us to make any amendments to your return transport, we will make the best suitable alternative arrangements and advise you as soon as we are in a position to do so.
>
> Source: Thomson Al Fresco Summer brochure 2005

The representative would ensure that these conditions were met and set in motion the paperwork to arrange compensation.

The second extract illustrates how Thomson accepts their liability for the facilities and services of their suppliers being below acceptable local standards. Again this relates to their responsibility under the Package Travel Regulations.

> ### Our liability to you
>
> As all our suppliers comply fully with relevant local and national laws, we accept responsibility for the proven acts and omissions of our employees, sub-contractors and local agents when acting in accordance with their duties to us. Although we do not control the day-to-day operation of our suppliers, we accept responsibility if it is proven or accepted that facilities or services which form part of the holiday and which we contract to provide are deficient or below acceptable local standards. However, please bear in mind that in some countries local standards will not be the same as in the UK, and it is not always within our control to impose our own standards.
>
> Source: Thomson Al Fresco Summer brochure 2005

Domestic and European drivers' hours

Regulations regarding driving hours are very strict and apply across Europe. Drivers of vehicles with 18 or more seats on national journeys, or 10 or more on international journeys, are subject to European Union Drivers Hours legislation and must record their hours on a tachograph. There are some exemptions to these rules, for example, for journeys under 50 kilometres. However, these drivers are still covered by UK legislation, for example, the Transport Act of 1968.

> **Key concept**
>
> **Tachograph** – this is an instrument that measures when a vehicle is stationary and when it is moving. It also measures speed and distance travelled. It is used to ensure that drivers comply with the law and its records can be demanded by police at any time.

The regulations state that a driver is entitled to a 45 minute break after four and a half hours of driving or 15 minute breaks totalling to at least 45 minutes during a four and a half hour period.

There is a maximum of 9 hours actual driving per day, this can be increased to 10 hours twice a week. A rest period between working days is normally 11 hours but there are variations on this allowing split rest periods. The rules are complicated and can be found in full at www.coach-tours.co.uk. As far as the holiday representative is concerned, they need not know the rules in detail but should have them available for reference should they need them. The rep must be aware that excursions must be planned incorporating the required driver rest periods and also that delays might take a driver over hours.

Health and safety

A direct responsibility is placed on tour operators for the safety of their customers under the Package Travel Regulations. Tour operators are legally responsible for the components of the package – transfers, hotels etc., if negligence is proved. As the holiday representatives are in the resort they are in a position to carry out regular health and safety checks on behalf of the tour operator. Before a property is contracted the tour operator will carry out a full survey of health and safety and make recommendations to the hotel management about any changes to be made. The tour operator must make sure that suppliers make adequate health and safety provision as the tour operator is liable if something is wrong, not the supplier.

These are some of the things the reps might check:

* fire safety – for example campsite couriers would walk round and see that campers do not have candles lit inside their tents and properly reps would check that fire doors are not blocked and that notices are in place

* swimming pools should have notices with depths marked

* balconies must have sufficiently high railings

* hygiene in accommodation and restaurants should be of a high standard

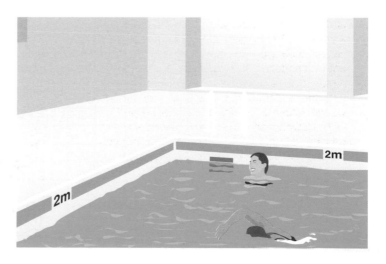

* food safety
* pool safety
* general safety
* beach safety
* legionella management
* children's clubs
* incident management.

The FTO also provides a safety-training video and courses on health and safety.

Documentation

Holiday representatives have to deal with quite a lot of paperwork to make sure they help the tour operator comply with the legal requirements. This is in addition to paperwork for excursions and sales. In training, the reps are shown how to complete all the forms.

Health and safety

Health and safety check forms are issued and if defects are found these must be reported. An example of a defect form is given here.

* gas and electricity should be provided safely
* safety features on coaches should be checked and pointed out to passengers
* appropriate flags for sea bathing should be displayed.

The Federation of Tour Operators (FTO) has devised a code of practice which gives advice on health and safety matters including:

* fire safety

Health and Safety Defect Report

Property _____ Company _____ Area _____

List other participating companies: _____ Date _____

The summary below should be completed at properties where any health and safety issues have been highlighted on the health and safety audit.

DEFECT DESCRIPTION	REPORTED TO	DATE	ACTION TO BE TAKEN	TARGET DATE	ACTION TAKEN	DATE
Management Effectiveness						

I confirm that a representative of Fabulous Holidays has reported the defects, detailed above, to me.

COMPLETED BY _____ SIGNED _____

Make up your own health and safety defect form and carry out a health and safety check of an area of your school or college.

Risk assessments

Holiday representatives will sometimes have to carry out risk assessments, for example a children's representative often takes children on

outings and they must make sure that the new environment is safe. Below is an example of a form that's used for wildlife activities.

Theory into practice

Imagine you are taking a group of children on an outing in your locality. Design a form similar to the example and carry out a risk assessment on the area to be visited. Discuss your findings with your group.

WILDLIFE ACTIVITY RISK ASSESSMENT

Activity name	Activity on/off site (delete as applicable)
Assessed by	Distance of walk
Date of Assessment	Recommended age group

For off-site walks please write a description of the intended route:

Please note:

- ✓ All supervised walks must use public and not private land/footpaths
- ✓ Children must be accompanied by parent/guardian on all off site activities
- ✓ Activities just for children are always based on the property
- ✓ Before taking a group off site inform your fellow couriers of your route

Don't forget:

- ✓ Phone numbers of nearest emergency services
- ✓ Office phone number
- ✓ Your consent forms

For the activity you intend to carry out please consider and identify any hazards and what safety measures you will take. Prior to the activity check out the route/venue. Using the form, mark the hazards you see. Write down whether the risk is LOW, MEDIUM or HIGH and note what safety measures you will take. Fill in any additional hazards. Remember, these may relate to the environment, people, nature of activity and any tools or equipment

HAZARD Here are some hazards you may find/look for others	RISK Low, medium or high	SAFETY MEASURE What can I do to reduce the risk
Mud and debris		
Uneven/holes in ground		
Steep slopes		
Fallen trees		
Litter		
Stinging/prickly plants		
Poisonous plant or fungi		
Water		
Wild animals		
Stinging/biting insects		
Adverse weather		
Possible diseases		
Medical conditions		
Clothing of participants		

Other risks:

Accident reports

If an accident occurs then the representative will fill in an accident report. Here is an example. Note that it includes guidelines for completion.

Consider this...

It is very important to have records of accidents as there may be insurance claims later.

REPORT OF AN ACCIDENT OR DANGEROUS OCCURRENCE

Notes on how to use this form are included at the end of this form

A. **Person making the report**   Property _____

Name _____

Your role on the property _____

B. **Date, time and place at which the accident took place. It is important that you be as precise as possible in completing this section.**

Date of Accident _____ Time _____

Address where the accident took place: _____

Specific location where the accident took place: _____

Was a photograph of the location taken: **YES/NO**

Normal activity carried out at this place: _____

Why was the injured person there at the time? _____

C. **The injured person**

Name _____ Ref No. _____ Pitch No _____

Address _____

Nature of injury or conditon and part of the body affected: _____

D. **Witnesses**

Name _____   Name _____

Address _____   Address _____

E. **Describe the event and how it happened. Please refer to the note below. Draw a sketch if appropriate.**

_____

_____

_____

_____

_____

_____

_____

_____

NOTES ON HOW TO COMPLETE THIS FORM
1. Please be as clear and precise as possible when completing this form.
2. In section E, you are asked to state only the facts relating to the incident, not opinions as to who is at fault. Details you must include are: what happened; information relating to any police involvement in the matter; and action taken by yourself or any other person involved in this matter. You should also include a sketch of what happened, in the space provided on this form.
3. Fax one copy **immediately** to the Operations Department and one copy to your Area Manager.

Theory into practice

Design your own form or copy the one shown on page 72 and fill in an accident report for the following accident:

You are a representative in Fuengirola in Spain. You happen to be visiting a hotel when an accident occurs and you are called to the scene. A child has slipped while running near the pool and fallen into the water. The child was rescued from the water by Jo, the lifeguard, and seemed to have a slight concussion and a broken leg. The lifeguards called the ambulance and the child went to hospital escorted by her parents.

Customer service reports

The holiday representative will also have to complete forms if there are customer complaints and if any compensation is given. Customers and representatives will both sign these forms. An example of a customer complaint form is given later in this unit.

Communication techniques

It is essential that holiday representatives are good communicators. That is their role, they are with customers for most of the time and must be able to speak and listen effectively to give good service. You have studied customer service as part of your BTEC programme and so you are already very aware of how to use effective communication skills. In this unit we are going to discuss how those skills apply to the role of the holiday representative and practise some of them.

Assessment activity 13.3

Helena is a holiday representative on Majorca. Her company is a major tour operator and employs over 200 representatives on the island. There are four managers covering the areas north, east, south and south west. In addition, there are several team leaders. Helena is what is known as a 'prestige' representative. This means she takes care of 'prestige' clients, that is, those in high quality, expensive accommodation. She has 10 or 11 properties to look after. Her contract is a renewable six-month contract. She lives in the middle of the island and is provided with a car and a mobile telephone. She gets one day off a week but is on call continually in order to provide a constant service to her discerning and demanding customers.

Apart from her day off, she holds a welcome meeting every day and visits customers at their properties by appointment. She is expected to sell excursions but these are guided by professionals apart from evening excursions. Helena must accompany two of these a week. Twice a week she is on airport duty, one of these shifts is at night from 10pm until 1am unless flights are delayed in which case the shift is as long as is necessary.

Helena undertook training in the UK followed by a further 10-days' training on Majorca. Much of the training related to health and safety and legal issues. Part of Helena's role is to carry out health and safety checks once a month on each property. She checks things like balconies, fire safety, gas and electricity supplies and pool safety. These reports are logged and sent to head office.

If a customer complains she completes a complaint form and this is copied to head office. One of the main problems Helena faces is overbooking where hoteliers have overbooked rooms. She is allowed to put guests in superior accommodation for the first night of their holiday until she has time to sort out the problem. She is also allowed to give guests compensation for complaints, such as free car hire or a free excursion.

1 Explain in general terms Helena's legal responsibilities.

2 Explain why health and safety checks are an important part of her job.

3 What is the point of giving customers superior accommodation or other compensation in cases of overbooking or other complaint? These tasks may provide evidence for P2.

4 Compare Helena's legal responsibilities with those of a children's rep. How do their legal responsibilities affect their role? This task may provide evidence for M2.

Verbal communication

This may be formal or informal. If you are presenting a welcome talk or a speech on a tour, you will be communicating formally. When you are chatting with colleagues or customers you will use informal communication.

Communicating with different types of customers

For some holiday representatives there may be few occasions where formal communication is needed. If you were an 18–30 type holiday rep the emphasis would be on informality with customers. However, if a complaint or difficult situation arose the representative might have to adopt formal communication to underline the seriousness of a situation.

Children's representatives have to communicate with children and would not expect to use formal communication with them. They should be especially aware of the tone of their voice and ensure it is not too strident, which could be construed as angry by small children and thus frightening. It is important to speak clearly and in plain English. A courier is likely to have children of different nationalities in their group. They might not understand English so the courier has to be quite innovative and imaginative to help them understand, using tone of voice and body language.

Voice level

If you are talking to a group of people you will need to use a microphone or project your voice. On a coach a representative would expect to use a microphone. At a welcome meeting it is likely that you would have to project your voice to be heard. Both need practice and a representative's training will include this. You should always begin by making sure everyone can hear you.

Listening

When you are communicating with an individual you should make sure you are listening as well as talking. Show that you are listening by using the active listening techniques you have learnt about. If you don't listen you will not understand what the customer needs.

Active listening – this is the process of demonstrating to the candidate both verbally and non-verbally that the information is being received. It is done by maintaining eye contact, nodding and agreeing in appropriate places.

Communicating with suppliers

Examples of suppliers to the holiday representative are hotel employees, airport workers, drivers and tourist guides. They should be treated with courtesy and consideration at all times. Sometimes the representative will be communicating with the supplier by telephone and should remember the supplier might not speak English.

Elizabeth had to speak to suppliers every day as part of her job as a chalet host.

'I had to order food for the chalet from our local suppliers. I had to do this every day so the food was fresh and I had to do it by telephone – in French. Well, it was good practice. It was much more difficult to understand people when I couldn't see them. There were no non-verbal clues that you normally have. My list of food would be in English so before I picked up the telephone I made sure that I had looked all the words up I didn't know and written down the French. After a few days I knew the name and voice of who I should speak to so that made it easier. I always started with "This is Elizabeth from Chalet Juliette" so they knew who I was. After we got the wrong quantities a couple of times I asked them to repeat the order to me at the end so I could check it.'

Good techniques for telephone communication – even in English!

* Prepare what you want to say – write it down if you need to

* Introduce yourself

* Make sure you are speaking to the person who can help you

* Speak clearly

* Speak slowly

* Listen

* Don't forget to smile.

Non-verbal communication

It's not what you say, it's the way that you say it. Our body language gives a lot away. Holiday representatives have to assume that they are always on view. Even if it's a day off at the beach there may be customers around so they have to think about the image that is being presented. On a property visit even before they meet the customers, they should be walking tall and looking ready for business. In presentations on the coach or at the welcome meeting all eyes are on the representative so it is important to give off the right signals. Remember the following body language points:

* head held high

* good posture

* no hands in pockets

* no fiddling with jewellery or hair

* make eye contact

* smile.

Next time you are in class look around you and note the body language of the group. Can you tell what they are feeling? What about the tutor? What about you?

Written communication

Completing forms, writing reports and putting information together are all part of the holiday representative's job.

Notice boards

The notice board is an important means of communicating with the customer. It is situated in a central location such as the reception area of their hotel or apartments. If a guest needs to find out how to contact the representative or remind themselves of the visiting times they should find the information on the notice board. The representative can use the notice board to give details of excursions and to advertise special events. Guests will also use the notice board to check details of their return transfer and flight, even though these details should also be communicated individually to each customer.

The presentation of the information on the board gives an impression of the representative and the company. If it is poorly presented with spelling mistakes and scraps of paper then the company does not look professional.

Some points to remember when presenting a notice board:

* word process information
* use a clear font
* use colour
* use headings
* make sure spellings are correct – any doubts, use a dictionary or check with someone reliable
* do the same with punctuation
* laminate posters and information sheets
* take down out-of-date information.

Departure details
Flight BL 2031

Please note for those people leaving on Monday 3rd February, the coach will be arriving at the hotel to pick you up at 9.20.

Please leave your cases at the reception desk ready for transfer by 9.00 that morning.

An example of a notice

Assessment activity 13.4

You are a holiday representative working in Ibiza in San Antonio for the summer season. It is your responsibility to set up and maintain the notice board in the Hotel Florida. Prepare the notice board making sure you include the following:

* a heading with the name of your company
* your photo and contact details
* visiting times
* emergency contact details
* departure details for guests for the next Tuesday
* a list of excursions and days
* a poster advertising a forthcoming 'flamenco' evening
* weather report.

This task could provide information towards P4.

Information books

This file of local information is prepared by the holiday representative at the beginning of the season. It is time consuming to produce but if it is done well it saves the representative work as the guests can find useful facts and information without having to contact their representative constantly. The file is kept in a reception area for easy reference.

A tour operator may have a set style of presentation for the file and will probably state what information should be in it. Here are some general guidelines for contents:

* representative details including contact numbers and visiting times
* any local regulations
* local transport
* beach distance and directions
* shopping information
* sunburn warnings
* medical contacts
* currency and exchange
* telephoning instructions
* excursion details
* potted history of the resort

* recommendations for restaurants
* departure details
* useful expressions in the local language.

A representative may not have to start from scratch to find this information. Previous representatives will have put together an information file. The Internet can be used to find the local tourism website. Guidebooks and the local tourist office are also sources of information. Representatives should get to know the resort and investigate restaurants and local haunts. It is a good idea for a holiday representative to do research before they go to their resort so that they are well prepared.

The same points for presentation apply as for the notice board.

Assessment activity 13.5

Remember that, as before, you are in San Antonio working as a holiday representative. Produce an information book suitable for guests of 18–30 staying in the Hotel Florida. Make sure you include everything listed above. Limit the number of excursion details to four trips.

This task could provide evidence towards P4.

Situations

We are going to consider some of the situations in more detail where a holiday representative has to use their communication skills and you will be able to practise your own skills.

The transfer
Preparation

* Rep gets a copy of the departures and arrivals for their accommodation.
* Checks the documentation and times of pick-ups at the hotel.
* Puts departure information on the notice board.
* Checks which transfers they are responsible for.

Arrivals

* Goes to arrivals and checks status of arriving aircraft.
* Checks coach numbers for return to resort.
* Greets arriving passengers, checks them off list and directs them to coach.
* Makes their way to assigned coach.
* Checks the right people are on the coach.
* Gives welcome and information commentary during transfer.
* Checks everyone into their accommodation.
* Says goodbye to the driver and finishes.

Consider this...
What information do guests want or need to know when they are on the coach after arrival?

The transfer commentary
* The representative introduces him or herself and the driver.
* Extends a warm welcome from the representative and from the company.
* Gives the local time, route and how long it will take.

* Explains safety features of coach.
* Gives out welcome packs.
* Gives some local information.
* Provides information about weather conditions, changing money, drinking water, sunburn.
* Gives information about checking in at the hotel.

Departures

* Arrives at the first pick-up point in good time and in correct uniform.
* Meets the driver and checks the coach is clean and tidy.
* Gets off at each pick up and goes to reception to greet and check off departing guests.
* Introduces him or herself.
* Checks passengers have paid bills, returned keys etc.
* At the last pick up does a head count as an extra check.
* Gives information about how to check in and flight details.
* At the airport thanks the passengers for holidaying with the company and goes to find out where the check-in desk is.
* Informs passengers of location of check-in desk and makes sure passengers take all their belongings.
* Stays at check-in looking after any problems until everyone is through.

Hotel reception

CASE STUDY

Sophie's transfer

Sophie has been working in Ibiza until very recently but has just moved to Marbella to work as a transfer representative. This is the transfer commentary she gave on the way from Malaga airport to accompany guests on their way to Marbella. The guests are all staying in 4 and 5-star properties.

'Hello everyone I'm Sophie and this is your driver,' (talks to driver to ask his name) 'and this is your driver Jaime.

'Has anyone been to Marbella before? Come on shout out if you've been before!

'Welcome to the Costa del Sol on behalf of The Luxury Holidays Company.

'It's 5 am here so set your watches. We'll be in Marbella in about 40 minutes so you've got time for a bit of shut-eye if you're tired after your journey.

'There is an emergency exit at the back of the coach and one at the front and there are safety belts on the seats. Please use them.

'I'm going to come around with your welcome packs now.' (Sophie distributes the welcome packs which are personalised – she gets to a young couple half way down.) 'I don't seem to have one for you – are you on the right coach?' (They reply that a rep directed them to this coach and Sophie soon realises they are on the wrong coach). 'I'm going to put you in a taxi to your hotel at the first stop. I am sorry – she was a silly cow wasn't she?'

(Back at the front) 'OK everyone just a few bits of information about life on Ibiza – great fun, loads of clubs, do put the sun lotion on, it gets very hot. Don't drink the water, stick to vodka' (laughing).

'What about a bit of a sing song before we get there?'

1. **Comment on Sophie's commentary and say how you would change it.**
2. **Role play the scene and show the right way and the wrong way of doing the commentary.**

Welcome meeting

The welcome meeting normally takes place the morning after the guests arrive. They will then have recovered from their journey and be eager to learn about their new surroundings. The meeting will take place in a hotel lounge or bar and complimentary drinks are usually served, depending on the time of day.

It is important to be well prepared for the meeting. The representative should do the following:

* be there in good time in correct uniform

* make sure the room has a suitable layout with enough chairs

* ensure drinks are ready

* have cue cards and visuals ready

* have any documentation ready

* know which guests to expect.

The following points should be covered in the meeting:

* the representative introduces herself, welcomes the guests and makes sure she knows their names

* refreshments are served

* asks if everyone has settled in

* information sheets on excursions are distributed

* information given on hotel facilities, e.g. changing money, swimming pool, restaurant times, safes

* local information given e.g. on transport, beaches, restaurants, shopping, telephoning and medical information

* guests are told about location of notice board, information file and representative's visiting times and contact details

* explanation and selling of the programme of excursions

* bookings for interested parties

* thanks and farewell

* individual questions answered.

Selling the excursions

This is a difficult skill at first. The holiday representative has to sell the excursions in order to earn commission and fill up the tours. However, the guests do not want to sit all day listening to detailed talks about tours. A meeting which is too long is counter productive and it should be limited to 30–45 minutes. The best way to sell the excursions is to present guests with a leaflet with full details of excursions so that they can refer to it later. The representative should give a brief outline of the various excursions, in an enthusiastic and interested manner. The rep might point out those tours which sell out quickly and need to be booked early. This is a good closing technique. Having done this the representative should allow guests to leave the meeting and invite to stay those who want to book excursions immediately or get more information.

Assessment activity 13.6

Prepare and carry out a welcome meeting for a resort of your choice. You can use San Antonio again if you choose. One or more of your group should carry out a critical evaluation of your meeting. Swap roles and repeat the exercise.

Tour guiding

The holiday representative often has to act as a tour guide. This can be a nerve wracking experience. Not only does the rep need to look after the guests as in the transfer situation but they also need to provide interesting and relevant information about the places being visited. The key to success in this situation is to carry out thorough research into the places being visited so that the information can be presented with confidence. Good research enables the representative to answer questions.

The following points will help you if you are acting as a tour guide:

* comprehensive research

* keep a guidebook to hand in case of difficulty

* practise your microphone technique

* present the information at the appropriate time (not two minutes after you passed a site of interest)

* keep the information clear and concise

* don't make things up

* if you don't know the answer to a question, say so and find out later

* have some little stories about the area ready in case you get stuck in a traffic jam

* don't forget practical issues – when people get off for a break make sure they know what time to come back and where to find the coach, make sure they take all their belongings

* point out the safety and comfort features on the coach and be aware of customers with special needs.

Consider this...

Are there any trips arranged for students in your college or school? Why don't you ask if you can guide the trip? It's a great opportunity to practise and may provide you with some assessment evidence.

Assessment activity 13.7

This is an opportunity to practise your tour guide skills. You have been called in to replace a Blue Badge guide on a London tour. The map below shows the various tour routes (you may also like to look at the map on the website: www.theoriginaltour.co.uk).

1 Study the map of London showing the tour routes. Choose a section of the route which includes 5 major attractions which you will describe from your coach. Research and prepare a commentary including information about your chosen attractions.

2 Role play the tour with your colleagues acting as passengers. They should be informed about the tour route so that they can prepare questions for the tour guide.

3 You stop for a photo opportunity by the Thames. Make sure the whole group knows exactly how long they have before they get back on the coach.

4 One of your passengers is deaf and cannot hear your commentary. How would you make sure they get as much enjoyment as possible from the tour?

5 A protest is taking place and holding up your tour. It seems to be about animal rights and although peaceful the protesters are in the way. How will you occupy the tour party until the protesters move on?

6 It's the end of the tour. Thank the party and bring the tour to a close.

These tasks could provide evidence for P3 and P5.

Effective and professional performance could provide evidence for M3 and D2.

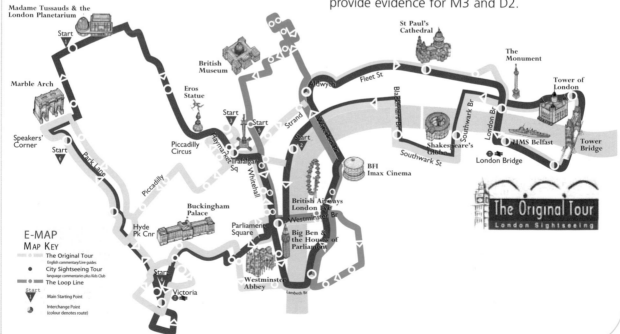

Social and customer service skills

Good social skills, customer service skills and personal presentation together add up to a high calibre of service and professional image for a holiday representative.

Personal presentation

Holiday representatives are the face of the company and the way they present themselves reflects the company image. The tour operator will provide a uniform for their representatives and this should be worn during working hours. It should be worn with appropriate accessories and should be clean and ironed. Even if the uniform is informal, for example shorts and a T-shirt, these guidelines still apply.

Personal presentation is not just about what is worn. It is also about grooming and bearing. Being well groomed means always being clean and fresh smelling. This seems obvious but is more difficult to maintain in hot climates and in stressful situations. Nails should be clean and unbitten. If varnish is worn it should not be chipped. Hair should be neat and clean. Long hair should be tied back for work.

Bearing is about the way people hold themselves. It is about presenting positive body language and showing confidence (even when a situation is difficult). Holiday representatives have to learn to present a calm and controlled bearing even if things are going wrong.

The holiday representative should show respect for their customers, colleagues and their company and never speak in a denigrating way about any of them – unlike Sophie whom you met earlier!

It is also important that the holiday representative treats everyone equally regardless of their accent, race, religion, age or gender. The holiday representative can be a role model for young people on holiday who have ambitions to be a representative in the future.

Social skills

You know if someone has good social skills. They have a knack of making everyone feel at ease in their presence and give out a warmth that makes other people feel important. It is true to say that some people do this naturally – it's their personality – but we can all learn to do it. Those who have poor social skills are often concerned about what people are thinking of them and feeling shy. This fear prevents them from opening up and talking to others. If you haven't got good social skills, you won't be a good representative.

What can be done to improve social skills?

* Don't worry about what people think about you.
* Concentrate on making others feel comfortable.
* Smile at people.
* Ask people their name, remember it and use it.
* Listen positively to others.
* Use appropriate language.
* Ask people questions about themselves.

Lifeguards in uniform

Customer service skills

Social skills and customer service skills are both needed to provide memorable service but it is possible to have one without the other. For example, a holiday representative can be charming and make us feel very welcome but if they don't do anything about our problem, they haven't fulfilled their customer service role.

On the other hand a representative might provide a new room immediately when a guest is unhappy with the first one, but if they are surly and off hand then the guest will be left feeling uncomfortable about complaining.

The customer service situations that a holiday rep will have to deal with include:

* providing information

* dealing with queries

* handling complaints

* dealing with customers with special needs

* dealing with non-routine incidents like crime or illness.

You have already studied the types of information a rep routinely supplies by preparing an information file and a welcome meeting. When you deal with queries you might be asked for non-routine information that you have to go and find out about or you may be given a request for something out of the ordinary.

Handling complaints

People on holiday are likely to complain if facilities do not match up to their expectations or if something goes wrong. Remember that reps are expected to solve as many complaints as they can in the resort so that the customer is satisfied and does not pursue the complaint once they get home. Companies do work hard to minimise complaints but there is no doubt that every rep will be on the receiving end of many complaints whoever they work for, particularly if the weather is poor. ABTA say they receive over 18,000 holiday complaints per year – in theory these are the complaints that were not resolved by tour operators and customers went to ABTA. However, some customers may go straight to ABTA without writing to their tour operator, as the organisation is so well known. Tour operators keep records and statistics on complaints but these are not in the public domain.

Customers are told in booking conditions that they should report complaints to their rep and then the rep has an opportunity to resolve the complaint. The following extract from the Thomson Alfresco brochure demonstrates this point.

The complaint, if handled well, is an opportunity to give excellent customer service and turn the complainant into a very happy, loyal customer.

* The rep should listen to the complaint, remembering active listening techniques.

* Complaints should not be taken personally, they are usually not about the reps themselves but about situations.

* The complaint should be summarised and reiterated to the customer to make sure it is understood properly by the rep.

* The rep should empathise with the customer's situation without admitting any liability for the complaint.

* The customer should be told what the rep is going to do about their complaint and when.

* It is essential that the rep stays calm and professional.

* A solution should be agreed with the customer.

* Appropriate records should be made.

Common complaints

Here are some common complaints with possible solutions.

Complaints about the hotel

There could be a range of complaints about the hotel – about rooms, the pool or the restaurant food and service. All these complaints can be resolved by the hotel so the rep needs to establish a good relationship with the duty management and with the respective heads of housekeeping, restaurants etc. and report problems to the appropriate department. Reps should ensure that the customers are satisfied with the response to their complaint.

CASE STUDY

'I won't go into the exact details, all I will tell you is that the service was appalling and one of the restaurant "specials" was spam in gravy…enough said! Anyway…. after about 4 days of horrible food and service I complained to the rep in our resort. She was very helpful and said that she would sort things out with the restaurant manager. In spite of that, even though she tried, the restaurant situation still didn't improve. We then wrote out a customer complaints form (essential to do in resort if you intend on complaining when you get home – you need your rep's signature).'

1. **Could the rep have resolved this complaint so that it was not pursued on return to the UK? If so, how?**
2. **What would the rep do if she thought the customer's complaint was not valid?**

Complaints about travel

The most common of these is flight delay which is beyond the control of the reps. The best way to handle it is to apologise for the delays without admitting any liability on behalf of their company e.g. 'I am sorry your flight was delayed, you must be very tired.' Passengers should be kept fully informed of delays and the reasons for them. Reps can also ensure that passengers receive food and drinks according to entitlement under the Denied Boarding Regulations.

Other complaints might be about length of transfers. In this case, the rep should reassure passengers that the holiday will be worth the journey.

Key concept

Denied Boarding Compensation Regulations – these are new regulations in 2005 and offer compensation for cancellations, delays and overbooking by airlines.

Complaints about excursions

Again customers have different expectations. If everyone complains about an excursion, then it may be that it really was poor value or badly managed and in this case it might be appropriate to give a refund. If customers complain about too few stops then the rep can ask the driver to make more or explain politely that there isn't enough time.

Empowerment

Most tour operators allow their reps to give compensation in resort for complaints to allow them to resolve as many situations as possible. Monetary compensation is avoided but not forbidden. Reps should be allowed to make changes of accommodation where necessary and to offer free excursions or car hire as compensation for valid complaints.

HOTEL FACILITIES COMPLAINT FORM

- Please complete this form AS SOON AS POSSIBLE following a customer complaint regarding the facilities.
- It is essential you bring the matter to the attention of the hotel management with a note of any action to be taken.
- The hotel management must sign this form in acknowledgement of the complaint.

Property _____ Date _____

Brief Summary of Complaint _____

_____

_____

_____

_____

Customer Name: _____ Ref. No: _____

_____ _____

Reported to member of Hotel Management: _____

Action to be taken with agreed Timescale: _____

_____

_____

_____

_____

Signed on behalf of the Hotel: _____

Signed Staff Member: _____ Date: _____

Assessment activity 13.8

Role play the following situations ensuring you use appropriate social and customer service skills. Take it in turns with members of your group to play rep and customers. Your aim is to deal effectively with the situation and end up with satisfied customers.

1. You are working as a holiday representative in a ski resort, La Plagne, which is located in the Alps in France. You are holding your welcome meeting and it is going very well but you are aware of a couple whose body language indicates that they are unhappy about something. They are not smiling or showing any enthusiasm about anything you say. When you have finished talking about the excursions and invite questions, they begin to complain loudly about their chalet, in particular, the standard of cleanliness and the attitude of the chalet hosts. They say that their pillowcases were used and they found sweet wrappers under the bed. The rest of the group is listening with interest. What will you do?

2. You visit one of your assigned chalets in La Plagne to find that a member of the party has a leg in plaster. It seems he broke his leg and was airlifted off the mountain. It was day one of a seven-day holiday. He does not want to go home but he needs you to help him with his insurance and suggest things for him to do for the rest of the week. You must also complete an accident form (see page 72 for example). Deal with this situation.

3. Some of your guests stay in a hotel and you make a visit most days. You are unhappy to see Mrs Allan waiting for you on your arrival. She has already complained twice about the sauna in the hotel. She likes to have a sauna when she comes off the slopes and on three occasions in the last week it has not been working. You have reported it to hotel management twice but nothing has been done. Your task is to appease Mrs Allan and to fill in a complaint form (see page 84 for an example of a customer complaint form).

These tasks may provide evidence for P5 and P3 if appropriate communication, customer and social skills are used effectively.

A merit grade may be awarded where there is consistent use of effective skills.

A distinction grade may be awarded where learners consistently project a professional manner and where confident and positive communication skills are also consistently used.

Improving customer service skills

As with social skills there are ways of improving customer service skills:

* deal with questions immediately – don't put things off

* try to anticipate customers' needs before they ask

* do research so that essential information is at your fingertips

* if you don't know say so but also say you will find out straightaway and do so

* make sure you know how to deal with non-routine situations, for example, medical emergencies

* if you refer a situation to a colleague or supplier, still follow up and make sure the outcome was satisfactory.

Theory into practice

Hold a brainstorm session as a group. Use your experience and imagination and think of all the possible things that could go wrong with customers at the Hotel Florida in San Antonio. Make a group list and discuss how you would handle each problem.

1 Describe three different kinds of reps.

2 What does a tourist guide do?

3 Which piece of legislation is most important for a rep to know about?

4 Name two other Acts which reps should be aware of.

5 What kind of things are checked in a health and safety check?

6 Who is liable for negligence, the tour operator or the supplier?

7 What points relating to body language should a rep consider at a welcome meeting?

8 What information should be included on a notice board prepared by a rep?

9 What is the purpose of a welcome meeting?

10 Why is personal presentation important for reps?

11 What is meant by social skills?

12 What would happen if a rep gives poor customer service?

13 What forms of compensation might a rep give to a customer when they have had a valid complaint?

UNIT 13 ASSESSMENT ASSIGNMENT

Part 1

Travel News 21 September

No more reps?

Reps everywhere are wondering how safe their jobs are as tour operators search for more cost cutting measures. Is the service of a rep really essential? Aren't customers confident enough to look after themselves on holiday? After all many of them are managing to book holidays over the Internet without using a travel agent. Can't they book their own excursions and hire cars as well?

At the moment it's just accommodation-on-arrival deals that seem to be targeted with both Thomson and Cosmos suggesting they might do away with reps on these deals. But where will it end? Surely some customers choose well-known tour operators just because they offer excellent service through their reps. What about the legal aspects of the rep's job? Who is going to check health and safety in the resort? Some tour operators are arguing that late bookers tend to be less well off and have lower expectations than other customers – so they don't need reps – or they don't pay for them.

This article recently appeared in *Travel News*

You work as a holiday representative for a tour operator and your boss is horrified at the tone of the article. She has been asked to respond at a forthcoming Travel Market, a trade exhibition where she will be giving a presentation to members of the trade including tour operators. She needs to present the case for holiday representative services and you are to help her by preparing her notes. The notes can be in the form of cue cards with supporting notes or in the form of information sheets which she can then form cue cards from.

You are to cover:

- A detailed description of the role and responsibilities of a property representative and another type of representative.

- The representative's legal responsibilities and the legal responsibilities in relation to health and safety.

  This information provides evidence for P1 and P2.

- A comparison of the roles and responsibilities of the two representatives.

- An explanation of how their legal and health and safety responsibilities affect their roles.

  This information provides evidence for M1 and M2.

- Give arguments for the case that holiday representatives enhance the customer's holiday and the potential effects of the representative's failure to provide an appropriate level of service.

  This task provides evidence for D1.

Part 2

Your boss is so pleased with the work that you did for her for her presentation that she agrees to post you to your chosen resort for the summer season – Palma, Majorca!

You are expecting a very busy season and these are some of the duties you are faced with.

1 To prepare for the season you are to produce an information file on Majorca and Palma in particular. This will be left at the hotel reception for guests' reference.

2 Prepare a notice board with information for your guests.

3 A customer wishes to book an excursion by coach to the local market. It costs 10 euros per person and there are three people in the party. Complete the booking form.

   NB. Your tutor will provide the booking form.

   Tasks 1 and 2 and 3 provide evidence for P4. A Pass grade is awarded if appropriate communication techniques are used.

4 Part of your role is to collect guests from the airport and transfer them to their hotel. Prepare and carry out the transfer speech you will give on the coach.

5 Prepare and carry out a welcome meeting for your guests.

6 A guest at the welcome meeting asks you if there is a water park in Majorca. Respond to this enquiry.

   Tasks 4, 5 and 6 provide evidence for P3. A Pass grade is awarded if appropriate communication techniques are used.

   Task 6 can also provide evidence for P5 as long as appropriate social and customer service skills are used effectively.

7 A customer is unhappy with her accommodation. She says the room is not clean and is too small and she does not consider that it reaches the standard of a four-star hotel which it claims to be. The hotel is full. Decide what to say to this customer and deal with her.

8 The lifeguard has pulled a child, one of your customers, from the pool. The child is alive but almost blue. His mother is hysterical. You have been called from the lounge where you were meeting some other guests. Deal with the situation.

Tasks 7 and 8 provide evidence for P5. A Pass grade is awarded if social and customer service skills are used effectively.

NB: These situations should be role played.

A Merit grade for part two is awarded if the learner consistently deals effectively with a range of customers in different types of situations (M3).

A Distinction grade is awarded for part two if the learner consistently projects a professional company image in all communications with customers and shows confidence and a positive attitude when dealing with customers (D2).

UNIT 15

Incoming and domestic tourism

Introduction

Most of your studies have been concerned with outbound tourism from the UK. In this unit we will focus on incoming tourism and domestic tourism. The aim is to develop your knowledge of the UK tourism product and understand its importance to our economy.

You will identify the differing needs and expectations of incoming and domestic tourists. You will examine the popularity and appeal of the UK to incoming and domestic tourists and look at and interpret statistics and identify trends in the number and nature of visits. We will study the different organisations involved in incoming and domestic tourism and determine their roles in attracting tourists.

We are also going to investigate heritage tourism and its role in attracting incoming and domestic tourists, looking at specific examples and their themes and status. It is recommended that you visit heritage attractions if you have the opportunity.

You should already be familiar with the VisitBritain website. It is invaluable as a resource for this unit and it is recommended that you refer to it as you study this unit. You should also familiarise yourself with the government's national statistics website.

How you will be assessed

This unit is internally assessed by your tutor. A variety of exercises and activities is included in this chapter to help you develop your knowledge and understanding of incoming and domestic tourism and prepare for the assessment. You will also have the opportunity to work on some case studies.

After completing this unit you should be able to achieve the following outcomes:

→ differentiate between the needs of and expectations of incoming and domestic tourists

→ examine the popularity and appeal of the UK to both incoming and domestic tourists

→ examine the role played by different types of organisations involved in incoming and domestic tourism

→ investigate heritage tourism within the UK.

Needs and expectations

Definitions

Domestic tourism

You will note in the tourism definition that people are only tourists if they stay in a place outside their usual environment. This means that people on day trips are not officially tourists and statistics count those who have at least a one-night stay. These domestic tourists spent over £26.4 billion in 2003.

However, day-trippers spend money in the tourism sector and boost the economy so it is important to measure the value of their spending. This is measured in the UK Day Visits Survey. Tourism visits are defined as trips which last three hours or more and which are not taken on a regular basis. These day visitors spent almost £30 billion in 2003, even more than those on overnight stays, so you can see why this must be taken note of.

Incoming tourism

Overseas visitors or incoming tourists to the UK spent about £11.9 billion in 2003.

Tourism is an invisible export. This means if tourists spend their money in the UK it brings the same benefit to our economy as if they buy goods exported from the UK in their own country. By the same token when we travel abroad we spend our money in another country and this equates to buying imported goods in the UK. The government would prefer us to spend our money in our own country and take our holidays here rather than go abroad, so the government promotes domestic tourism. It also wishes to encourage more overseas visitors to come to the UK. It attracts these tourists through various organisations which you will study later in this unit.

Balance of payments

The impact on the economy of incoming and outbound tourism is recorded in the balance of payments. Each sector of the economy is measured in terms of its imports and exports. A happy situation for our economy is where there is a surplus in the balance of payments rather than a deficit, that is more money coming in than going out. Unfortunately the travel services balance shows a deficit (£15.8 billion in 2003) and has done for some years as the graph opposite shows.

This is because so many of us choose to go abroad for our holidays and not enough people are coming to the UK to make up for the outbound travel. Transport has its own balance figure, separate from travel services.

Travel Services Balance

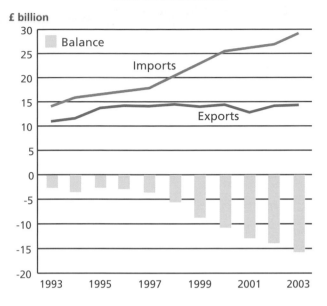

£ billion

Source: Office for National Statistics

Needs of the visitor

Food and drink

Tourists need access to a range of eating places, from cafes and bars to haute cuisine, whether they are domestic or incoming tourists. Domestic tourists are familiar with the cuisine in the UK and understand opening times and licensing laws.

These can cause confusion to foreign visitors who are surprised when the pub they are drinking in has a bell ringing at ten minutes to eleven and last orders called. These licensing laws are being reviewed and may come into line with the rest of Europe.

Tourists also need catering facilities to be available at transport hubs and on transport.

Transport

Tourists, like all of us, need a safe, efficient and clean transport system. Most domestic tourists travel by car (71% of day trips are taken by car according to the Day Visits Survey). The car traveller needs an adequate, uncongested road network and services at regular intervals en route.

In terms of public transport, domestic tourists are familiar with our systems and are more likely to get to grips with booking tickets on different forms of transport than overseas visitors. Overseas visitors are much more dependent on public transport than domestic tourists. Driving is not such a popular option as drivers have to contend with driving on the left and steering wheels on the right in hire cars. Transport systems which met the needs and expectations of incoming tourists, especially those coming from countries with excellent train services, would certainly meet the needs of domestic tourists.

Incoming tourists need:

* good public transport directly from airports to cities and towns – Heathrow and Gatwick are quite well served but some regional airports are not

* access by lift and escalator, space for luggage

* clear information about services – across transport systems

* the ability to buy tickets which can be used for through journeys across transport systems

* catering on route, for example, buffet cars on trains.

At the end of 2004, the Department of Transport launched a new website. The aim was to provide everything you need to know about getting round Britain in one place. It forms part of the government's integrated transport strategy. Travellers can enter in their departure point and their destination and get a breakdown of the journey by public transport with details of trains and buses, times and even walking times between connections. Information for air routes is also given. Details of the equivalent car journey can also be found for comparison. Some have already criticised the website saying it does not have complete information but it is still in its infancy. The website has a budget of £40 million allocated up to 2006.

Our example shows the route by public transport for a visitor arriving at Gatwick and travelling to Manchester.

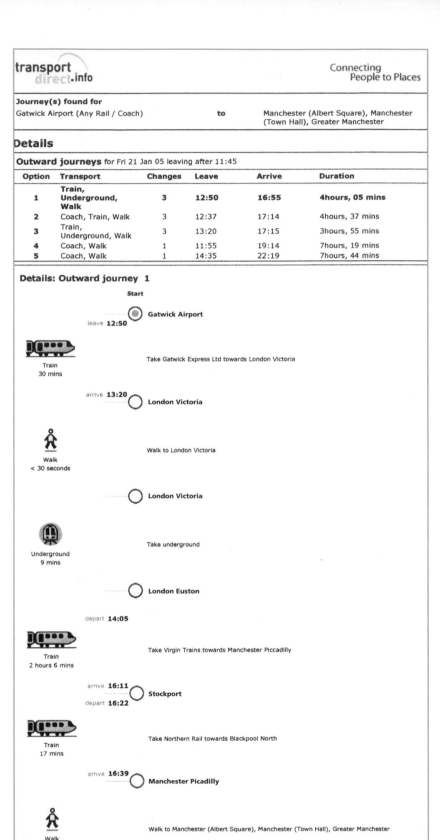

transport direct.info

Connecting People to Places

Journey(s) found for

Gatwick Airport (Any Rail / Coach) **to** Manchester (Albert Square), Manchester (Town Hall), Greater Manchester

Details

Outward journeys for Fri 21 Jan 05 leaving after 11:45

Option	Transport	Changes	Leave	Arrive	Duration
1	Train, Underground, Walk	3	12:50	16:55	4hours, 05 mins
2	Coach, Train, Walk	3	12:37	17:14	4hours, 37 mins
3	Train, Underground, Walk	3	13:20	17:15	3hours, 55 mins
4	Coach, Walk	1	11:55	19:14	7hours, 19 mins
5	Coach, Walk	1	14:35	22:19	7hours, 44 mins

Details: Outward journey 1

Start

leave **12:50** Gatwick Airport

Train
30 mins Take Gatwick Express Ltd towards London Victoria

arrive **13:20** London Victoria

Walk
< 30 seconds Walk to London Victoria

London Victoria

Underground
9 mins Take underground

London Euston

depart **14:05**

Train
2 hours 6 mins Take Virgin Trains towards Manchester Piccadilly

arrive **16:11** Stockport
depart **16:22**

Train
17 mins Take Northern Rail towards Blackpool North

arrive **16:39** Manchester Picadilly

Walk
16 mins Walk to Manchester (Albert Square), Manchester (Town Hall), Greater Manchester

arrive **16:55** Manchester (Albert Square), Manchester (Town Hall), Greater Manchester

End

Access to information

The website discussed above has helped domestic and incoming tourists have access to transport information. The Internet has helped all travellers in planning their journeys and holidays. Incoming tourists need information on transport, accommodation, attractions and events. The VisitBritain website and the national and regional tourism board websites and their links allow incoming tourists to do a lot of research before they arrive in the country.

Travel agents can be a good source of tourist information

Incoming tourists may also require information in their own countries. The provision of overseas offices by VisitBritain is one means of providing this information. Tour operators in overseas countries are also a source of information about the UK.

Domestic tourists need the same information and can get it from travel agents, tourist boards, direct from attractions and from Tourist Information Centres.

Incoming tourists cannot always access information in English. It needs to be available in their own language. VisitBritain has added to its local language websites facility with new websites for the Czech Republic, Greece, Hungary, Malaysia and Thailand.

Quality assurance

All tourists have a right to know that the transport and travel services that they use meet particular quality standards. The quality assurance scheme used for accommodation in the UK is described on page 206 (Unit 19).

It is unlikely that incoming tourists will want to know the details of such a scheme, rather they want to know that three-star or four-star-rated accommodation can be relied on to be of a particular standard wherever they go in the UK or elsewhere.

Incoming tourists will also use guides for quality recommendations on places to visit and for restaurants. These may be international guides such as Michelin or Fodor.

VisitBritain is coordinating a review of inspection services in the UK. The aim is to encourage participation in quality assurance schemes and to drive up quality of products.

Health, safety and security

The UK has stringent health and safety legislation so tourists can expect to be as safe or safer than they would be in their own country. This applies to security also. However, people tend to behave differently when they are on holiday and may not be as aware as they normally are of difficult situations. People who are unfamiliar with their surroundings and the culture are more vulnerable to crime than others. Domestic tourists may also be more vulnerable when visiting a part of the country they are not used to. The Metropolitan police have issued advice for tourists visiting London and an extract is shown here. You will note that much of the advice relates to common-sense precautions for any large city.

- Keep your bag or camera where you can see them by wearing them in front of you, not over your shoulder. This is especially important if you are in a crowded area such as on a bus or an underground train.
- When in restaurants, bars, theatres or cinemas never leave your bag on the floor or over the back of your chair. Keep it where you can see it.
- Only buy theatre or concert tickets from reliable sources and not from 'touts' in the street.
- If you're out and about at night on foot try to keep to busy, well-lit areas.
- When travelling by bus or train try to avoid using stations in isolated places. When possible sit near the driver on buses, and on trains try to make sure you sit in a compartment where there are other people.
- Always use licensed mini cabs or black cabs. Mini cabs should always be booked in advance. Unlicensed cabs and rogue drivers may compromise your safety. To find licensed mini cab firms in your area, call Transport for London on 020 7222 1234 or visit www.tfl.gov.uk.
- Be particularly vigilant when using ATM cash point machines. Be aware of anyone behind you and if the machine appears to have been tampered with in any way do not use it and report it to the police or bank immediately.
- Take extra care when crossing the road. Always remember to look both ways as traffic may be coming from a different direction than you are expecting.

Source: www.met.police.uk

Interpretation of language and awareness of culture

The British are not best known for their linguistic abilities and yet our incoming tourists cannot always be expected to speak English. They need to have information readily available in their own language. This does not often happen, even with common languages like French and Spanish. Few restaurants provide translated menus and transport information is not often available in other languages. Hotel staff with languages are only found in large cities. In addition, cultural differences between visitors and UK residents should be recognised.

The sector that performs best in terms of language interpretation is the attractions sector where, in order to appeal to incoming tourists, information in the form of leaflets and tapes is often in several languages.

The importance of welcoming visitors in their own language is recognised by the 'Welcome Excellence' training programme provided for tourist staff by tourist boards. The course also raises awareness of cultural differences. Here is an example from the Welcome International course language module.

The objectives are that by the end of the training, you will be able to:

* meet, greet and inform visitors in nine languages – Arabic, Chinese (Mandarin), Dutch, French, German, Italian, Japanese, Norwegian and Spanish
* be able to help visitors with a range of requests
* promote your facilities and services
* enhance the positive image of your organisation
* make overseas visitors especially welcome – so hopefully they will want to return.

Consider this...

If you travel in the Netherlands, you will find that everyone speaks English including the shop assistants, railway staff and ice cream sellers at a theme park. Imagine you are a French person with no English visiting the UK. Where do you think you would find French spoken?

Expectations

Customer service

Visitors to the UK expect a high level of customer service and generally receive it. Breakdown of customer service usually occurs when there are language difficulties.

Cost

The UK has a very high cost of living in comparison to most nations. In addition, our economy has seen several years of boom and sterling is very strong against the euro. This means that travelling to the UK is very expensive for other Europeans, particularly those with developing economies, e.g. Latvia and Slovakia. In 2005 sterling was at a record high against the dollar so that the UK was also very expensive for American travellers. (Conversely, UK travellers going to the US at this time found it very cheap as they got almost two dollars for each pound.) There is no doubt that incoming tourists perceive the UK as expensive and that some visitors are deterred by the cost. Some costs may surprise incoming tourists, for example the high cost of public transport compared to their own countries.

Domestic tourists also may expect different areas of the country to be more expensive than others and they will expect transport costs to be high.

Interaction

Incoming tourists will expect to interact with UK residents during their stay. Some types of visit lend themselves more readily to this such as staying in a home with a host family or participating in an activity. Business tourists will interact with their colleagues.

Products and services

VisitBritain employs a series of marketing campaigns promoting England as a series of products based on different themes, activities and experiences. Visitors often have a very traditional view of England and the UK and expect to see beefeaters, red London buses and black taxis, and of course they can. The marketing campaigns show what else is on offer and aim to attract more tourists.

Business tourism is a very important product for the UK both for domestic and incoming tourists. It brings in a lot of revenue but also allows regeneration of urban areas when hotels are built for business tourism. In seaside areas, resorts which might be lifeless in the winter are often used for conferences out of season. London and Cardiff have been pinpointed by the government as locations for the development of major international conference facilities.

Consider this...

What were your own expectations the first time you went to London? Were they correct? If you have never been to London, think of somewhere else you have been to and what your expectations were.

Part of the role of VisitBritain is to encourage British people to spend more on tourism in England throughout the year. It is fairly straightforward to work out how many people go where, how often and how much they spend. This is quantitative data. It is much more difficult to determine why people choose the destinations and activities they do as this involves qualitative research. VisitBritain carried out some research in 2004 to try and establish who England's customers are and what their expectations are. The study was entitled 'Destination England – How well does it deliver?' The British public was grouped into 8 main segments as shown in the pie chart below. The labels describe the type of people and the percentage relates to the percentage of the population in that category.

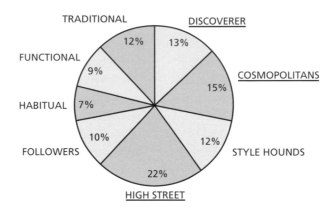

Three of the groups were chosen as specific targets for marketing campaigns. They were chosen on the basis of taking frequent short breaks and on the likelihood of their receptiveness to enjoy British marketing campaigns.

The three chosen groups are described below.

SEGMENT	CORE VALUES	MARKET SIZE AND LIFESTAGE	HOLIDAY HABITS
Cosmopolitans	Independent, individual risk-takers who seek new experiences and challenges, both physical & intellectual	15% of the population, with high ethnic representation. Relatively young, average income is £26K and over a third of them are post-family.	On average take over 4 short breaks a year. Enjoy wide variety of types of holiday, especially activity/themed holidays.
Discoverers	Independent of mind and keen on value for money. Little influenced by style or brand, but value good service.	12% of the population, predominantly C1 with average income of £25K. Most likely to be aged 26–35, with kids at home, and high Internet users.	Likely to take bargain break/late deal rather than package holiday. Much more likely to weekend in England than abroad.
High Street	Fashion victims (rather than pioneers) who care what others think. Will pay more for quality as long as tried and tested.	21% of the population, predominantly ABC1 with average income of £22K. Physically active, representing wide range of ages.	Attracted to bargain breaks and unlikely to go off the beaten track. Much more likely to take long holiday abroad than in England.

Another function of VisitBritain is to attract overseas tourists. An important market is Japan. VisitBritain provides market profiles of different countries to aid organisations who wish to market to them.

This extract describes two market segments from Japan.

ACTIVE SINKS AND DINKS

- Global segment – SINKS (single income no kids).
- Aged 25–49 (majority female).
- Segment size approximately 12.8 million.
- Income £12,000–£40,000 per annum.
- Well-educated.
- Still living at home or living alone – good disposable income levels.
- Women 35–44 yrs higher interest in visiting Europe.
- Very work focused – interested in travel, very IT literate.
- Influences on travel – TV programmes, lifestyle magazines, the Internet and word-of-mouth recommendation especially important.
- Desire for self-improvement, more creative, self-expression – women in this segment interested in short courses e.g. aromatherapy and in beauty products and services, tea making and English language short programmes.
- Branded products (Burberry's, Louis Vuitton, Pringles, Hermes etc.) very popular.
- Skeleton packages – flights, hotels, some minimal land-arrangements – strong appeal.

MODERN POST-NESTERS

- Global segment – Empty nesters
- Aged 50+
- Segment size approx 16.5 million
- Income £42,000–£52,000 per annum
- Married – may have adult children living at home, who are not the main focus of their lives
- Interested in the world around them – politics, economics, environment, community, plus personal focus on health, self-fulfilment and being creative
- Interested in travel – needs to be more than standard package
- Travel information sources mostly via direct mail from travel agents, travel brochures, TV programmes, word-of-mouth recommendation especially important.
- First-timers mainly take package tours – can be very upmarket
- Repeat visitors to the UK are increasingly choosing B&Bs and home-stays
- Enjoy gardens, culture and heritage, nature, walking, self-expression, personal experiences
- Those aged 65+ hold 80% of Japan's personal savings.

Source: Office for National Statistics

1 Choose one of the British groups of tourists described and one of the Japanese groups. Describe their needs and expectations in terms of facilities/products transport, customer service, cost, interaction with hosts, quality assurance, language and health, safety and security. Write this up as an information sheet.

   This task may provide evidence for P1.

2 Compare and contrast the needs and expectations of the British tourists with those of the Japanese tourists. You might present this as a comparative chart with comments.

   This task may provide evidence for M1.

Source: National Statistics: Overseas Travel and Tourism First Release

Popularity and appeal

Popularity

Visitor flow for incoming and outgoing tourists

Remember that in order to avoid a deficit in the travel balance we need to encourage more tourists to come into the UK than travel abroad. In 2004 there was a record high of 27.2 million incoming tourism visits, an increase of 6.6% on 2003. The value of this business to the economy is £12.3 billion. This news was particularly pleasing to the industry members as incoming tourism had suffered for a few years with the effects of 9/11, foot and mouth and the downturn of the Asian economy.

Meanwhile in the same period, UK outgoing tourist visits also rose to 63.5 million visits. The number of visits to western Europe hardly changed but visits to North America rose by 15 per cent possibly, reflecting the strength of the pound against the dollar. The chart shows overseas residents' visits to the UK and UK residents' visits abroad.

Consider this...

How do you think we know how many visitors come to the UK? The data is collected in the International Passenger Survey for the Office of National Statistics. A sample of people is questioned at airports and seaports. People travelling outbound are also questioned. Around 250,000 interviews are carried out per year representing 0.2% of all travellers.

Generating countries

It is visitors from eastern European countries and from long-haul destinations outside the US who have provided the increase in visits of incoming tourists. The expansion on the European Union with 10 new members in 2004 has meant that residents of those states have easier access to European travel. Asian tourists are returning as the Asian economy improves.

The table shows the top five overseas markets for the UK in 2003.

Country	Visits (000)	Country	Spend (£m)
USA	3,346	USA	2,315
France	3,073	Germany	820
Germany	2,611	France	694
Irish Republic	2,488	Irish Republic	681
Netherlands	1,549	Australia	535

Source: International Passenger Survey, Office for National Statistics

There are a number of points that can be noted from these figures.

1. The countries generating the most visitors are not necessarily those who generate the most expenditure. Australia is ninth in position in our overseas market and yet ranks fifth in terms of expenditure. This is important as high spending tourists are more valuable to us.

2. Four out of the top five are our neighbours. It is easier and more convenient for them to travel to the UK than for other nations.

3. The Irish Republic ranks high as there is a strong VFR (visiting friends and relatives) market between Southern Ireland and the UK.

Visitor flow within the UK

Day visits represent the largest segment of domestic tourism with 60 per cent of expenditure. Remember that these figures are recorded separately in the Day Visits Survey. Between 1996 and 2002, domestic tourism expenditure in England increased by 14 per cent. The most popular and fastest growing sector is the leisure breaks sector.

Domestic tourism expenditure includes expenditure as a result of resident visitors travelling within their country and occurs en route, at the place visited and in advance on spending for the trip.

In 2003 UK residents took:

* 70.5 million holidays of one night or more spending £13.7 billion

* 22.3 million overnight business trips spending £6.1 billion

* 34.3 million overnight trips to friends and relatives spending £3.4 billion.

Source: UK Tourism Survey

The UK Tourism Survey is very detailed and shows information such as number of tourist trips, number of tourist nights, spending, breakdown between England, Scotland and Wales and purpose of trip. You can find the survey data at Star UK (www.staruk.org.uk).

Key UK destination regions

The distribution of domestic tourism is measured by region with the south west of England attracting most tourists, closely followed by the south east. The north east attracts the least number of domestic tourists.

DISTRIBUTION OF DOMESTIC TOURISM BY GOVERNMENT OFFICE REGION 2003			
	Trips Millions	Nights Millions	Spend £ Millions
West Midlands	10.8	25.9	1,633
East of England	11.8	37.6	1,654
East Midlands	9.6	28.0	1,352
London	14.3	32.8	3,212
North West	16.0	44.4	2,615
North East	4.8	13.3	824
South East	20.7	60.1	2,999
South West	22.8	92.1	4,263
Yorkshire & the Humber	13.1	35.8	1,930
Total England	121.3	371.9	20,560
Total UK	151.0	490.5	26,482

Source: UK Tourism Survey

Similar figures are available for incoming tourists from the International Passenger Survey. You can find this online at the government's national statistics site. It is difficult to make exact comparisons as the regions are defined by government area in the UK Tourism Survey and by tourist board area in the IPS. However the popularity of regions is much the same for incoming tourists as for domestic tourists except that London and the south east are more popular with overseas tourists. It is also of interest to see which towns and cities tourists most like to visit. The following chart shows the popularity of our towns and cities.

OVERSEAS VISITORS TO THE UK	
Top Towns 2003: Visits Rank City/Town	Visits (000)
1 London	11,700
2 Edinburgh	770
3 Manchester	740
4 Birmingham	720
5 Glasgow	420
6 Oxford	360
7 Cambridge	310
8 Bristol	290
= 9 Brighton/Hove	270
= 9 Liverpool	270
11 Cardiff	250
= 12 York	210
= 12 Nottingham	210
= 12 Bath	210
15 Newcastle-upon-Tyne	200
16 Coventry	180
= 17 Leeds	170
= 17 Inverness	170
= 19 Chester	160
= 19 Leicester	160

Visits figures are rounded to nearest 10,000
Excludes day visits

Source: International Passenger Survey, Office for National Statistics

London is popular with overseas tourists

Average length of stay

Domestic tourist trips tend to be short in length with more than half of trips lasting one or two nights. This is explained by the growth of short leisure breaks and the decline of the traditional British seaside holiday. Business tourism trips also tend to be short.

The table shows the duration of domestic tourism trips for 2003.

DURATION OF ALL TOURISM TRIPS 2003	
UK Residents	% of Trips
1 night	29
2 nights	27
3 nights	15
4 nights	9
5 nights	5
6 nights	3
7 nights	6
8–13 nights	3
14 nights	2
15+	*
Average number of nights	3.25

Note: *less than 1%   Source: UK Tourism Survey

Theory into practice

Choose one of the towns in the chart above and try to find out the visitor numbers for that town. You should be able to find these on their local government website or via the Tourist Information Centre. Produce a short report with charts on numbers of visitors, length of stay, purpose of visit etc. Draw conclusions from your findings. Ask your tutor to check your work.

Visitor numbers to attractions

The Survey of Visits to Visitor Attractions is conducted annually by the national tourist boards of England, Northern Ireland, Scotland and Wales. It monitors trends in the visitor attraction sector. Separate surveys are carried out for each country. You can access these surveys through the national statistics website. The Association of Leading Visitor Attractions (ALVA) publishes its own statistics as shown below.

VISITS MADE IN 2003 TO VISITOR ATTRACTIONS IN MEMBERSHIP WITH ALVA			
SITE	**TOTAL VISITS**	**CHARGE/FREE**	**% +/−**
Blackpool Pleasure Beach	6,200,000	F	−3.5%
British Museum	4,584,000	F	−0-5%
Tate Modern	3,895,746	F	−16%
Natural History Museum	2,976,738	F	−3%
Science Museum	2,886,850	F	+6%
Victoria & Albert Museum	2,257,325	F	+2%
Tower of London	1,972,263	C	−3.6%
Eden Project	1,404,737	C	−19%
Legoland Windsor	1,321,128	C	−4%
National Maritime Museum	1,305,150	F	+8%
Edinburgh Castle	1,172,534	C	+1%
Tate Britain	1,106,911	F	+4%
Kew Gardens	1,079,424	C	+9%
Chester Zoo	1,076,000	C	+2.5%
Canterbury Cathedral	1,060,166	C/F	−4.5%

Source: Association of Leading Visitor Attractions

The statistics do not show how many domestic tourists, day visitors and incoming tourists visit but only the total. Individual attractions may be able to estimate what percentage of visitors is from overseas and certainly many actively market to incoming tourists.

Trends and influences

Approved destination status

There are several emerging markets which can be targeted to increase incoming tourism. These include the EU new member states already mentioned and increasing numbers of visitors from the rest of eastern Europe. VisitBritain also predicts that visitor numbers from Asia will grow. China is a good example of an emerging market as in February 2004 the UK, alongside several other European countries, was granted 'approved destination status'.

CASE STUDY

It is estimated that there are about 25 million Chinese people with enough money to travel abroad. The UK has only 0.6 per cent of this market, whereas Germany and France each have acquired more than 1 per cent. VisitBritain has a branch in Shanghai and the staff there work with public relations and advertising companies to promote Britain.

Virgin Atlantic has a general manager for China and he says the company is ready to take advantage of the approved destination status and has developed a package to sell in China.

The target for the UK is to attract 1 per cent of the Chinese market. This would generate an estimated £1 billion and create 25,000 extra jobs in tourism.

1. **Find out how many Chinese people are currently visiting Britain.**
2. **Find an example of an attraction, an airline or a tour operator who has special facilities or services for Chinese visitors.**
3. **Write up your findings as a newspaper article.**

Key concept

Approved destination status is granted by the Chinese authorities to countries the Chinese people may visit as groups. Travel agents in China are authorised to deal with designated agents in the host country.

Apart from making it much easier for Chinese citizens to travel to these countries, this status also has the advantage of allowing destination countries to open offices in China to promote travel to their country.

Exchange rate

The exchange rate will continue to exert an influence on visitor numbers. Rates to watch are sterling/euro and sterling/dollar. An improvement in the strength of the dollar could bring a greater rise in US visitors.

Low-cost airlines

Many new low-cost airlines are starting up, bringing increased services between eastern Europe and the UK. In addition, established low-cost airlines are adding new services to Europe allowing tourists to travel cheaply to the UK. Such services also increase outbound travel.

Terrorism

Terrorism is an important factor in travel. If there were major terrorist activity in the UK the incoming tourist trade would be severely hit. Terrorist attacks in other countries can damage international travel in general as people fear travel and feel more secure in their home environment.

Theory into practice

Find an example of a marketing initiative from VisitBritain or VisitEngland to promote incoming tourism. Report back on the campaign to your group. Draw up ideas for a campaign to promote your own area to domestic tourists from other parts of the country.

Appeal

The appeal of the UK lies in the following areas.

Features

There are varied landscapes and geographical features. It offers coasts and beaches, beautiful countryside areas and the mountains of Scotland and Wales. In addition it has superb cities with plenty of cultural experiences.

Attractions

Thousands of visitor attractions cater for every taste and many are free, including all the national museums.

Special events

Events are put on to add interest at attractions or to present music, theatre or carnival. Some examples are given later in this unit.

Facilities and services

Accommodation is available for all ranges of budgets with good standards of quality. Transport facilities, although expensive, are available throughout the UK.

Image

The image of the UK as a country with strong traditions and welcoming to tourists adds to its appeal.

Climate

Unfortunately, our climate does not appeal to many tourists, although they may be lucky and enjoy good summer weather. Snow in Scotland in the winter may attract skiers to Aviemore.

Accessibility

You saw that our near neighbours generate most visitors to the UK. Accession to the EU has added to the appeal of the UK for new member states. Low-cost air travel, including low transatlantic fares, makes the UK more accessible to all. Emerging markets such as China and India will generate more visitors as air travel agreements between those countries and the UK come into play.

Cost

Appeal on the basis of cost is determined to an extent by current exchange rates and is, therefore, variable.

Needs and expectations

Appeal is very personal to each tourist or group of tourists. It depends on individual needs and expectations, some of which are discussed in the first part of this unit. The success of a destination lies in its tourism professionals being able to understand the needs and expectations of visitors and satisfying them.

CASE STUDY

A survey by the European Tour Operators Association investigating the appeal of Europe to tourists found that the criteria that most influenced their decision to visit were scenery, culture and history. The full list of criteria included in the survey is given here. The priority order is the order given by the tourists before their visit. The order changed slightly when the tourists were again questioned following their visit. You will note that 'welcoming' and ' gastronomic' were rated higher, for example.

ETOA SURVEY: INBOUND VISITORS TO EUROPE		
Priority Order	Before coming to Europe	After coming to Europe
1	Scenic	Historic
2	Cultural	Scenic
3	Historic	Cultural
4	Easy to travel to	Diverse
5	Secure	Easy to travel to
6	Good value	Welcoming
7	Diverse	Secure
8	Welcoming	Gastronomic
9	Clean	Clean
10	High quality service	Good value
11	Gastronomic	Good shopping
12	Good shopping	Fashionable
13	Fashionable	High quality service

Source: European Tour Operators Association

Types of organisations

As the UK is made up of different countries, there are several national organisations responsible for the development of tourism in the UK. They sometimes have overlapping responsibilities so it can be difficult to remember who does what. These national organisations are all part of the public sector but work closely with other sectors to fulfil their roles of developing and promoting tourism. In this section we will find out who these public bodies are and their role. We will also explore other organisations involved in incoming and domestic tourism and, in turn, examine their roles.

Government departments

The main roles of government departments are setting policy and providing funds for implementation of policy.

Tourism responsibility

The Department for Culture, Media and Sport (DCMS) has responsibility for tourism policy in the UK. This policy was determined and published in 'Tomorrow's Tourism' in 1999. In 2004 the policy was updated in 'Tomorrow's Tourism Today'. The department determines the responsibilities and actions of public and private sector organisations in key areas such as marketing and quality. DCMS has greater control over public sector organisations in tourism than in the private sector. This is because the department provides much of the funding for tourism organisations. For example, the grant for 2004/05 to VisitBritain for promoting Britain overseas was £35.5 million. Further money was granted for domestic marketing and for the specific marketing of England as a destination.

The responsibility for the development of Scottish tourism lies with the Scottish Executive. Tourism comes under the remit of the Department for Education and the policy is published in 'Tourism Framework for Action'. In Wales it is the Welsh Assembly which has responsibility for tourism. In Northern Ireland the government Department for Enterprise, Trade and Investment (DETI) develops the tourism strategy. Each of these government departments funds its national tourism offices.

Department of Transport

Other government departments may be involved in tourism more indirectly. The Department of Transport has to provide the infrastructure for tourists to travel around. It has been heavily involved in developments at Stonehenge as proposals include widening of a major road.

Airport development relies on the department's involvement as public transport links are included in development proposals. The Home Office determines policy on immigration and visa requirements.

National tourism offices

The tourist boards in the UK are VisitBritain, Wales Tourist Board, the Northern Ireland Tourist Board and VisitScotland.

They are responsible for attracting incoming and domestic tourists, marketing of destinations, developing new products, research projects and providing information both to tourists and to the travel trade.

VisitBritain

In the introduction to this unit you were recommended to use the website of VisitBritain for your research. This body is the statutory organisation for tourism for the whole of the UK. It does not concern itself with outbound tourism but seeks to market Britain to the rest of the world and England to the British. Note that in terms of domestic tourism, VisitBritain markets England and not Scotland, Wales and Northern Ireland. It has to work very closely with the national tourist offices of these countries in order to achieve its aims of promoting the whole of Britain to the rest of the world and to persuade the Scottish, Welsh and Irish peoples to take holidays in England.

Here are the aims of VisitBritain as laid out in its website:

Overseas Customer: To promote Britain overseas as a tourist destination, generating additional tourism revenue throughout Britain and throughout the year

Domestic Customer: To grow the value of the domestic market by encouraging British residents to take additional and/or longer breaks in England

Tourism Industry: To help the British tourism industry address international and domestic markets more effectively

Government: To provide advice to Government and devolved administrations on matters affecting tourism and contribute to wider Government objectives

Strategic Partners: To work in partnership with the devolved administrations and the national and regional tourist boards to build the British tourism industry

Staff: To achieve all goals by making efficient and effective use of resources and by being open, accessible, professional, accountable and responsive.

Source www.visitbritain.com

To promote Britain abroad, VisitBritain has 25 offices covering 31 different markets. It also employs staff overseas in these offices. They have to work with the travel trade in their area to promote the UK. They are in competition with other countries vying for the tourism trade. Besides the funding given to VisitBritain by the DCMS, the organisation raises money itself through partnerships and activities.

CASE STUDY

A VisitBritain campaign

In October 2004 VisitBritain held an international business tourism event 'Discovery', in Wales. The event was sponsored by the Wales Tourist Board and Celtic Manor Resort. It was supported by Connect Global. The purpose of the event was to promote business tourism in Britain and attract corporations to hold their meetings, conferences and exhibitions in Britain, benefiting the local and national economy by millions of pounds.

Connect Global is a commercial organisation which represents worldwide destination-management companies and promotes them to the event buyer.

The Celtic Manor Resort has a purpose built convention and business centre. It is situated in Gwent, Wales, off the M4.

1. **Why is VisitBritain working with other organisations on this event?**
2. **Give reasons for the involvement of Celtic Manor Resort and Connect Global.**
3. **Find out what a destination-management company is.**

Wales Tourist Board

The Wales Tourist Board is the national tourist organisation for Wales. It reports to the Minister for Economic Development of the Welsh Assembly government. It also receives funding from the Assembly. The role of the Wales Tourist Board is to:

'support the tourism industry and to provide the appropriate strategic framework within which private enterprise can achieve sustainable growth and success, so improving the social and economic well being of Wales.'

Source: Wales Tourist Board

To assist in marketing, Wales is divided into 12 marketing areas. Examples include the Isle of Anglesey, Snowdonia and Pembrokeshire.

The Northern Ireland Tourist Board

Northern Ireland also has its own national tourist office, the Northern Ireland Tourist Board. This is the body responsible for the development, promotion and marketing of Northern Ireland as a tourist destination. It also advises the government on the formulation of policy on tourism in Northern Ireland.

VisitScotland

VisitScotland is the national tourist organisation for Scotland, supported and funded by the Scottish Executive. The Scottish Executive recognises the importance of promoting tourism in Scotland and has funded extra marketing activites.

Regional tourist boards

Regional tourist boards were set up to carry out the development and promotion of tourism in the regions. Traditionally they represented the public sector and implemented national policy. They aim to attract both incoming and domestic visitors to their region as this extract from the VisitLondon website illustrates.

'VisitLondon is the official visitor organisation for the capital. Our aim is to promote London as the world's most exciting city by marketing to domestic and overseas leisure and business visitors, as well as Londoners themselves. VisitLondon is a partnership organisation which also acts as a voice for the London tourism industry.'

Source: www.visitlondon.com

The role of tourist boards has changed a great deal in recent years and now they have a key role in bringing together public and private sector parties in the tourism business. This role is summarised in this extract from the Tourism South East website.

'Tourism South East is the only organisation with a specific interest and responsibility for tourism across the region and it plays a key role in building understanding and support between the different sectors.

'Part of this key role is to liaise with and lobby government departments, local authorities and other tourism bodies. Tourism South East works closely with VisitBritain and the South East England Development Agency, and consults extensively with our members, either in meetings or via a membership magazine.'

Source: www.tourismsoutheast.com

The Internet has changed the way that the tourist boards present themselves to the public. Many of the boards now have two websites, one is aimed at consumers with lots of information about destinations and attractions in their region. Some of the tourist boards have changed their names on their consumer websites to make them more attractive in marketing terms and easy for overseas visitors to understand, e.g. VisitLondon rather than the London Tourist Board. Technology has been a benefit to the boards as it means potential visitors can find out information from the Internet wherever they are in the world. This enables them to research and plan their visit. The second website is generally aimed at businesses and tourism trade partners with information about how to market their products and take advantage of the tourist boards' services.

The activities of regional tourist boards are wide ranging and also cover:

Training

Many of the courses provided are under the 'Welcome to Excellence' brand. The courses are available to all tourism employees at a reasonable fee (usually paid by the employer). There is a specific course 'Welcome International' for welcoming international visitors.

Research

Research services may be surveys carried out on behalf of tourism businesses or mystery shopper services covering Tourist Information Centres.

Quality

This includes inspecting accommodation and determining quality grades.

Development

The tourist boards employ business advisers who will give advice to tourism businesses and also inform them of any grants they may be eligible for.

These are the tourist boards in England.

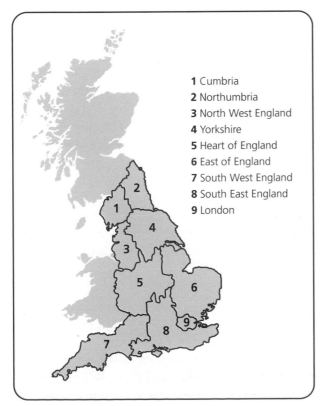

1 Cumbria
2 Northumbria
3 North West England
4 Yorkshire
5 Heart of England
6 East of England
7 South West England
8 South East England
9 London

English Regional Tourist Boards

* Cumbria Tourist Board
* Northumbria Tourist Board
* North West Tourist Board
* Yorkshire Tourist Board
* Heart of England Tourist Board
* East of England Tourist Board
* London Tourist Board
* South West Tourism
* South East England Tourist Board.

Scotland has 14 Area Tourist Boards which have been established since 1996. These Tourist Boards are responsible for Tourist Information Centres at local level. They also undertake marketing activities at local level and work with partners in the private sector. They aim to bring together the public and private sector and to link national and local tourism policy. Wales has three regional tourist boards. These are North Wales Tourism, Mid Wales Tourism and South and West Wales Tourism.

Regional Development Agencies (RDA)

These agencies were set up by the government to promote sustainable economic development in England. They have strategic responsibility for tourism in their regions.

The aim is for businesses to lead development and promote economic regeneration in the areas where this is needed. Eight of the nine English RDAs do not report to the DCMS but to the Department of Trade and Industry (DTI). The London RDA reports to the government department for London.

The Regional Development Agencies Act 1998 sets out the purposes of the RDAs:

* to further economic development and regeneration
* to promote business efficiency, investment and competitiveness
* to promote employment
* to enhance development and application of skills relevant to employment
* to contribute to sustainable development.

The projects differ across regions as they should fit the particular needs of a region. The RDA sets out a strategy for its region – a regional Economic Strategy. The money to finance these projects comes from various government departments and is put into one budget. Then the RDAs decide how to spend the funds. As tourism is a means of bringing economic benefit to an area then the RDAs often decide to back tourism projects.

CASE STUDY

Advantage West Midlands is one of the English RDAs. Much of this RDA's work concerns business and community projects as it is concerned with economic development and community regeneration. Sometimes this work will include projects related to tourism. The Royal Shakespeare Company in Stratford is in Advantage West Midland's area and Advantage is working alongside other funding partners to raise money for a £100 million development project at this world-famous venue. The proposal is to redevelop the theatre retaining the original art deco building but with a new 1,000-seat theatre inside.

1. Visit the RSC website to find out who the other funding partners are. Why doesn't Advantage West Midlands provide all the funding?
2. Find out who the RDA is for your region. What tourism projects are they involved in? Choose one and report on it to your group.

A similar set up to the regional development agencies exists in Scotland. This is the Scottish Enterprise Network. This includes Scottish Enterprise National, situated in Glasgow and 12 Local Enterprise Companies (LECs) from the Grampians to the Borders. Like VisitScotland these bodies are funded by the Scottish Executive. The northern and western parts of Scotland are covered by the Highlands and Islands Enterprise based in Inverness.

Northern Ireland has a Department for Regional Development which produces a regional development strategy but no similar network of development agencies. There is also an organisation called 'Invest Northern Ireland' whose role is to promote local business and economic development within Northern Ireland. In Wales the Welsh Development Agency promotes economic development and growth throughout Wales.

Tourist Information Centres

A network of Tourist Information Centres (TICs) covers most towns and cities in the UK. Their role is to provide information and services at a local level. They are funded from the regional tourist board and by the local authority. Most TICs have had cuts in funding in recent years and have had to become more enterprising to be, to some extent, self-financing. They can make money by selling souvenirs in their shop, by charging for maps etc., by selling tours and by organising conferences as a separate arm to their business.

This extract from the Cambridge TIC website gives you an overview of their role and the services they offer.

'We can help with local accommodation, public transport, conference services, events, U.K holiday information, walking tours of Cambridge, maps & guidebooks, information for those with disabilities, Cambridge souvenirs, tickets to view the world-famous King's College Chapel, chauffeured punt tours, sales of the Great British Heritage Pass & much, much more!

'Looking for that perfect place to stay? Booking accommodation in Cambridge could not be simpler!

'Just call our advance accommodation booking service and speak to one of our friendly reservations team.

'For that perfect Cambridge gift or souvenir. Why not take a look around our extensive gift shop.'

Source: www.visitcambridge.org

1. **Summarise the role of the TIC from the information given here.**
2. **See if you can organise a group visit to your own TIC.**

Local authorities

Local authorities are responsible for delivering services to local communities. They also have to make plans which implement national policy and take care of economic, social and environmental issues in their area. Tourism is just one of the services of concern to local authorities. Others include:

* social services
* education
* libraries
* fire
* highways
* refuse collection and disposal
* leisure services.

Central government allocates funds to local authorities to pay for some of this work. The rest has to be raised through local taxation (council tax) and business rates.

Local tourism projects can be of economic benefit to an area and the local authority will include tourism plans in its local plan. It is likely that there will also be a Tourism Strategy.

It should be noted that policies do not always promote the growth of tourism even though the national policy is for the growth of tourism. If we look at Cambridge again we will see that the tourism policy is very much one of management and selective development. This is because the local authority recognises that it has a role in conserving the historic city centre and too many tourists result in congestion and environmental problems, such as potential damage to old buildings.

This point of view of conservation is reflected in the local plan for Cambridge summarised here:

'The policies in the local plan have to be land-use based. In the tourism section of the local plan they:

* allocate sites for hotels

* control changes of use to and from tourist accommodation, balancing the need to provide additional accommodation with the need to retain family homes, and protecting the amenities of residential properties

* support new attractions that complement the character of the City, while resisting those which would bring in additional visitors.'

Source: Cambridge local plan, Cambridge City Council

The reason for allocating sites for hotels is that without enough hotels, visitors do not stay in the area and tend to be day visitors. Day visitors do not spend as much money as those who stay.

Membership organisations

Youth Hostel Association

Most people have heard of the Youth Hostel Association (YHA) even if they have not stayed in one of their establishments. The association has a long history of providing budget accommodation mainly for young people, although people of all ages can stay in the hostels. There are 227 hostels in England and Wales (Scotland and Ireland have different youth hostel associations). Most of the youth hostels are in rural locations, but there are some in cities, for example there is one in Manchester city centre. Many of the members of the association are domestic tourists but the YHA also attracts foreign visitors, from over 80 different countries. To ensure that international links are maintained the YHA is a member of the International Youth Hostel Association, which has 4,000 youth hostels across 60 countries.

Here is the aim of the YHA extracted from its website.

> 'To help all, especially young people of limited means, to a greater knowledge, love and care of the countryside, particularly by providing hostels or other simple accommodation for them in their travels and thus to promote their health, rest and education.'
>
> Source: Youth Hostel Association

CASE STUDY

The YHA produced a five-year plan in 2001. These are some of the aims of that plan:

- to increase youth hostel use from 2.1 million to 3 million overnights
- increase membership from 300,000 to 500,000
- raise YHA's profile
- work more actively with a wider range of partners
- help guests get the most out of their visit to town and country, with youth hostels as a gateway to the local area.

You can read all the aims and the full plan at www.yha.org.uk

1. **Find out the measures YHA are taking to increase membership and therefore visitors.**
2. **Find out what types of partners YHA works with.**
3. **What progress has been made on the plan?**

It would be interesting for you to research this case study by visiting a local youth hostel and arranging a talk for your group. Otherwise you can find the information on the YHA website.

English Heritage

This body is sponsored by the Department for Culture, Media and Sport and is an Executive non-departmental public body. Its official name is the Historic Buildings and Monuments Commission for England. The organisation also works with other government departments as their work also affects heritage. An example is the Department for Environment, Food and Rural Affairs which takes care of policy on rural issues. The government provides funding for English Heritage but it also earns revenue from the historic properties.

The organisation looks after over 400 properties for the nation and maintains registers of England's most significant historic buildings, monuments and landscapes.

The role of English Heritage is described on its website:

> 'English Heritage works in partnership with the central government departments, local authorities, voluntary bodies and the private sector to:
>
> - conserve and enhance the historic environment
> - broaden public access to the heritage
> - increase people's understanding of the past.'
>
> Source: www.english-heritage.org.uk

National Trust

The National Trust differs from English Heritage in that it is completely independent of government. It is a registered charity and therefore a voluntary organisation. It was founded in 1895 by three Victorian philanthropists who were concerned about industrialisation and set up the trust to acquire and protect threatened coastline, countryside and buildings.

This is still the role of the National Trust today. It protects over 200 historic houses and gardens and 49 industrial monuments and mills. It also owns more than 248,000 hectares of countryside and almost 600 miles of coast for people to visit and enjoy.

The Trust also has a role in managing the environment, developing best practice and acting as a source of advice on environmental issues.

Hotels and other accommodation providers

Hotels and other accommodation providers wish to attract incoming and domestic tourists. Those hotels in international groups often have an advantage as they can market globally and visitors to the UK who are familiar with a brand in their home company may look for it here. Smaller establishments can use the services of tourist organisations to help them promote themselves to tourists.

Transport operators

Airlines and ferry companies cater for outbound and incoming tourists but UK-based companies have to make greater marketing efforts in foreign countries to establish their reputation. Some low-cost airlines have had success in this way to the extent that they have established bases in other countries, for example Ryanair has a base in Frankfurt-Hahn.

Inbound-tour operators are less familiar to you than outbound ones as their marketing activity takes place overseas attracting tourists to the UK. These tour operators are represented by Ukinbound, a trade organisation. It has over 260 members in all sectors of tourism.

Interaction between different organisations

It is essential that different organisations work together for mutual benefit in attracting incoming and domestic tourists. To illustrate this we are going to look at 'First Stop York', which is a partnership of several organisations, some of which are public, some private and some voluntary. This began some years ago with the establishment of a tourism strategy group consisting of core organisations, for example, the city council, the chamber of commerce, York Visitor and Conference Bureau. This group laid down broad strategic goals for tourism.

First Stop York includes the following partners:

City of York Council

Many council departments are involved in issues which impact on tourism, for example, environmental health, planning and city centre management. The Economic Development Group in the council looks after budgetary requirements within First Stop York and leads on development of policy. It also collates tourism research information for York.

The council represents the local authority and must make sure policies reflect national decisions. They also have to make sure that health and safety matters are taken care of and that taxpayers' money is well spent.

York Tourism Bureau

This is a non-profit-making organisation which looks after the marketing of York on behalf of First Stop York. It has 480 members who pay an annual subscription used for marketing purposes. This organisation has responsibility for running the Tourist Information Centres in the city.

Yorkshire Tourist Board

This is the area's regional tourist board. Its role concerns marketing, development and training. It has to make sure national and regional policy is reflected in what happens in York and may give grants and advice to individual companies or projects.

York and North Yorkshire Chamber of Commerce

There is a national network of chambers of commerce. Their role is to provide a forum for business people to meet. In York many retail members of the Chamber link to First Stop through their chamber of commerce. Linking with First Stop gives individual members a voice in decision-making.

York Hospitality Association

This association represents around 100 members of the hospitality industry in and around York. It publishes a quarterly magazine and runs a hospitality awards scheme.

York Hoteliers

A group of managers from the main York hotels who meet to discuss working together on research, marketing and communication. They would wish to have influence on First Stop policy.

Assessment activity 15.3

In this activity you should find out more about the following organisations:

- VisitBritain
- your Regional Development Agency
- your Regional Tourist Board
- your Tourist Information Centre
- National Trust.

Describe the role of each of them in relation to incoming and domestic tourism.

This task may provide evidence for P4.

Explain how these organisations increase the appeal and popularity of the UK to incoming and domestic tourists.

This task may provide evidence for M2.

Analyse how these organisations interact with each other to meet the needs of incoming and domestic tourists.

This task may provide evidence for D1.

Heritage tourism

There is a great deal of recognition of the importance of our heritage in terms of tourism policy. We have seen that the National Trust and English Heritage have the protection of heritage at the heart of their work.

The DCMS has a designated heritage minister and in 2001 published a statement of government policy on the historic environment entitled 'A Force for our Future'. The report sets out five specific tasks:

* providing leadership
* realising educational potential
* including and involving people
* protecting and sustaining the historic environment, and
* optimising its economic potential.

DEFRA also acknowledges heritage and its significance in tourism in its publication *Economic Goals and Objectives*. This extract comes from the section on objectives for the eastern region.

Attractions

As heritage is so important in terms of appeal to tourists, we will look at heritage tourism in more depth and study some specific examples of the different types of heritage tourism.

Heritage tourism includes tourism activities such as visits to sites of historical importance, scenic landscapes, natural areas and locations where historic events occurred. Tourists are interested in heritage so that they can learn about the culture and past of a country or region in an enjoyable way.

Theory into practice

Go back to the chart of leading visitor attractions on page 101 and try to decide which of these attractions could be termed heritage attractions. The following descriptions of types of categories might help you.

Monuments and ruins

The Ancient Monuments and Archaeological Areas Act of 1979 gives protection to nationally important archaeological sites as Scheduled Ancient Monuments. There are about 19,000 entries listed. The list includes sites such as prehistoric standing stones, Roman forts, medieval villages and wartime pill boxes. English Heritage advises the government on the conservation of ancient monuments.

Cities and towns

Some cities and towns have traditionally been on the 'tourist trail' for incoming tourists. London is the most popular but overseas visitors are usually keen to see places such as Bath, Stratford, Oxford and Edinburgh. Indeed package holidays are available for tourists which take in these towns and cities in one visit.

Castles and palaces

The Tower of London

Some of these are royal palaces. Unoccupied royal palaces are looked after by the Historic Royal Palaces Agency, a charitable organisation set up by DCMS. The organisation must care for the upkeep and conservation and also manage public opening.

The palaces it takes care of are:

* The Tower of London
* Hampton Court Palace
* Kensington Palace State Apartments
* Royal Ceremonial Dress Collection
* The Banqueting House
* Whitehall
* Kew Palace with Queen Charlotte's Cottage.

Visitor centres

Visitor centres give tourists an opportunity to get an overview of what is on offer at an attraction in an especially built environment. They usually have an exhibition illustrating the attraction's features, a cafe and a shop. Sometimes tourists go to the visitor centre and don't bother going to the actual attraction.

An example is the Loch Ness Visitor Centre which has a cinema and an exhibition about the monster sightings as well as a shop and a restaurant. You can appreciate that it might be difficult for tourists to see the actual monster.

'The first documented sighting of a creature in Loch Ness was by St Columba in the 6th century A.D. Only in recent times has the spectacular phenomenon of 'Nessie' become internationally known.

'The Exhibition presents you with the up-to-the-minute facts and fully documented evidence from photographs, descriptions and film footage, together with an account of the area's unique historical and cultural background.'

Source: www.lochness-centre.com

Churches and cathedrals

The DCMS has responsibility for our ecclesiastical heritage. It also sponsors the Churches Conservation Trust. This body was set up in 1969 to preserve churches no longer needed for regular worship but which are of architectural, historical or archaeological importance. There are over 300 of these churches looked after by the Churches Conservation Trust.

Tourist visits to churches are very popular, in fact, churches are much more popular with tourists than they are with worshippers. According to the *Christian Science Monitor* there are only about 4 million regular worshippers in our churches but visits to churches by tourists are estimated at about 20 million.

Museums and galleries

The UK's national museums and galleries receive more than 30 million visitors a year. Admission is free and this is an incentive to visitors. Museums not in public ownership can, of course, charge.

Gardens and parks

Some of our parks are designated national parks. These are explained later in this unit. In addition there are many botanical parks in the UK, possibly the most famous is Kew Gardens near London. Also in London there are several royal parks, for example, St James Park and vast areas of heath such as Hampstead Heath. The heaths are most popular with local people for recreational activities and walking but some are also attractive to tourists. Greenwich Park with its observatory is one of the most popular London attractions.

Events and festivals

Our many music festivals are more likely to attract domestic rather than incoming tourists. In the summer 'V' festivals in Reading and Leeds attract rock music lovers to those areas. Glastonbury is a famous music festival. In addition, events such as the Notting Hill Carnival attract domestic tourists to London at the August

Daffodils in St James's Park

Bank Holiday. Other events feature pageantry or historical anniversaries. VisitBritain uses such events whenever possible to aid in its marketing to tourists. Often the marketing campaigns link events and attractions to a theme to give added impetus to the campaign.

Themes

Themes are a useful way of homing in on a group's interest so that a package of events and attractions can be suggested to help them make the most of their stay in the UK or a region of the UK. Here are some examples of themes.

Industrial

> ### CASE STUDY
> Industrial towns are turning to tourism and competing with old favourites such as Bath and Stratford.
>
> Bolton was home of the 'spinning mule' invented by Samuel Crompton and now entices tourists to visit. Bolton advertises its Reebok stadium and the award winning Octagon Theatre. Industrial heritage is celebrated with tours of Warburton's bakery and the local bedpan factory! Councillors express delight that the continuing promotion of Bolton as a tourism destination is attracting interest and visitors from as far afield as Australia, Canada and America. Sunderland was once famous for glass production but now tells tourists 'You're in for a surprise the next time you visit Sunderland.' The city is promoted as a base to visit the region including the seaside. It offers the National Glass Centre, a riverside art trail and new Winter Gardens.

Choose a town which is exploiting its industrial heritage in its tourism marketing. Explain how it uses the industrial theme to attract visitors. Gather information and photos which can be used for a display.

Literature

Literature is another theme adopted by VisitBritain. Anniversaries are a useful tool in forging a campaign. Thus, the 150th anniversary of Charlotte Brontë's death inspired an exhibition for the summer of 2005 at the parsonage in Haworth, her home. Similarly, in the Lake District it was 100 years since Beatrix Potter bought her farmhouse Hill Top, near Lake Windermere. This is a National Trust property open to the public. A famous children's book *The Railway Children* is 100 years old and this was marked by a series of events at the National Railway Museum.

Society

A theme can centre on a location rather than events such as the activities planned to attract more visitors to Cardiff in 2005. These included the Royal Horticultural Society Spring Flower Show at Bute Park, an international festival of musical theatre at the Wales Millennium Centre and the Cardiff Mardi Gras, a gay and lesbian festival at Cardiff Castle.

Military

SeaBritain was a campaign designed to run for a whole year celebrating Britain's naval history and coastal locations. Each month a different destination was highlighted to attract visitors.

Royalty and tradition

Many tourists from overseas are fascinated by our royal family and the pomp and ceremony that goes with it. Remember that many of our visitors are from republics and therefore have no royalty. There are numerous royal palaces to visit and some of them put on events to attract people. Every Sunday the 400th anniversary of Guy Fawkes' attempt to blow up Parliament are celebrated with visitors able to watch interpreters in costume recreating the event.

Theory into practice

There are lots of possible themes that could be used to attract tourists. Others might be history, agriculture, education or religion. Choose one of these and plan a campaign to attract either incoming or domestic tourists to your area. Decide which particular events and attractions might be included in your campaign.

Protective status

Many of our heritage attractions are given special status to protect them from development or too many visitors.

National Parks

About 9 per cent of the land area of the UK is designated as national park. These parks were created in the 1950s and 60s because of their special features such as beauty, or ecological features. They also are of value in providing recreational areas for visitors. In England and Wales there are ten National Parks.

In recent years there have been some new national parks designated. One was Loch Lomond and another, the Trossachs National Park, the first one for Scotland.

The parks are not publicly owned. In fact, areas of them are owned by private landowners. The National Trust owns about 12 per cent of the Peak District National Park and more than 25 per cent of the Lake District. It also owns areas of other parks.

National Park Authorities run national parks and are given funding to do so by the government. The Authorities have powers to control development and manage tourism.

Areas of Outstanding Natural Beauty (AONB)

This is a landscape which has such great beauty that it is important to protect it. It may be coastline, water meadow, moors or downland. There are 41 AONBs in England and Wales. About 18 per cent of the countryside of England and Wales is protected in this way. The AONBs are important national resources and were given further protection under the Countryside and Rights of Way Act of 2000.

UNESCO

The United Nations Educational, Scientific and Cultural Organisation (UNESCO) seeks to encourage the identification, protection and preservation of cultural and natural heritage around the world considered to be of outstanding value to humanity. It does this under the World Heritage Convention of 1972 and has over 700 World Heritage Sites designated worldwide. UNESCO is a global organisation and not specific to the UK. In the UK the DCMS makes sure that the UK complies with the convention. It can also nominate sites in England as potential World Heritage Sites. Nominations in Wales, Scotland and Northern Ireland are made by the respective administrations.

The UK currently has 25 World Heritage Sites. Here are some examples:

* City of Bath
* Hadrian's Wall
* Heart of Neolithic Orkney
* Giant's Causeway and Causeway Coast
* St Kilda.

Theory into practice

Find the list of UK World Heritage Sites from either the UNESCO website or from the DCMS website. Make sure you know what and where each of them is. Choose one and try to decide what makes it outstanding. Discuss your findings with your group.

UNESCO's World Heritage mission is to:

* encourage countries to sign the *World Heritage Convention* and to ensure the protection of their natural and cultural heritage

* encourage States Parties to the *Convention* to nominate sites within their national territory for inclusion on the World Heritage List

* encourage States Parties to establish management plans and set up reporting systems on the state of conservation of their World Heritage sites

* assist States Parties in safeguarding World Heritage sites by providing technical assistance and professional training

* provide emergency assistance for World Heritage sites in immediate danger

* support States Parties' public awareness-building activities for World Heritage conservation

* encourage participation of the local population in the preservation of their cultural and natural heritage

* encourage international co-operation in the conservation of our world's cultural and natural heritage.

Source: whc.unesco.org

Heritage coast

32 per cent of English coastline is designated heritage coast. This means the coasts are protected to conserve their natural beauty. If possible access for visitors is improved. One of the most famous coasts, and the first to be designated, is Beachy Head in Sussex. Many of these areas of coastline are also part of a national park or an AONB.

Beachy Head

1 Why are day visitors important to the economy?

2 What is the balance of payments?

3 Explain the travel services balance.

4 What expectations about cost would incoming tourists to the UK have?

5 How is the International Passenger Survey carried out?

6 Why do France, Germany and the Irish Republic generate large numbers of incoming tourists to the UK?

7 Explain why China is an emerging market.

8 What is the role of the DCMS regarding tourism?

9 What is the difference between VisitBritain and VisitEngland?

10 What is the function of Regional Development Agencies?

11 Explain the difference between English Heritage and the National Trust.

12 How does having a theme for heritage tourism help attract visitors?

13 Explain what a National Park is.

14 Explain an ANOB.

15 What is the role of UNESCO?

ASSESSMENT ASSIGNMENT UNIT 15

The Department for Culture, Media and Sport has a new Minister for Tourism. You and your colleagues at VisitBritain are surprised at the appointment as the Minister has no experience of the tourism industry and does not appear to be very knowledgeable about it. At a preliminary meeting with the Chairman of VisitBritain, the Chairman tried to explain all the various research reports, marketing campaigns and organisational structures that VisitBritain is involved in to boost tourism but the Minister was very slow to understand and short of time. It was decided that a clear presentation should be prepared covering all the issues essential for a grounding in the work of attracting incoming and domestic tourists and that an afternoon should be set aside for the Minister to listen to this presentation.

The Chairman has asked you to prepare all the materials for the presentation.

1 The Minister did not seem to grasp that domestic and incoming tourists sometimes have different needs.

   Describe the needs and expectations of incoming and domestic tourists.

   This task may provide evidence for P1.

2 Compare and contrast the needs and expectations of incoming and domestic tourists.

   This task may provide evidence for M1.

3 The Minister should be informed about the popularity and appeal of Britain to tourists.

   Assess the popularity of the UK to incoming and domestic tourists. You should include graphs or charts with relevant statistics.

   This task may provide evidence for P2.

4 Describe the factors which give the UK appeal to incoming and domestic tourists.

   This task may provide evidence for P3.

5 Although the Minister understands the workings of the DCMS as it is the government department he is assigned to, he needs to understand the role of other organisations involved with incoming and domestic tourism.

   Describe the role of the different types of organisation involved in incoming and domestic tourism.

This task may provide evidence for P4.

6 Explain how these different types of organisations are able to increase the appeal of the UK to incoming and domestic tourists. Give examples of specific campaigns.

This task may provide evidence for M2.

7 Analyse how these organisations interact with each other to meet the needs of incoming and domestic tourists. You might include a chart to illustrate the interaction.

This task may provide evidence for D1.

8 The Minister is particularly interested in how heritage enhances the appeal of the UK to tourists. He expects some new funding to be available to promote heritage attractions and is so enthusiastic that he has just joined the National Trust and English Heritage.

Describe different types of heritage attractions in the UK, giving specific examples of each type.

This task may provide evidence for P5.

9 Explain how the travel and tourism industry uses heritage themes to increase the popularity of the UK to incoming and domestic tourists.

This task may provide evidence for M3.

10 Analyse the significance of heritage tourism to incoming and domestic tourists.

This task may provide evidence for D2.

NB: Tutors should decide whether students should carry out all or parts of the presentation but all materials should be submitted.

Conferences, exhibitions and events

Introduction

In this unit you will examine the conference, exhibition and event industry and how it relates to travel and tourism. You will get the opportunity to organise your own conference, exhibition or event and develop practical skills. Such a project is very challenging but also enjoyable and should result in a great sense of achievement.

You will learn about the different kinds of conferences, exhibitions and events, their venues, the personnel involved in organisation and buying. You will also look at the trends and issues affecting the industry.

Planning and staging an exhibition, conference or event will help you develop your organisational and teamwork skills, show your initiative and solve problems. You should aim to work conscientiously, pay attention to detail and consider other team members and their role.

We will study methods of evaluation so that, after the event, you will have the opportunity to carry out a full appraisal of the event and your own performance in its planning and staging.

How you will be assessed

This unit is internally assessed by your tutor. A variety of exercises and activities is included in the unit to help you develop your knowledge and understanding of conferences, exhibitions and events and prepare for the assessment. You will also have the opportunity to work on some case studies.

After completing this unit you should be able to achieve the following outcomes:

→ examine the conference, exhibition and event environment in the UK
→ plan a conference, exhibition or event
→ stage the conference, exhibition or event
→ evaluate own performance and the success of the conference, exhibition or event.

The conference, exhibition and event environment

Types

Trade fairs

Product launches and events to raise public awareness

Events are held to launch new products or new company names or to raise awareness of existing products. An example was the launch in Toulouse, in January 2005 of the Airbus 380, a huge aircraft

The World Travel Market is held annually in London and is probably the best-known travel-related trade fair. It attracts visitors from overseas as well as the UK. In recent years it has moved to the ExCeL venue in east London. Trade fairs provide an opportunity for industry members to meet up and conduct their business. They also give an opportunity to find out about latest developments in the industry.

The British Travel Trade Fair is held in Birmingham in the spring at the National Exhibition Centre (NEC). This is how the British Travel Trade Fair promotes itself.

'British Travel Trade Fair is the UK's premier annual business-to-business travel and tourism event, attracting 300 exhibitors and 3,000 domestic and international travel trade professionals over two days at Birmingham's NEC.

'BTTF provides a key forum to establish new business contacts, exchange ideas, expertise, and experiences, and to lay the foundations for the future success of the industry at large.'

Source: www.britishtraveltradefair.com

Trade fairs are important events in the travel industry

capable of carrying up to 850 passengers. Premiers of France, Spain and Germany were invited. Tony Blair represented the UK. Airline heads like Richard Branson were there and members of the international press covered the event.

Political conferences

The most famous are the party political conferences held each year by our leading political parties. The Conservative Party Conference is held annually in Brighton, Labour in Blackpool and Liberal Democrats in Bournemouth. It is not mere coincidence that they are held in these seaside towns. Our seaside resorts heavily rely on conference business outside the summer holiday season.

Business meetings

Many business meetings are held on work premises as part of the working day. However, there are occasions when this is unsuitable:

* where a group of staff need uninterrupted time to discuss policy or issues – they may hire a room in a local hotel

* when a supplier needs to meet a customer – when only two or three people are involved in a meeting they can meet in the lounge of a hotel or airport without any charge.

Team-building events

These are usually arranged as staff development exercises to bond teams and get them to work more effectively. When we think about these, outward bound, physically demanding courses come to mind. These are fun but not suitable for everyone. Other types of team-building activities are available and there are companies which specialise in running them.

CASE STUDY

This is an example from a team-building events company, Sandstone.

Romanbar

Probably our most 'out-and-out fun' team-building activity. Certainly a very popular one!

When you want a session with some real team-building flavour, why not try a full-bodied business simulation? In a Romanbar session, product sampling isn't the only aspect that involves the participants! In the idyllic setting of Oldetown, Devashire, each team starts a wine bar within the franchised Romanbar family.

Collectively, they must be competitive enough to wrestle business away from the pre-existing competition. Individually, each team will want to be the best.

Teams make their first decisions and the venture begins! Their deliberations are computer analysed and the results fed back on a 'weekly' basis in the form of profit and loss statements, balance sheets, cash-flow statements and general information on the state of the business.

But no business or service is only about facts and figures, of course. It's also about knowledge, skill and application. Our experts help you learn to become wine connoisseurs, tell different cheeses apart, show off your physical prowess against the other bars in the cheese rolling race, recognise a large range of cocktails etc.

Your new-found expertise converts prospective customers into revenue. Most participants tell us that their favourite part is learning flair bar-keeping skills from our own flair specialist. Move over Tom Cruise! Romanbar participants are catching up fast!

Source: www.sandstone.co.uk

1. **Determine the objectives of a Romanbar team-building activity for a team of staff who work for a reservations call centre.**

2. **What advantages does this kind of activity have over a physical team-building session?**

You could organise a team-building event for your group. You can find out about activities in your local area. What about devising your own team-building course and running it for another group of students?

A group of students on an outward bound course

Corporate hospitality

Corporate hospitality refers to the provision of hospitality and entertainment to customers of a company. It is done to develop good relationships with customers and to encourage new business. For example, a company might hire a marquee at Wimbledon and invite business guests to watch the tennis and have drinks and strawberries and cream in the marquee. Many sporting venues provide facilities for corporate hospitality and it is a lucrative market for them.

Sales exhibition

Most exhibitions have the aim of generating new sales and attracting potential customers. Examples in travel and tourism include the Travel Technology Show. Such a show would not be of interest to the public but would attract trade customers who need to update technology in their

CASE STUDY

Many sporting venues provide facilities for corporate hospitality

'Game, Set and Match to Corporate Hospitality'

At Wimbledon, fans can queue up and get tickets on the day – or can they? At a match last season, thousands of seats were empty and fans who had been queuing in the rain did not get in. Only 500 seats had been reserved for those who queued. The rest of the seats, they were told, were full. Officials blamed the bad weather for the empty seats but critics said corporate hospitality was to blame. The seats are bought by companies and given out to their customers. If it's raining they don't turn up. A marquee at Wimbledon costs thousands of pounds but companies think it is worth the expense to entertain their top clients.

Choose a sporting venue in your area, for example, the football club. Find out what corporate hospitality packages are on offer and what they cost. Make notes and comment on whether they represent value for money.

business. This particular event boasts over 100 suppliers exhibiting.

Further examples of sales exhibitions are the holiday and travel shows held annually in Glasgow and Manchester. Exhibitors at these events are potential holidaymakers, from the general public. These are known as consumer exhibitions rather than trade.

Many people attend shows on products or themes which interest them as a leisure activity. An example is the Ideal Home Exhibition. With this in mind, exhibitors provide entertainment, free samples etc. to attract more visitors, but the ultimate aim of the exhibition is to sell.

Annual conferences

Annual conferences may be held by a single company to bring their employees together or they may be organised to bring interested professionals together to discuss industry issues.

Travel Insight is an example of an industry conference. It is aimed at travel marketers and discusses a number of key marketing topics, for example consumer behaviour. Delegates or their employers pay to attend and are attracted because high level speakers attend the conference. In 2005 Travel Insight had speakers from British Airways, Ryanair and E Bookers amongst others.

Fund raisers

Some organisations hold fund-raising events and donate the funds to their chosen charity. Such events have several benefits:

* they raise money for charity

* they allow staff to work together for a common cause

* they get useful publicity for the company.

Some charities are proactive in using tourism to help them raise funds. The charity 'Mind' organises, alongside travel professionals, a series of treks, for example in Cuba. Participants raise money from sponsors to pay for the trip and to donate money to the charity.

A fund-raising event is one of the easiest events for you to organise. Make sure it is linked to travel and tourism in some way.

Venues

Purpose-built centres

In 2003 18 per cent of conferences were held in purpose-built centres. National exhibitions are held in purpose-built centres as they are so large and they need to be in venues that accommodate large numbers of visitors and are accessible by all modes of transport.

We have several purpose-built exhibition and conference centres in the UK. You have probably heard of the National Exhibition Centre (NEC) in Birmingham, our biggest venue. You may have heard of Olympia and Earls Court in London and GMEX in Manchester. In Glasgow, there is the Scottish Exhibition and Conference Centre.

Hotels

Hotels are the most popular venues for conferences with 58 per cent of them held in hotels in 2003. All hotels want to cultivate the business market and will provide conference and meeting facilities. In addition, local sales exhibitions are held at hotels. Examples include wedding fairs and property exhibitions.

Academic venues

Academic venues are ideal for conferences and meetings as they have all the necessary facilities inbuilt. Student rooms can be used to accommodate delegates and catering facilities are readily available. Lecture rooms provide room for

large numbers of people with audio-visual facilities for speakers. Universities and colleges are pleased to have the opportunity to hire their premises and facilities outside term time.

Sporting venues

We have already mentioned sporting venues in terms of corporate hospitality. They often provide conference and meeting facilities in order to make use of the facilities when sport is not taking place.

Theory into practice

Manchester United is known as an organisation with great business acumen. Part of its business activity involves a complex of function rooms for social or business use.

Visit the Old Trafford website and find out what kind of facilities are offered and what they cost. Decide on an event you might hold there and write some notes on the products and services you would hire.

Unusual venues

Many venues not traditionally used for conferences and events are vying for the lucrative conference trade; 12 per cent of conferences were held in unusual venues in 2003. The advantage of holding a conference at a more unusual venue is that it adds an extra incentive to attend for the delegates and the conference can be combined with corporate hospitality. Examples include Xscape, a snow centre where conference rooms and facilities are available and delegates can go skiing as well, and London Zoo, where events or conferences can be hosted.

Civic venues

Civic buildings usually have board rooms and meeting rooms where council meetings are held. When not in use for these purposes they may be hired out to local businesses for meetings.

Buyers

Buyers for conferences, events and exhibitions are the different types of customers. The customers for a conference are the delegates who attend – they are usually corporate customers as they represent their companies. The organisers of the conference are also buyers. They are buying the services of the venue or the conference-organiser company.

These buyers or customers may be domestic, that is UK based, or international. The UK conference market's international customers are mainly from the US, Germany and France. Emerging markets are China because of 'approved destination status' granted to the UK and other European countries. Central American countries such as Panama, Nicaragua and El Salvador have had rapid growth in their economies and are likely new customers for UK conferences.

Buyers at exhibitions and events fall into two main categories. Firstly there are the exhibitors. These are the buyers of space and stands and they are the main source of income for the exhibition organisers. Secondly there are the people who attend the exhibition and usually pay an entrance fee. This is the second strand of income for the exhibition organisers.

The exhibitors may be companies, government organisations such as VisitBritain or trade associations like the Federation of Tour Operators. Of course, the nature of exhibitor depends on the type of exhibition.

Those attending the exhibition may be corporate customers or members of the public or a mix. Again this depends on the type of exhibition or event.

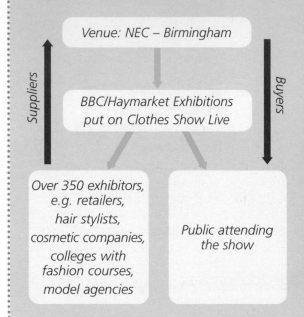
Suppliers

Venue-finding agencies

Most organisations involved in venue finding offer the service as part of an extended range of services. Once the venue has been confirmed and booked for the client they will offer a conference-organising service too. Venue-finding agencies build up databases of contacts and find suitable venues to match the clients' requirements. They do not charge clients for the venue-finding service as they earn their fees on commission from the venue. However, they need to offer more services than venue finding as it is easy for customers to trawl the Internet themselves and find suitable premises.

Some Tourist Information Centres offer venue-finding services. They have excellent knowledge of local venues and can advise on suitability. The service allows them to make some extra revenue in commissions and they can offer other services to organisers and delegates, for example, souvenirs of the area, visits to attractions or walking tours.

Conference organisers

Around one-third of conferences are booked by a professional conference organiser or venue-finding agency. Organising an event or conference is very time consuming and within a company it may be that a busy member of staff has this task on top of their normal duties. Conference organisers take the stress away from companies who merely tell the organiser what their requirements are and allow them to do all the work. The service they offer will include:

* offering a choice of suitable venues
* putting together a delegate package
* making all bookings
* liaising with the venue
* organising catering
* organising signage
* booking accommodation
* arranging speakers
* booking transport
* arranging audio-visual equipment.

Exhibition organisers

There are several large exhibition organisers in the UK. UK-headquartered Reed Exhibitions is the world's leading organiser of trade and consumer events, with a portfolio of over 420 events in 32 countries. Reed has 13 travel and tourism exhibitions in its portfolio and is responsible for organising the British Travel Trade Fair and the World Travel Market. In France they also run the International Luxury Travel Market and in Dubai, the Arabian Travel Market.

This is how Reed explains its role on its website.

> 'At Reed Exhibitions we don't just organise trade shows. We see our role as that of a relationship broker, identifying, targeting, attracting and matching the needs of buyers and suppliers at our shows. We maximise business and networking opportunities through associated conferences, features, events and sponsorship opportunities.'
>
> Source: www.reedexpo.com

There are also smaller companies successfully operating in exhibition organisation. An example is John Fish Exhibitions Ltd which was formed in 1992 which has annual exhibitions in Manchester and Glasgow attracting 77,000 and 50,000 visitors respectively.

Audio-visual suppliers

For meetings and conferences the venue usually supplies any audio-visual equipment required. Sometimes more sophisticated equipment and technicians are needed and then a specialist company may be hired. Venues or conference organisers have contacts with such companies or they can be found easily on the Internet. The services they offer may include:

* conference production
* set design (where a themed event is desired)
* graphics
* multimedia presentations.

Catering suppliers

Most venues have in-house catering supplies and will not allow organisers to use outside contractors, particularly hotels. Where such services are not on offer the organiser will have to seek another contractor.

Large exhibition centres provide different kinds of catering, for example, at the ExCeL Exhibition Centre in London a number of sandwich bars, cafes and restaurants are provided on site for the benefit of visitors and exhibitors alike. In addition, stand catering is available, where exhibitors can order catering items for their stands from an on-site shop. The shop delivers the

Catering at an exhibition centre

goods directly to the stands. The shop will also offer coffee machines, napkins, cups etc.

IT suppliers

Exhibition centres will provide for the IT needs of their clients as this example from ExCeL demonstrates.

'Nothing is left to chance by our experienced IT support team – ExCeL InTouch – which is able to facilitate a number of requests and ensure that everything runs smoothly on the day. And your Event Manager will happily facilitate all requests, which means fewer things for you to coordinate and worry about.

- Wireless registration
- Web casting
- Speaker networks (speaker presentations broadcast simultaneously to a number of meeting rooms from a central control room).'

Source: www.excel-london.co.uk

At smaller venues, companies will normally expect basic IT needs to be met and will expect to bring in anything further required.

Security personnel suppliers

For an event, security personnel will be needed and there are specialist agencies who provide security. They can take charge of crowd management, car parking, entry control, front of house security and safety issues. At a large event it is worth getting a specialist company to oversee security as they will also be able to advise on what is required for a particular event.

Trends and issues

Market growth

Research by the British Association of Conference Destinations (BACD) shows that the UK conference business was worth about £7.7 billion in 2003, up from £7.2 billion in 2002. This is in terms of direct spend by organisers. The value rises even more when indirect spend in bars, restaurants, on entertainment and transport by delegates is taken into account. Most venues reported an increase in business over the previous year. Venues managed to hold an average of 386 conferences in 2003, an increase of 32 per cent on 2002.

The peak months for conferences in 2003 were September and October. The quietest months were August, January and December.

Impact of technology

> **Key concept**
>
> **Video-conferencing** allows two or more people in different locations to link up and communicate by video.

Video-conferencing

The advent of video-conferencing did not have the expected impact on conferences and business meetings. It seems that people still prefer to meet and talk face-to-face. With video-conferencing, the camera focuses on the person who is speaking so it is impossible to gauge reactions of the rest of the meeting and to get an instinctive feel for the meeting. It is least suitable for large meetings.

The Internet

However, other forms of technology have impacted on the conference market. Organisers of conferences and events are more easily able to search for suitable venues on the Internet rather than rely on the services of a venue finder or events company. Not many suppliers have adopted online-booking systems to date but this is rising fast.

Wireless technology

Wireless technology will impact on businesses as it is possible to set up a network for delegates to use in a meeting or conference. Delegates will be able to comment or ask questions using their computers and will be able to do so anonymously if they choose.

Growth of budget meeting facilities

There is a trend for meetings to become smaller and shorter. The reasons are so that companies can control spending, so that more frequent and flexible meetings can be held and because employees are reluctant to spend long periods of time in meetings they feel are not always relevant to them. This trend has led to companies choosing smaller and cheaper venues for meetings and often seeking out the more unusual venues.

Assessment activity 16.1

1 Study a city or major town in your own area and find out what conference, event and exhibition provision is available. Examine different types of venue and events and consider who the suppliers and buyers are at the venues. Write up your findings in the form of pages that could be posted on a Tourism Information Centre website for the town.

   This task may provide evidence for P1.

2 Analyse the trends and issues affecting the conference environment as described above.

   This task may provide evidence for M1.

3 Evaluate how the conference environment described above has responded to trends and issues.

   This task may provide evidence for D1.

Planning the conference, exhibition or event

Initial considerations

Feasibility

Carrying out a feasibility study may involve some research. Some conferences take place on a regular basis but delegates may be consulted to ensure the content is relevant. If a new venue or type of event is to be tried then research should consider:

* suitability of venue in terms of capacity and facilities

* location and access

* cost

* time available for planning

* whether the event will meet planned objectives.

Theory into practice

Carry out a feasibility study to decide if your ideas for an event are feasible. Do not underestimate the time you will need to plan your event. Beware of taking too long to determine what type of event you will have. Limit yourselves to one or two class sessions to decide

---

Objectives

The objectives of the conference or event must be clear from the outset. In the case of a conference it is usual to communicate the objectives to the delegates. The objectives should be tested against the SMART theory to make sure they are feasible.

Key concept

SMART objectives stands for:

Specific – clear and concise

Measurable – how will we know if we achieved them?

Achievable – must have the skills and resources to achieve them

Realistic – not overly ambitious

Timed – deadlines.

One group of students organised a day trip to a go-cart track. They had all managed to find sponsors based on the number of laps they managed to achieve. They had to organise transport and the entrance to the track. They managed to have the track to themselves as they were a group. They took lots of photos and wrote a press release which they sent to the local newspapers. The funds raised were donated to charity.

What do you think were the objectives of this event?

Theory into practice

You will have to determine the objectives for your own conference or event. You might find it useful to do this as a group. You can record the objectives individually and then you can determine your own personal objectives depending on your role in the planning and staging of the event.

Venue

The following venue factors must be considered when planning a conference, exhibition or event:

* capacity
* accommodation and quality
* facilities
* availability for specific dates
* access for visitors
* parking
* cost.

Once a venue has been chosen, the size of room needed must be determined and the organiser will also be given a choice of layouts for the room. Different layouts are suitable for different degrees of formality in meetings. Conferences for large numbers of delegates will need theatre-type layouts to ensure there is room for everyone and that they can all see speakers. The Moat House Hotels offer a wide range of conference and meeting room layouts:

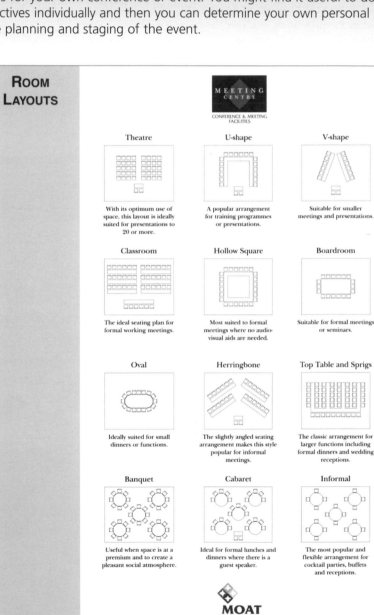

ROOM LAYOUTS

MEETING CENTRE
CONFERENCE & MEETING FACILITIES

Theatre — With its optimum use of space, this layout is ideally suited for presentations to 20 or more.

U-shape — A popular arrangement for training programmes or presentations.

V-shape — Suitable for smaller meetings and presentations.

Classroom — The ideal seating plan for formal working meetings.

Hollow Square — Most suited to formal meetings where no audio-visual aids are needed.

Boardroom — Suitable for formal meetings or seminars.

Oval — Ideally suited for small dinners or functions.

Herringbone — The slightly angled seating arrangement makes this style popular for informal meetings.

Top Table and Sprigs — The classic arrangement for larger functions including formal dinners and wedding receptions.

Banquet — Useful when space is at a premium and to create a pleasant social atmosphere.

Cabaret — Ideal for formal lunches and dinners where there is a guest speaker.

Informal — The most popular and flexible arrangement for cocktail parties, buffets and receptions.

MOAT HOUSE HOTELS

Which venue are you going to use for your own event? You may be thinking of using a room at your school or college as it will be free. This is fine, but consider contacts you have at other venues. One group of students borrowed a whole theatre for a day and put on a fashion show. Another group organised their event for children in a local primary school. The local council allowed another group to put on a Christmas fete in a hall at the local Guild Hall. Remember too that your conference, exhibition or event must be related to travel and tourism.

Once you have a venue, you need to decide what kind of layout is most suitable for your event and include it in your plan.

Staffing

Staff are needed to meet the visitors and establish their needs. They should be able to identify potential customers and deflect others. Such staff are important because European Travel Trade Fairs Association (ETTFA) research shows that 60 per cent of visitors will walk away from a stand if they are not greeted within one minute. In addition, sales staff are needed who actually sell to these customers, once identified. These should be the usual sales team.

Equipment

At a conference the basic equipment needed is presentation material, that is, a flip chart, markers and an overhead projector. Many speakers arrive with Powerpoint presentations and they will expect a screen and projector to be provided. They may require Internet access. It is usual to provide pens and paper for delegates and water should be on the table.

More sophisticated equipment like video-conferencing or computer networks will have to be specially ordered.

At an exhibition or events, all kinds of specialist effects may be required from lighting to graphics. These could be provided by a specialist company.

Certain types of event require a licence. You can get a Public Entertainment Licence from the local authority if you need one. You do need one for any kind of dancing, theatre or sporting event. If you want to play music you need to contact the Performing Rights Society. If you intend to run a raffle then you need to check the regulations and make sure you do not have to register with the Gaming Board. You can find out all the details by looking at the websites of the relevant bodies.

Make a list of all the equipment you will need for your event. If you are holding a conference think about what you want to give the delegates. Have you thought about asking your marketing department if they have any college pens or diaries that they will give you? If you are holding an exhibition you should be able to borrow boards or stands within your school or college. You will need to know what the equipment costs for your budget. The list of equipment will go into your plan.

Health, safety and security

The Health and Safety at Work Act lays out a duty of care towards members of the public visiting an establishment. Thus, a conference or exhibition organiser must 'ensure, so far as is reasonably practicable' that visitors are not exposed to health and safety risks. In addition, the Occupier's Liability Act (1984) places a duty of care on occupiers to see that a visitor will be reasonably safe in using the premises for the purposes for which he is invited or permitted by the occupier to be there.

An HMSO publication is available called *The Guide to Fire Precautions in Existing Places of Entertainment and Like Premises* (known as the Yellow Guide).

If an organiser brings in outside contractors to a venue, for catering, for example, then the organiser must make sure that the contractor complies with health and safety legislation.

Here are some of the points relating to health and safety that should be considered.

Take note of these points when planning your own event.

Room layout

When designing the layout make sure that everyone will be able to get out if necessary. Make sure that exits and gangways are not blocked and that there are no obstacles for people to fall over.

Delegate numbers

Every conference or exhibition room has a maximum capacity which should be displayed in the room. The capacity is determined by the size of the room and by ability to exit in a fire. A room with many fire exits will be allocated a larger capacity than a room with only a few. Organisers must make sure the maximum capacity is not exceeded and bear in mind that if there are many wheelchair users then the overall capacity is reduced.

Delegate flow

Entrances, exits and reception areas must be able to cope with numbers of visitors arriving at the same time. Consideration should be given to the movement of people around the building, to toilets, dining rooms etc. If necessary, people should be guided in smaller groups.

Car parking facilities for delegates with impaired mobility should be provided

Special needs

Organisers have to consider access for people with impaired mobility or other special needs. The Disability Discrimination Act should be taken account of.

Signage

Signs may be needed at various points around the building, particularly in venues where several events are taking place at the same time. Organisers should remember that signs may also be needed to guide people to a venue.

Risk assessment

The Management of Health and Safety Regulations have specific requirements regarding risk assessment and it is necessary to carry out a risk assessment in relation to persons visiting an establishment.

Carrying out the risk assessment:

✱ Who is at risk?
- people attending the event
- organisers
- outside contractors working at the event.

✱ What are the possible hazards?
- tripping or slipping
- manual handling injuries
- bad housekeeping
- electrical problems

- fire hazards from heaters or smoking
- food hygiene.

✳ How can the risk be minimised?

- remove the hazard e.g. no lit candles, no blocked gangways
- minimise the hazard e.g. provide fire extinguishers, train in lifting techniques.

For example, at the Leeds Festival organised by Mean Fiddler, no campfires are allowed on site. This reduces the risk of fire and is a condition of the festival licence from Leeds City Council. Patrols are carried out to make sure fires are not lit and there are fire observation towers.

✳ What is the level of risk?

- very low
- low
- medium
- high
- very high

A risk assessment form should be completed and kept.

Contingency procedures

Key concept

Contingency plan – a plan you have ready to deal with things that go wrong.

The risk assessment will identify some hazards but there are many things that can go wrong which do not fall into the category of hazards. When planning a conference, exhibition or event it is always best to think of everything that could possibly go wrong and prepare for it. The most common problem at conferences is the late arrival or cancellation of speakers. Good planners confirm with their speakers the week before and the day before the conference and make sure times and transport details are confirmed in writing. It is such attention to detail that may prevent problems. At a very large exhibition it may not be so noticeable if one or two exhibitors cancel. However, exhibitors may have problems if their products, props or outside contractors let them down.

Theory into practice

Imagine you have invited a group of 15 eight year olds to participate in an afternoon of games in your sports hall. Carry out the risk assessment by copying the form layout shown below.

HAZARD	RISK LEVEL	SAFETY MEASURE	WHO IS RESPONSIBLE?

Theory into practice

Produce a contingency plan for your own event. Use this form to help you.

WHAT IF?	CONSEQUENCES?	WHAT SHOULD WE DO?

Contract supplies

The venue may not be able to provide everything the organiser desires, or the organiser may just want something different. In that case the organiser will look to outside contractors to provide extras. They might order:

* carpeting for stands and exhibition areas
* flowers
* food and drink
* transport, e.g. taxis or buses to shuttle delegates from one venue to another
* accommodation – may be provided at hotels nearby the venue in a separate arrangement.

A stand at an exhibition

Theory into practice

In your case, you may be operating on a very small budget but that doesn't mean you can't use contract suppliers to provide what you need for your event. Some suppliers might be prepared to provide you with supplies on a sponsorship basis. This means in return for you promoting their name and logo in your programme and in your publicity they will give you what you need. Be warned, however, that this is very hard to achieve and you need some very determined and persuasive students on the case. Also, you must deliver what you promise in terms of publicity. Examples of successful sponsorship for student events include the provision of decorative balloons at an event, hairdressing and make up at a fashion show and T-shirts for sports events.

Financial

Rates

Venues calculate rates for delegates on a day basis or on a residential basis. Such rates will usually include accommodation, meals and use of facilities if at a hotel. Conference organisers may add a percentage onto these rates to add to their profits.

The average daily delegate rate achieved by venues for conferences in 2003 was £47.30 and the average 24-hour/residential rate was £167.20. The packages can always be enhanced when extra funds are available.

Exhibition space

When booking space at an exhibition, suppliers have to take into account the cost of stands and space. The best positions, for example, at the top of escalators, cost more as do the larger stands. Companies have a budget allocated annually which must cover all the shows at which they wish to exhibit. This budget must cover the cost of hospitality on the exhibition stand as well as any props.

A holiday home company exhibiting at the National Holiday Home Show has the following costs to consider:

* cost of stand
* wine and appetisers on the stand to offer customers
* props inside the holiday homes
* purchase of garden chairs, table and parasols to add ambience to the stand
* hire of greeters (meet customers and direct to sales personnel).

In addition, the company is likely to provide corporate hospitality in the evenings in terms of dinners out and entertainment.

CASE STUDY

The Moat House Hotels offer the following conference and meeting facilities delegate rates:

PRICES, PACKAGES AND EQUIPMENT

MEETING CENTRE
CONFERENCE & MEETING FACILITIES

DAILY DELEGATE PACKAGE

Main meeting room
Morning coffee and biscuits
Conference lunch
Afternoon tea and biscuits
Table refreshments
Table stationery

Overhead projector and screen in main meeting room
Flipchart and marker Pens
Meeting Centre Toolkit
Service and VAT

RATE: £55.00 per Delegate   £67.00 per Delegate and a Round of Golf

24-HOUR DELEGATE PACKAGE

All elements of the daily delegate package PLUS:
3-course dinner
Accommodation
Full breakfast
Use of Club Moativation health and fitness club

The contact on the day for residential conferences will receive a complimentary upgrade to a Crown bedroom or a complimentary round of golf subject to availability.

RATE: £175.00 per Delegate   £190.00 per Delegate and a Round of Golf

36-HOUR DELEGATE PACKAGE

This includes all elements of the daily delegate and 24-hour packages, with an extra discount built in.

RATE: £210.00 per Delegate   £225.00 per Delegate and a Round of Golf

ENERGISER BREAKS

Only £25.00 per 30 min. session, per group.

Why not take time-out to invigorate your meeting with a workout? Qualified instructors can put you and your colleagues through your paces in either the gym or your meeting room. Or unwind in the pool, sauna, steam room and spa - towels are provided. The Energiser Breaks can be as relaxing or energetic as you like and there's no need for sports clothing.

SNACK PACK - the working lunch option

As an alternative to your conference lunch why not choose between:
Snack Pack Original or Snack Pack Plus
Both offer:
• A choice of filled baguettes or ciabatta bread
• Packet of Walkers crisps
• Seasonal Fruit
• Cadbury's confectionery
• A choice of Pepsi, Diet Pepsi or 7-up with the SNACK PACK ORIGINAL
• An 18.75cl bottle of wine or a can of Heineken with the SNACK PACK PLUS

SPECIAL DIETARY REQUIREMENTS

Our chefs are able to cater for vegetarian, vegan and other special dietary needs.

MOAT HOUSE HOTELS

Cambridgeshire

You are going to use the Moat House for a small conference to discuss the next year's business plan. You have 12 staff but it is not essential that they all attend. However, some may be upset if they are not invited. You have a budget of £2,000 for the event. Decide whether it is to be a day meeting or a residential and what you will offer the delegates. Draw up a chart showing how you have spent the budget. Compare your plan with those of your colleagues.

Space and stands are very expensive as the Stand Application Form for the World Travel Market indicates (see below). Those suppliers on a limited budget may opt to share a stand.

ExCeL, London, 14 - 17 November 2005
2005 pricing information and Stand Application Form

If you have not already submitted your space requirements for 2005 please complete and return this form to: **EXHIBITOR BUSINESS LOUNGE.**

Post to: **World Travel Market Sales, Reed Travel Exhibitions, Oriel House, 26 The Quadrant, Richmond, Surrey, TW9 1DL United Kingdom**

Fax to Graeme Barnett: **+44 (0) 20 8334 0596**

Visit our website: **www.wtmlondon.com**

Space
We wish to reserve _____ square metres of stand space

Stand
We will require the following stand option (tick box):

Option 1 ☐ Space only at £268 sqm
Option 2 ☐ Shell scheme at £316 sqm
Option 3 ☐ Stand Package A   or   ☐ AA at £3,700
☐ Stand Package B   or   ☐ BB at £4,930
☐ Stand Package C   or   ☐ CC at £6,170
☐ Stand Package D   or   ☐ DD at £8,450

Double decker ☐ Space only sqm_____ @ £44

Location
We wish our stand to be located in the following region (tick box)

☐ Africa   ☐ Global Village*   ☐ Travel Technology
☐ Asia Pacific   ☐ Middle East   ☐ UK & Ireland
☐ Caribbean   ☐ North America
☐ Europe & Mediterranean   ☐ South & Central America

*for international companies with global representation

Registration
We wish to register _____ sharing companies at £56 each
After 12 August 2005: £68 each

Your main stand-holder registration will include:
Main stand-holder registration £140
After 12 August 2005: £160
All prices quoted above exclude VAT @ 17.5%

Sponsorship
☐ Tick here for details of WTM sponsorship opportunities

WTM Consultancy Service
Tick box if you would like further information on any of the following advisory services that are designed to help you achieve the best possible result at World Travel Market 2005:

☐ PR ☐ Group Travel Solutions ☐ Early Bird Discounts ☐ Meridian Club
☐ Stand Design & Management ☐ Marketing & Promotional campaigns

Charity Donation
☐ 'Just a Drop' is RTE's dedicated charity for the travel and tourism industry. Please tick the box if you would not like to make a £20 donation.

1. Who is selling the stand space?
2. What do you think is meant by sponsorship opportunities?
3. Explain the other services on offer.
Discuss your answers with your group.

Calculation of ticket costs

The second strand of revenue for exhibition companies is the entry fee. Exhibition organisers have to decide at what price to sell their tickets.

Remember too that many business customers will not be charged for entry to an exhibition as their custom is precious and if they do not attend then the exhibitors do not want to be there. For example, at the World Travel Fair, everyone who pre-registers gets in free. Of course, the organisers then have useful names and addresses for their future mailings. Some exhibitions are targeted at the public and in this case an entrance fee can be charged. The fee will depend on what customers will be prepared to pay and on how many visitors to an exhibition are expected. This is not difficult to calculate for an exhibition which is held regularly as previous visitor numbers are available.

Producing a budget

A budget must be realistic and include all costs and all sources of revenue. It should include an amount for contingencies.

Here is an example of a budget for a local outdoor festival.

OUTGOINGS

Site

Toilets:	£6,000
Fencing, radios etc:	£2,000
Recycling and litter:	£2,500
Site & park crews, vehicle:	£2,800
Crew food and drink:	£1,200
Total site	**£14,500**

Health and safety

Stewards, security:	£6,000
Gate crew, first aid, barriers:	£4,000
Total health and safety	**£10,000**

Entertainment

Bands:	£3,000
Stage and lighting:	£3,600
Marquees:	£5,000
Sound:	£900
Total entertainment	**£12,500**

Production

Signs:	£500
Insurance:	£600
Publicity:	£900
Phone, photocopying:	£2,000
Other production:	£3,000
Total production	**£7,000**

Council charges

Entertainment licence:	£3,000
Use of park:	£6,000
Park deposit:	£1,000
Total council charges	**£10,000**

Total expenses	**£54,000**

ESTIMATED INCOME

Stalls:	£20,000
Bar income:	£10,000
Gate donations:	£8,000
Muffin and magic stalls:	£3,000
Fun make-up stalls:	£400
Sponsorship:	£500
Loans:	£2,000
Donations:	£2,000
Programme:	£100
Park deposit:	£1,000
Total income	**£47,000**

Current estimated shortfall	*£7,000*

Here is a worksheet for you to copy that can help you prepare a budget for your expenses.

Total amount available:	Number of people attending:

Category	Amount budgeted
Venue cost	
Catering	
Entertainment	
Decorations	
Audio-visual equipment	
Printed materials and promotion	
Transport	
Gifts/souvenirs	
Overheads	
Contingency	

Theory into practice

You will have to produce a budget for your conference or event. This will form part of your plan. Estimate all the costs you will have and all the revenue. It is likely that you will be keeping costs as low as possible and using accommodation and facilities in your school or college as far as possible. Will you be able to charge for entry? It is unlikely if your conference is targeted at fellow students. If you are planning a careers conference you can expect the speakers to give their time for free as they may be keen to recruit.

You will have some expenses, for example, you should provide coffee and lunch for your speakers and you might wish to offer a drink to the delegates. If you have no funds available for your event, consider fundraising activities like sponsored walks and cake sales. Don't forget to ask your school or college if they have funds allocated for student events.

Operational plan

Roles and responsibilities

Everyone involved in planning an event must know exactly what they are responsible for. At organisational meetings, tasks must be assigned to personnel with agreed deadlines. Where tasks are not assigned to specific members of staff they will not happen.

These will vary depending on the type of event but areas of responsibility may include:

* venue liaison and booking
* administration
* finance
* fundraising
* marketing
* catering
* contracting speakers
* planning layout, delegate flow, signage etc
* methods of gathering feedback for evaluation.

Organisation on the day

In addition, people will have particular responsibilities on the day of the event. These may include:

* welcome and registration
* setting up the room/s
* food preparation
* guiding delegates and speakers
* taking photos

* meeting press
* hosting the event
* introducing and thanking speakers
* gathering feedback
* taking everything down
* clearing up.

Theory into practice

You should determine the roles and responsibilities of each group member at the beginning of the unit, once you have decided on the nature of your conference or event. Be very specific and write job descriptions which you can include in your plan. Consider the strengths and weaknesses of group members when deciding who will do what and who will work well together in small groups. Decide whether you will have a chairperson for the project.

Timings

The operational plan for an event must be timed. Personnel will set up the day before where possible, otherwise they have to arrive in good time to set up. When delegates or visitors arrive, they will gain a poor image of the company or event if preparations are still underway. Delegates attending a conference must be informed of programme timings and time of registration before the event. Visitors to an exhibition must be aware of opening times. It is good manners to provide speakers with a full programme of speeches, not just their own and a list of who the other speakers are.

Registration format

At a conference there is an attendance list which delegates should sign to confirm their presence. Badges should be provided for delegates as it cannot be presumed that they all know each other and they will hope to network – which badges enable them to do.

At exhibitions it is usual to collect all details of visitors. At a large event like the World Travel Market a system of pre-registration online or by post enables visitors to arrive with tickets. This

means reception halls are not clogged with people filling in forms, although there is a provision for people to resister on arrival as well.

Programmes

These will be prepared in advance and can be as simple as a sheet with times and locations of seminars or meetings or, for an exhibition, a full catalogue of exhibitors and their location within the venue. These catalogues can be sold to provide extra revenue. They sometimes carry advertising.

Assessment activity 16.2

Your group has decided to put on a Higher Education Fair at your school or college. The event will last one day at the beginning of July and will take place in the main hall. You are to produce a full plan for this event. This should be an individual piece of work although you may carry out group discussions. The following information will help you although you may add any other details you think are appropriate:

* roles and responsibilities of group members
* target audience – all students in the schools and colleges in the area who may be interested in entering HE in the next two years – you cannot expect them to pay to attend
* exhibitors – you will need to invite HE establishments to attend – you will not have to pay them
* room layout – must allow visitors to look round all stands in safety – determine maximum capacity
* equipment – consider stands, tables, chairs for exhibitors, lighting
* catering – should provide drinks and possibly lunch for exhibitors. You could have drinks and snacks on sale for visitors (consider contracting to your cafeteria)
* marketing – invitations to exhibitors with response forms, marketing to schools and colleges, press release
* decoration of hall and signage needed
* budget needed
* programme for visitors listing exhibitors and location
* operational plan for the day.

Your plan may provide evidence for P2.

Staging the conference, exhibition or event

Contracts

Venue suppliers and suppliers of services contracted will require a contract to be drawn up with the particulars of what has been ordered and the terms of the contract.

Venue contract

The contract with the venue will specify times and dates that are booked and will lay down the conditions of the booking. These cover payments and schedule of payment, cancellation procedure and any other requirements that the venue wishes to include such as the venue retaining ultimate approval of any external suppliers whom the organiser might wish to hire.

Other types of contract

If any services from outside contractors, such as catering and audio-visual services are booked, then these too require a contract. For an exhibition, personnel for security or waiting duties may be needed. These staff will need a contract laying out their duties and hours and days of work.

Sometimes venues have preferred suppliers. These are people they are accustomed to working with and consider reputable. They can recommend them with confidence to their clients.

Marketing

Publicity and advertising

Unless the event is a very small conference or meeting, it will require publicity or advertising. The two are often used together in a campaign. The publicity for an event has, of course, been planned in advance, and hopefully the press releases have resulted in press interest and they have turned up to the event. This should never be assumed and it is a good idea to put on some pressure by reminding the press a couple of days before that the event is happening.

Even if press do not attend, a photographic record of the event can be made and a further press release sent out with photos after the event. This would still be useful publicity. The photos can be posted on a website.

We will consider some examples of publicity for different types of events.

A conference for company staff

All this requires is an internal email or invitation for staff to attend. Posters and leaflets advertising the event can be distributed throughout the company.

A national conference for travel professionals

It is necessary to inform potential delegates of the event. This can be done by placing advertisements in professional travel journals. Press releases with information about the event can be sent to journals too. These have the benefit of generating free publicity – if they are used.

A national trade exhibition, for example, the World Travel Market

As soon as one of these major trade fairs finishes, work begins on planning the next. A website is constantly updated giving information about dates and exhibitors. Press releases are sent out to all the travel trade press, particularly in the weeks leading up to the fair. These give news updates and information about competitions to entice visitors. Adverting is placed in travel trade journals. Mailshots are sent to all the people who attended the fair in the previous year with their pre-registration information.

A national consumer exhibition, for example, Clothes Show Live

This is a very popular, successful show and therefore can afford a large adverting budget. Money is spent on a television advert as well as press advertising. Mailshots are sent to schools and colleges who have previously sent groups to the show. In addition, a publicity team generates press releases and news items to create press interest.

This example shows an extract from the advertising and public relations campaign for 'The Hotel Show' held in the United Emirates.

Theory into practice

Prepare a press release for a sponsored run which is being held at your school or college to raise money for charity. Use headed paper and include a picture that a newspaper could print. Make sure you have all the details of:

- what is happening
- where it is taking place
- the date
- the times
- contact details for further information.

Guest lists and invitations

Conferences and corporate events require the drawing up of a guest list and design of invitations. These should be sent out in good time before the event. Organisers of major exhibitions send out invitations a few months in advance. This will be too long for your project. Your aim is to send out invitations in good time – so that recipients' diaries are not full – and not too early so that your guests have time to forget about your event or lose interest.

Sponsorship

Sponsorship is a very good idea as it gives kudos to an event if a well-known brand provides sponsorship and it also relieves the budget. Drinks companies such as Moët & Chandon or Evian or Kronenbourg often sponsor events to push their brands – but it is unlikely they will sponsor yours!

Sponsors may send a representative to make sure their logo, name and products are being presented properly. The representative should be given VIP treatment at the event. When setting up the event the organiser must consider the sponsor's needs and incorporate them into the room plan.

This example shows how TravelMole runs its 'Fast conference' service by using sponsors. This means that three or four different sponsors pay for the costs of a conference on current issues in travel and tourism and then delegates can attend for free. This enables them to discuss reaction to events like the tsunami in the Indian Ocean in 2004.

Silver Sponsors receive:

- company logo, 100-word profile and live link to your website from the TravelMole Fast Conferences website (this site will be promoted via email marketing and banner advertising)
- company logo and profile of 150 words included in the delegate pack
- acknowledgement by the TravelMole chairperson during event opening
- free attendance for one company delegate
- opportunity to be included in post-event promotion, including editorial summary.

Package value: £500

Source: www.travelmole.com

Guest list/list of delegates

This should be available at reception for guests to be welcomed and signed in. Guests may have reserved seating.

Operation

The day of the event has arrived and the whole team is on tenterhooks. Even people who plan events constantly get anxious on the day as they hope that everything runs smoothly. Hopefully, the excellent planning means that everything will go well.

Communication on the day of the event

Members of the organisational team may need to contact each other around a building or on different sites. Walkie-talkies are an efficient means of contacting personnel but everyone involved should know where they are meant to be at all times. It is a good idea to appoint a couple of people as runners. They can do all the errands and pass on messages and will be invaluable.

Principles of customer service

At a conference, exhibition or event it is important to offer excellent customer service and to remember that customers may be internal, for example, colleagues, employees or contractors.

Problem solving

As no event is ever the same as another, organisers must be able to show initiative and solve problems. Of course, experience helps, and once a particular problem has occurred it can be incorporated into the contingency plan, but there will always be something unexpected.

Contingency plans

A contingency plan should be written and available. It allows organisers to check contingency procedures and gives them confidence. Organisers need to know when the contingency plans come into play, that is, what the trigger is. For example, if an event is to move indoors in case of rain, does a shower trigger the move or a downpour? Absolutely every detail of an event should be written down and everyone should know where the plans are and what the timetable for the day is.

Evaluating the conference, exhibition or event

It is very important that the issue of evaluation is not left until the end of the event or conference. At this stage it is too late to request feedback or design a questionnaire. For this reason, decisions on evaluation must be incorporated into the planning stages. The criteria for evaluation have been determined throughout the process of planning. Aims and objectives have been set.

Types of evaluation

Meetings

The team of organisers meet following an event and go through every detail and analyse it. They are very critical and look for areas which can be improved next time.

Questionnaires

These are a useful tool for gathering feedback. They have to be prepared well in advance and the usual rules of questionnaire design apply. The organisers must determine who the respondents of the questionnaire will be, for example, at a large exhibition it would not be feasible to ask everyone to complete a questionnaire but a sample could be completed.

Observation

Members of staff who are working at an event can be involved in feedback by noting comments of visitors and watching people's reactions to events.

Statistics

Quantitative information about numbers of visitors is easily acquired and allows organisers to make comparisons with the same event in previous years or with comparative events.

ILTM 2004 VITAL STATISTICS
• 980 exhibiting companies
• 320 stands
• 884 exhibiting delegates
• 750 VIP Hosted Buyers flown in from 52 countries
• 180 additional buyers paying Euro 250 entrance fee
• 34,000 appointments pre-arranged between sellers and Hosted Buyers
• 3 trading days
• 1 luxury travel conference
• 2 official evening functions (Hotel Martinez, Majestic Barriere)

Source:iltm.net/postshow

This example shows the vital statistics from the International Luxury Travel Market Fair held annually in Cannes. These statistics provide an overview but are then broken down further and analysed in a post-show report.

Reviews

The newspapers and relevant publications should be checked every day for reviews of exhibitions or events. Reviews are copied and kept for future reference.

People involved

The organiser should consider using feedback from different groups of people and not just the organising team. In this way, different points of view are aired.

Delegates

It is customary for delegates at a conference to fill in an evaluation form. The example shown below is from a seminar organised by local government to encourage sustainable business practice. You can see that the format is very simple but gives the organisers a clear idea of the success of the seminar.

Tourism SustainBiz

Gales Brewery – 12th October 2004

In order to continually improve our service, we welcome your feedback. Please complete this form and hand it in before you leave. Your opinion is valued!

Name: _____   Company: _____

The overall objective of the SustainBiz event is to offer examples of best practice and provide practical advice on ways to make your business more sustainable. Do you think we have met these objectives? YES / NO (delete as appropriate)

If not, why? _____

Please tick the appropriate box:	V. Good	Good	Average	Poor
1. Booking arrangements				
2. How effective was the seminar format				
3. Presentations & content				
4. Topic relevance				
5. Standard of delegate packs				
6. Standard of catering & refreshments				
7. Overall event				

Would you be willing to discuss ways around some of these problems in a small group in the months following this meeting?

Yes ☐   No ☐

Following today's seminar, do you feel better equipped to make practical changes to your business in order to make it more sustainable?

Yes ☐   No ☐

Further Comments:

Thank you for participating in this event and for taking the time to give us feedback.
Please hand this form to an EHDC representative as you leave or fax to 01730 234169

Clients and suppliers

Clients or suppliers invited to an event such as corporate hospitality can be invited for their view on how it went. Of course, having been invited they can be expected to be complimentary but observation of behaviour and enjoyment during the event will give a good indication of how it is going. At an exhibition, visitors and suppliers can participate in a questionnaire or can complete feedback forms provided around the venue. They will probably require different questionnaires as they will be evaluating different aspects of the exhibition.

Staff and organisers

Meetings of planning teams following the event will aid a critical evaluation of its success.

Points for consideration

* Were the objectives met?

* Objectives relating to numbers of visitors are easy to measure. It is more difficult to measure issues such as 'raising awareness'. Delegates can be asked if they consider that the objectives of the conference were met on their feedback forms.

* Was the venue suitable and the event well designed?

* Were the roles and responsibilities allocated appropriately?

* Were legal requirements met?

* Was the budget met?

* How were my own performance and skills?

* Was the programme suitable?

* Was the evaluation system a success?

* What were the areas for improvement?

* What improvements are recommended?

CASE STUDY

A group of students at Trenchtown College started their Conferences, Exhibitions and Events unit in September at the beginning of the term. They were allocated 3 hours a week of class time with a tutor for the unit which was to be completed by February. This meant that their event must take place by the end of January at the latest to allow time for full evaluation. They were fortunate in that the local Tourist Information Centre had asked them to help in a consultation process with local tourism businesses to aid with the writing of the Trenchtown tourism strategy. The idea was that the students would organise a one-day conference in January. All details of the organisation of the conference would be left to the students but on the day, discussion and seminar activities would be led by Tourist Information Centre staff.

Planning

The students thought they had plenty of time to prepare. The first couple of meetings went very well. As a group they determined the objectives of the event and then they decided who would be responsible for what and wrote their job descriptions. Graham, their tutor, told them to keep a log of their contributions and to keep copies of whatever they did. They started their logs and were very happy with themselves.

- Sunita and Saul were responsible for finding tourism businesses to be represented at the conference as were Tony and Sean.

- Annika and Phillip were in charge of catering – there was to be morning coffee and lunch on the day.

- Lizzie and Selma were in charge of administration and finance.

- Raj was to organise a venue.

- Marcy and Chris were the marketing team.

- Helena and Marcus were to oversee the project as chair and deputy chairperson.

- James and Chitra took responsibility for health and safety and equipment.

Four weeks in

Graham, the tutor, had taught the group how to run a formal meeting and they were doing this weekly with an agenda, minutes etc. It was now the end of October and the students realised that although they had roles, job descriptions and minutes of meetings, they had not actually progressed their event. No one had arranged a venue, contacted any businesses or done anything outside Graham's class. They realised that each of them needed deadlines for specific tasks and that they needed a timeline of planning for the whole event. They spent three hours doing their timeline with dates set for each task. They felt much better. The next week they came to class and still no one had done anything, after all, they still had nearly three months.

- Helena and Marcus had a talk with Graham and he told them to be more forceful. They started to ask each team member to report on what they had done weekly.

- Sunita and Saul had contacted a whole list of businesses and had four positive replies, but Sunita had left the letters at home. She would bring them next week to show the group.

- Tony and Sean were going to contact some businesses – soon.

- Raj had sprung into action and booked a room in the college. It was fine although not their first choice as that had just been booked the week before.

- Marcy and Chris had drawn up a beautiful poster. The others weren't sure what to do with the poster or who it was for.

- Annika and Phillip spent three hours a week planning the lunch menu and how much it would cost. Sometimes they went to Sainsbury's to check prices. However they had, as yet, no money to spend and nothing much else to do before the event.

The weeks went on and slowly and surprisingly, with a lot of help from Graham, they had delegates; they raised some money to buy the food for lunch by having a series of cake sales; James and Chitra had done a risk assessment. Marcy and Chris wrote a press release and sent it to local papers. The meetings were a bit of a shambles as Helena and Marcus – who had been a couple – split up. There was a lot of arguing with members of the group shouting at each other. Sunita was away a lot so Saul found the delegates by himself. Tony and Sean found one. Graham thought he might be in the wrong job but decided to persevere.

On the day

All but Tony turned up and they were early. This was just as well as the room had someone in it. This was sorted out and the group managed to set up in time using the layout plan they had prepared. Saul went to collect their AV equipment from the IT department. It all worked but there was a lead missing. Saul knew there was one in the staff room and found it. Graham appeared and said their delegates were arriving. They had forgotten to put anyone in charge of meeting them so Helena and Marcus went. Helena wished they had thought of having badges for the students and delegates. The conference went well and the Tourist Information people were very happy. At lunchtime, Annika and Phillip produced a wonderful buffet lunch although two delegates went out for lunch appointments as they had not been told lunch was on offer. They all stayed to clear up.

The following day

The group met to write thank you letters to delegates. Graham said they would start their evaluation and asked them if they had any feedback. They could have had a questionnaire, a delegate feedback form, asked the Tourist Information Centre staff for their comments or taken a video or some photos – but they hadn't thought about any of these options!

You could do better than this, couldn't you? Discuss the performance of this group and point out where they went wrong and the few things that went right. Show how they could have done things differently. Look critically at your own group so far and see if you are repeating any of their mistakes. Discuss how you can improve your own performance. Make notes on the discussion points and keep them for reference.

Theory into practice

Consider carrying out a group evaluation half way through the planning of your own project. This is called a formative evaluation and it will help you tackle any problems which are apparent. The easiest way to do this is to carry out a SWOT analysis as a whole group. Remember that this means identifying the strengths, weaknesses, threats and opportunities of the group so far. Don't forget to prepare other types of evaluation now e.g. questionnaires.

Repeat the SWOT at the end of the project and keep records of both.

The next stage of the group evaluation is to meet as a group and decide whether you have met your objectives. List all the objectives you set out at the beginning of the project and go through each one and comment on how successfully it was met. Use the list in 'points for consideration' to help you carry out your evaluation. Make notes and make sure you make recommendations for improvements in the future.

Self-evaluation

Reflect on the following and make notes.

* Did you achieve your personal objectives? (list and comment)

* How much did you contribute to the group objectives?

* Did you attend all the planning sessions?

* Did you meet deadlines?

* Have you improved your communication and organisational skills and if so, how?

* Did you work well in a team?

* Did you work well independently?

* Did you show initiative?

* What would you do differently in the future?

1 Explain the difference between a trade fair and a consumer fair.

2 Explain what is meant by corporate hospitality.

3 What kind of venue would be most suitable for a national exhibition?

4 Discuss the advantages and disadvantages of academic venues.

5 Explain 'Approved Destination Status' in relation to China.

6 What services do conference organisers offer?

7 Comment on market growth for the conference trade.

8 What is meant by SMART objectives?

9 Which Acts place a duty of care for visitors on the occupiers of premises?

10 What is the purpose of a risk assessment?

11 Think of five things that could go wrong at a conference.

12 What is meant by a delegate day rate?

13 Suggest some marketing activities for a National Exhibition.

14 What is a contingency plan?

15 Why is it important that evaluation is considered at the planning stage of an event?

ASSESSMENT ASSIGNMENT UNIT 16

Part 1

You recently gave advice to a company named Slovenia Tours who were hoping to set up an office in the UK promoting Slovenia as a destination to UK outbound tourists. They have been very successful in the holiday market and have returned for you for advice once again. They are now interested in the conference, event and exhibition market which is in its infancy in Slovenia. They see the development of their business in organising conferences in Slovenia for international businesses. They want to know how conferences and events are organised in the UK and what issues affect the market. They think that knowledge of the UK experience will help them build their business in Slovenia.

Produce a report in which you:

1 Describe the conference, exhibition and events environment in the UK. Include information on the types of events held, the venues, suppliers and buyers.
This task may provide evidence for P1.

2 Analyse trends and issues affecting the conference, exhibition and event environment in the UK.
This task may provide evidence for M1.

3 Evaluate how the UK conference, exhibition and environment has responded to trends and issues.
This task may provide evidence for D1.

Part 2

You and your colleagues are to put on a conference. The theme is to be 'Careers in Travel and Tourism' and you will invite all the travel and tourism students at your college or school to attend. You may, of course, invite other students if you wish. Although this is a group activity, all your evidence must be your own individual work and record your own individual contributions to the conference. Remember to consider evaluation at the early stages and not just at the end.

Planning

1 Produce a plan for the conference which must include:
- objectives for the conference
- choice of venue with reasons for choice

- list of equipment needed
- health, safety and security measures
- any supplies needed
- financial considerations
- an operational plan for the day of the conference.

You must also start a log of your individual participation in the planning and keep detailed records of everything you do.

This task may provide evidence for P2.

2 Continue your log to show your active participation in the staging of the conference.

Note any problems you face and how you deal with them.

This task may provide evidence for P3.

Evidence for Tasks 1 and 2 which shows a significant, positive and sustained contribution to the planning and staging of the event may provide evidence for M2.

3 Carry out a critical evaluation of the success of the conference. The evaluation should include:
- group evaluation
- self-evaluation.

This task may provide evidence for P4 and P5.

Evaluations that show feedback from a range of sources may provide evidence for M2.

4 Provide realistic and justified proposals for improvement in the planning and staging of the conference. Include proposals for improvement of your own performance.

This task may provide evidence for D2.

Visitor attractions

Introduction

The visitor attractions sector is an important component of the travel and tourism industry. It's the sector that provides the interest, excitement and activity for tourists when they visit a destination or when they venture out on a day trip.

In this unit you are going to find out about the different types of visitor attractions and the products and services they offer. You will explore the impacts of the attractions, both positive and negative on the communities which surround them and on a wider scale.

Many techniques are used at attractions to interpret exhibits and to aid the visitor's understanding of the attraction and we will look at some of these techniques.

You will investigate the appeal of different types of attraction to different types of visitor. You will determine what it is that constitutes appeal to a visitor at particular attractions and consider how the appeal can be increased.

Whilst studying this unit you will be encouraged to visit as many attractions as you can to aid your knowledge and understanding. You can easily visit attractions in your own locality but don't forget that you may be going on organised visits with your group or going on holiday with friends and family during your studies. Use these outings to take the opportunity to visit more attractions and compare their appeal. You are fortunate too, in that almost all visitor attractions have their own websites full of information. Some of them have prepared materials for students which you can download from the Internet. Remember that such materials are meant to aid your research and cannot be submitted as your own work.

Completing the assessment for this unit could provide evidence for other units, for example, Marketing or Customer Service. Make sure that you plan for this when you go on any visits so that you collect appropriate information.

This unit is internally assessed by your tutor. A variety of exercises and activities is included in this chapter to help you develop your knowledge and understanding of visitor attractions and prepare for the assessment. You will also have the opportunity to work on some case studies.

After completing this unit you should be able to achieve the following outcomes:

→ examine the range of products and services provided by visitor attractions

→ explore the impact of visitor attractions

→ examine a range of techniques used for visitor interpretation

→ investigate the appeal of visitor attractions to different types of visitor.

Visitor attractions and their products and services

In 2004 there was, for the first time, a Visitor Attractions Conference in the UK. This is to be an annual event and demonstrates the significance of this sector to travel and tourism and to our economy. In her speech at the conference, Tessa Jowell, Culture Secretary, said that large and well-placed visitor attractions are vital to tourism – the 'heart of our economic engine'.

A 'Survey of Visits to Visitor Attractions' is conducted annually by the national tourist boards of England, Northern Ireland, Scotland and Wales to monitor visitor and other trends. According to the survey, there are an estimated 6,400 visitor attractions in the United Kingdom.

This is an extract from the definition of a visitor attraction according to the survey.

'An attraction where it is feasible to charge admission for the sole purpose of sightseeing. The attraction must be a permanently established excursion destination, a primary purpose of which is to allow public access for entertainment, interest, or education; rather than being primarily a retail outlet or a venue for sporting, theatrical or film performances. It must be open to the public, without prior booking, for published periods each year, and should be capable of attracting day visitors or tourists, as well as local residents.'

Note the main points of the definition:

✳ it must be feasible for the attraction to charge admission – but many are free

✳ it must be permanently established – thus for the purposes of the survey, events such as the Notting Hill Carnival would be excluded

✳ must have a primary purpose of interest, entertainment or education – thus shopping centres are excluded even though they attract tourists

✳ must be open to the public for at least part of the year

✳ must attract tourists, not just locals.

The top five paid-admission visitor attractions in 2002 were:

✳ British Airways London Eye

✳ Tower of London

✳ Eden Project, St Austell

✳ Legoland Windsor

✳ Flamingo Land Theme Park & Zoo, Kirby Misperton.

The top five free-admission visitor attractions in 2002 were:

✳ Blackpool Pleasure Beach

✳ Tate Modern, London

✳ British Museum, London

✳ National Gallery, London

✳ Natural History Museum, London.

The Natural History Museum in London

The Visitor Attractions sector covers many different categories of attraction. They include museums, art galleries, historic houses and castles, churches and cathedrals, gardens, wildlife sites, leisure parks and other recreational facilities. For the purposes of this unit we are going to use the same categories of visitor attractions as the Survey of Visits to Visitor Attractions. These are shown in the table below. You can also see how many of each type of attraction participated in the survey in 2003 and whether the trend in visits is up or down.

Note that Blackpool Pleasure Beach tops the list of free-admission attractions but of course it is not free unless you choose not to go on any of the rides. Each ride is paid for individually.

Although all of the top five paying- and free-admission attractions are in England, the figures up to 2002 were compiled for the whole of the United Kingdom. After 2002, each national tourist board compiled its own separate figures. You can find out what these are by visiting the website of each national tourist board.

Theory into practice

Go to the websites of the national tourist boards for England, Northern Ireland, Wales and Scotland and find out what the top five paying and free attractions are in each country. Note them.

Check whether the English top attractions are the same as the ones mentioned on page 151.

The website addresses are given here to help you:
- www.visitbritain.co.uk
- www.visitscotland.com
- www.discovernorthernireland.com
- www.walestouristboard.com

ENGLAND VISIT TRENDS 2002–2003 BY ATTRACTION CATEGORY (%)		
Category	Attractions sample	% 03/02
Country parks	(87)	+9
Farms	(70)	+13
Gardens	(126)	+6
Historic houses/castles	(392)	+4
Other historic properties	(149)	−2
Leisure/theme parks	(41)	+2
Museums/art galleries	(657)	+1
Steam/heritage railways	(52)	+3
Visitor/heritage centres	(81)	+7
Wildlife attractions/zoos	(95)	+1
Workplaces	(108)	+6
Places of worship	(75)	−5
Other	(96)	−3
England	(2,027)	+2

Primary products and services

Whatever the visitor attraction the main reason for the visit is the primary product or service. If you visit a gallery it is to see an exhibition of art, if you go to a stately home it is to admire the beauty of the architecture and learn about our history. When we go to theme parks it is to have fun on the various rides.

The primary product or service can change from time to time but rarely changes completely. If it were always exactly the same then there would be little reason for visitors to come back again. So, museums hold temporary exhibitions to attract people back again and theme parks introduce new rides regularly to entice us back. The primary product and service serves to attract visitors but is not always the main source of revenue. In fact, we have already seen that some of our most popular attractions are free to enter. These are usually museums and they do receive public funding but they also have commercial activities to raise revenue. Those attractions that we pay to enter often have special offers with free tickets, sometimes in conjunction with other companies, for example rail companies.

Ancillary products and services

The role of ancillary products and services is to provide the services that customers require during a visit to an attraction and to raise money from these services. There are several benefits of providing such services:

* increase in customer satisfaction during the visit
* visitors are encouraged to spend more time at the attraction
* increase in revenue from secondary spend.

All visitor attractions have similar ancillary products. They include:

* toilets
* services for visitors with special needs
* car parks
* gift shops
* restaurants
* snack bars
* ice cream stands
* minor attractions that cost extra, for example, special exhibitions
* children's activities
* photos.

Corporate hospitality and room hire

Most visitor attractions hire out rooms for business seminars, special celebrations and even weddings. Although such services are ancillary to the main product they are a major source of revenue and visitor attractions try to make the most of these lucrative markets.

Types of attractions

We will look at each of the categories from the Visitor Attraction Survey to ensure you know what kind of attractions are included in each category and what their primary products are. We are going to study them in order of their popularity.

Museums/art galleries

The market research agency, MORI, carried out research in 2004 into visits to museums in Britain. It showed that in the previous year, 37 per cent of adults in Britain had visited a museum or gallery. This is more than visit the theatre or theme parks. A quarter of these visitors had been five or more times to museums in the year.

The survey showed what visitors liked to see in museums. This included topics like ancient history, how people used to live and local history. Exhibitions on these topics make up the primary product or service for museums.

These are the most popular museums and galleries in Britain. The top eight are in London.

* Tate Modern
* British Museum
* National Gallery
* Natural History Museum
* Victoria & Albert Museum
* Science Museum
* National Portrait Gallery
* Tate Britain
* Kelvingrove Art Gallery & Museum, Glasgow
* The Lowry Centre, Salford.

They all offer permanent exhibitions of artefacts and artworks but they differ according to the museum's speciality or leaning.

CASE STUDY

The Lowry Centre is an art and entertainment venue which opened at the newly renovated Salford Quays in 2000. Besides its art galleries it houses two theatres with performances of drama, dance, opera and music.

The Lowry Centre has some permanent exhibitions of the work of the artist Lowry. The displays are changed regularly to encourage visitors to return and see a different aspect of Lowry's work. In addition there are several shorter exhibitions per year, lasting up to three months. These are usually exhibitions of modern and contemporary art and themed exhibitions about the urban or industrial environment. Artists are sometimes invited to create new work especially for exhibitions.

Education is an important aspect of the gallery's work and activities are put on for visiting groups of children and community

The Lowry Centre, Salford

groups. There is a Community and Education team for this specific purpose and they deliver about 1,000 sessions per year.

The Lowry has a gift shop which sells art books and souvenirs including Lowry prints.

There are three different eating places for snacks or full meals. Other sources of additional revenue are guided tours at £2.50 per person, a family activities club and gift vouchers.

The Lowry is a new building and therefore was built with accessibility in mind. It provides car parking spaces for wheelchair users and theatre spaces. Disabled toilet facilities are on each level of the complex. Four wheelchairs are available free of charge. An infra-red hearing facility is available from the box office for theatre performances and there are some sign-language interpreted performances.

The two theatres and four conference rooms are available for seminar or conference hire with full equipment available. Rooms are available with views over the canals for wedding ceremonies and receptions.

You can find more information about the Lowry at www.thelowry.com.

1. **Describe the primary products and services at the Lowry.**
2. **Describe the ancillary products and services at the Lowry.**
3. **Explain why there are several temporary exhibitions each year.**

Country parks

There are over 270 country parks in England. The Countryside Agency was founded in 1999 by the government and is funded by the Department for Environment, Food and Rural Affairs (DEFRA). Its aim is to:

> 'conserve and enhance England's countryside, spread social and economic opportunity for the people who live there, help everyone, wherever they live and whatever their background, to enjoy the countryside and share in this priceless asset.'

The Countryside Agency has a role in supporting country parks through its renaissance programme, the aims of which are described below:

- To support the further development of the country parks network.
- To facilitate the exchange of information and good practice between country park practitioners and interested parties.
- To raise the competence of country park staff and their use of appropriate management tools.
- To identify funding and income-generation opportunities for country parks and promote these widely.
- To secure local authority commitment to country parks.

Source: www.countryside.gov.uk

Ashton Court Estate is a popular country park

Here are some examples of popular country parks in the UK which attract more than a million visitors a year:

* Strathclyde Country Park, Motherwell, Scotland
* Ashton Court Estate, Long Ashton, England
* Upper Derwent Reservoirs, Bamford, England
* Drumpellier Country Park, Coatbridge, Scotland
* Fairlands Valley Park, Stevenage, England.

The local authority manages country parks, for example North Lanarkshire Council is responsible for Strathclyde Country Park. They protect different types of landscape such as woodlands, wetlands and lakes and the wildlife that inhabit them.

Entry to a country park and many of its activities is free so visitors can go birdwatching, walking or cycling. However, there are some activities which are charged for to allow funds to be raised for further improvement to the park. Examples include watersports, hire of land and equipment and accommodation on campsites.

Historic properties

Here are some examples of the UK's most popular historic properties.

* Tower of London
* Edinburgh Castle, Edinburgh
* Windsor Castle, Windsor
* Roman Baths, Bath
* Stonehenge, Amesbury
* Chatsworth, Bakewell
* Tatton Park, Knutsford.

The Tower of London is managed by the Historic Royal Palaces Agency, alongside other unoccupied royal palaces. The Agency is responsible to the Department for Culture, Media and Sport (DCMS).

Windsor Castle is one of the UK's royal residences and is held in trust for future generations, so the Queen couldn't decide to sell it. The palaces – others are Buckingham and Sandringham – are royal homes, used for state functions and are also open to the public at certain times of the year. Windsor Castle is an official residence of the Queen and the largest occupied castle in the world.

Chatsworth is a beautiful stately home and is the home of the Duke of Devonshire and his family. The house is a major visitor attraction in Derbyshire.

There are two important organisations who look after heritage in the UK. These are English Heritage and the National Trust.

English Heritage reports to the DCMS. It has powers and responsibilities from the National Heritage Act (1983, amended 2002). English Heritage is funded in part by the government and in part from revenue earned from historic properties and other services.

The National Trust is a registered charity and completely independent of government. It relies for funding on donations and revenue from its properties. It has over 3 million members and cares for over 200 historic properties and gardens. The Trust exists to conserve its properties but has to attract visitors to them in order to raise funds to do its work.

It has come up with some interesting ideas to encourage visitors, including touring film locations. On the page opposite is the description of filming at Lyme Park from the National Trust website.

Stonehenge is a popular historic property

Lyme Park, Stockport, Cheshire
Pride and Prejudice (BBC)

The words 'Colin Firth' and 'Mr Darcy' took on new depth in 1996 when the BBC's six-part adaptation of Jane Austen's famous novel hit our television screens. If you were swept up with Darcy-fever, you weren't alone – video sales of the adaptation shot up as people who could not wait for the transmission of the last episode queued to buy. The magnificent Lyme Park, with its 1,400-acre deer park and 17-acre garden, is where they filmed the external scenes at Pemberley. (The internal views were shot at Sudbury Hall in Derbyshire – also a National Trust property.) The first view of the house is as breathtaking in real life as on camera. The famous pond (where Darcy takes his plunge) and other memorable places can be located with the National Trust's 'Pemberley Trail' leaflet, available at the garden kiosk.

Source: www.nationaltrust.org.uk

Consider this...

Can you think of any other film locations at visitor attractions? The National Trust website has lots more.

Assessment activity 18.1

Go to the English Heritage and the National Trust websites and identify three historic properties in your area.

Describe the products and services provided by each of the properties. Remember to distinguish between primary and ancillary products and services. Include facilities for special needs visitors and corporate hospitality.

Produce a fact sheet for each property.

This task could provide evidence for P1.

Leisure/theme parks

The UK market for theme parks reached 49.7 million visitors in 2003. Blackpool Pleasure Beach is the leading park with around 14.3 per cent of the total market share.

The Tussauds Group is a significant company in running theme parks. The group includes the following:

* British Airways London Eye
* Thorpe Park
* Alton Towers
* Chessington World of Adventure
* Warwick Castle.

The Tussauds Group acquired Heide Park, in Soltau, Germany, in 2003 as part of their expansion strategy. Heide Park is one of Europe's top theme parks.

Alton Towers has been transformed by the Tussauds Group and has a reputation for thrilling roller coasters, such as Oblivion, Nemesis and AIR. The Tussauds Group successfully enhanced the product offering at Alton Towers by opening two hotels, the Alton Towers Hotel and Splash Landings. The latter is themed and incorporates a water park. The addition of the hotels meant that Alton Towers became a short-break destination as well as a day-trip destination. The hotel also incorporates facilities and accommodation for corporate customers. This is of particular importance in the winter months when the theme park is closed.

Theory into practice

Find out more about the Splash Landings Hotel and the facilities offered for corporate customers at Alton Towers. Report back to your group.

Thrilling rides at Alton Towers

Gardens

These are some examples of the UK's most popular garden attractions.

* Eden Project
* Kew Gardens, Richmond
* Royal Botanic Garden, Edinburgh
* Wisley Garden, Wisley, England
* Botanic Gardens, Belfast.

The Botanic Gardens in Belfast is one of the most frequented parks in Belfast with events and band performances attracting visitors as well as the plant collections. It is owned by Belfast Corporation who paid £10,500 for it in 1895. There are collections of exotic flowers and plants and a beautiful palm house. The gardens are a famous landmark in Belfast and attract thousands of visitors.

Another botanic garden, Kew, has been designated a World Heritage Site.

Consider this...

What do you think the primary product is at a garden?

Wildlife attractions/zoos

The main attractions in this sector are zoos. Examples are Chester, London, Bristol and Edinburgh zoos. Also included are attractions such as 'The Deep' in Hull. Described as a submarium, The Deep celebrates and investigates the world's oceans. The Deep is a good example of a Millennium project. Half of its funding came from the Millennium project, that is lottery funding. Part of its remit is to carry out environmental research.

Farms

Farm attractions suffered immensely from a decline in visitors in 2002 with the foot and mouth outbreak. However, this part of the attractions sector has demonstrated a strong recovery and the most popular farms attract 200,000 to 300,000 visitors per year. Examples include the Cornish Cyder Farm in Penhallow and the Donkey Sanctuary in Salcombe Regis.

Some farms cater specifically for children and attract school visits.

Places of worship

Tourists on city visits often visit a church or cathedral but it is not often the sole purpose of the visit. They do not usually charge entry as people should be free to enter a church but they might charge for entry to a tower, for example. At King's College Chapel, in Cambridge, a charge is made so that the chapel is not overrun with visitors. The dwell time is short in a place of worship, the average is only just over an hour, less than in any other type of attraction. Popular places of worship for visitors are York Minster, Canterbury Cathedral, Westminster Abbey and St Paul's Cathedral.

Visitor/heritage centres

This category of visitor attractions has a variety of attractions within it ranging from Somerset House to Cadbury World and the World Famous Old Blacksmith's Shop Centre, Gretna Green – an exhibition built around the original blacksmith's shop. It houses an exhibition about run-away weddings from the first one in 1754.

CASE STUDY

This extract from www.gretna-area.co.uk explains the exhibition.

'The Gretna Green Story Exhibition reveals a fascinating chapter in social history. Why did people run away here? What happened when the angry relatives caught up with the eloping couple? When they returned home, were people punished for marrying this way? Intriguing questions. The answers can be found when you step back into Gretna Green's past. The story unfolds through a collection of audio and audio-visual displays along with memorabilia and artefacts from the hey-day of run-away weddings. The push button displays situated along the route of the exhibition bring the story to life as characters re-enact a part of Gretna Green's past.'

Who do you think would visit this exhibition?

Workplaces

Some workplace attractions form part of our industrial heritage like those in Bradford. Others are still working and provide a means of attracting attention to their products as well as making money from admission fees. These are the most visited workplace attractions in the UK.

* Poole Pottery
* Blakemere Craft Centre, Northwich
* Denbies Wine Estate, Dorking
* Cheddar Gorge Cheese Company.

Steam/heritage railways

Probably a type of attraction that particularly attracts enthusiasts, there are still quite a few steam railways in the UK. These include the North Yorkshire Moors Railway, the Severn Valley Railway and the Great Orme Tramway in Llandudno.

Health and safety in visitor attractions

Health and safety at visitor attractions in the UK is controlled by the Health and Safety at Work Act. The 'Code of Safe Practices at Fairs' which also applies to theme parks outlines the standards relating to ride operation. Obviously, theme parks take safety very seriously as the bad publicity resulting from an accident could deter visitors or even close the park. The British Association of Leisure Parks, Piers and Attractions (BALPPA) advises its members on relevant legislation.

The extract below from the New Pleasurewood Hills website emphasises the importance of ride safety at a theme park.

Accidents at theme parks are infrequent but can be serious or fatal when they do occur. There are many warnings placed at ride entrances advising those who have bad hearts, bad backs etc. not to ride. In 2003 an 81-year-old woman died following a heart attack on the Universe of Energy ride at Epcot, Florida. Theme park managers maintain that accidents occur because customers do not follow safety instructions. They say that more education about safety is needed and are targeting children with the safety message.

A 'Wild about Safety' campaign at Disney is designed to teach children to remain seated on rides and to keep their hands inside vehicles. At the British Airways Eye in London over 350 hours per week of maintenance and testing are carried out to ensure safety.

Health and safety is considered at all attractions, not only theme parks, and usually consists of avoiding accidents and providing on-site emergency procedures and first-aid facilities. Attractions have trained stewards on site who are in contact with each other via radio communication. Thus, they are able to communicate quickly in emergency situations and call relevant personnel.

If school parties make a visit to an attraction the responsible teacher will be expected to carry out a risk assessment prior to the visit. Attractions are keen for school parties to visit and therefore often issue health and safety guidelines and risk assessments to aid the teachers. On the next page there is an example of a risk assessment provided by the Eden Project for school groups.

'All attractions must obtain a safety certificate renewed annually which requires an examination report from an independent body of engineers. At New Pleasurewood Hills, Leisure Technical Consultants, a British company of engineers, conducts the survey and issues their report to enable us to apply for the safety certificate required for operation. BALPPA and the Health & Safety Executive hold copies of this certificate. Each year the machines are subjected to a variety of tests (including metal fatigue) on maximum stress to ensure the rides are safe and to enhance safety precautions. At New Pleasurewood Hills all attractions are inspected daily by the park engineers.'

Source: www.pleasurewoodhills.co.uk

Eden Project

Health and safety guidelines for school visits

We hope that you have an enjoyable and worthwhile trip to Eden. We have identified below the main hazards that could affect your visit and we ask that you cooperate fully with us to ensure the smooth running of your trip. Please study the guidelines below and feel free to contact us if you have any concerns or feedback.

General safety measures

- School staff are responsible for the supervision, welfare and behaviour of children at all times. Adult leaders should be aware of specific medical or behavioural conditions affecting group members.
- It is the lead teacher's responsibility to ensure that staff and children are fully briefed.
- Staff and children are divided into small groups to explore the site. If older children are allowed to explore in small groups adult leaders should set up regular rendezvous.
- All adult leaders should carry a list of the children in their group, and a comprehensive list of all staff and children present at Eden from their school.
- Eden staff trained in on-site emergency procedures and in dealing with vulnerable persons.
- Highly trained stewarding team with site-wide radio communications.
- 2 trained Paramedics, 1 on-site registered nurse and a large number of trained first-aiders.
- As far as possible all school groups are met, given an introduction to Eden which includes a health and safety briefing, and provided with a base room.

Location	Description of hazard	Likelihood	Seriousness	Control measures
Site-wide	Personal injury through slips, trips & falls.	Med	Low	• Daily inspection of paths, steps etc. • Verbal warning in introduction.
Lake, ponds, drainage ditches	Possibility of drowning	L	High	• Life buoys present. • Eden team to give verbal warning if inappropriate behaviour spotted.
Humid Tropics Biome	Heat exhaustion	L	M	• Schools advised on appropriate clothing and drinking water. • Emergency cool room, help points and drinking fountains in HTB.
Site-wide	• Allergic reaction to plants due to touch • Poisoning due to ingestion of poisoning plants	L	M	• Verbal warning given in introduction. • Signage discourages picking and touching plants. • Eden hazardous plants manual provides reference in emergency.
Site-wide	Personal injury from traffic/land-train	L	H	• Verbal warning given in introduction. • Site-wide vehicle speed restrictions. • Large vehicles escorted on-site. • Signage clearly indicating land-train route.
Education Centre	Allergic reaction to products used in schools, workshops	L	H	• No nuts included in any of the products used. • Food transported/stored in airtight containers. • Verbal warning to teachers/children.
Site-wide	Possibility of abduction/assault by members of the public			• On-site Emergency and Vulnerable persons procedures. • School staff responsible for location of their group at all times.

Eden Schools Team, April 2004

Security in visitor attractions

Security is also a consideration in two ways. Visitor attractions must provide a means of protecting their visitors and their property and also must protect their exhibits.

Exhibits are protected by many means from very sophisticated alarm systems in galleries to roped off areas and glass. Vulnerable items like tapestries are also protected from light and flash photography.

In some museums and galleries security searches are undertaken on visitors as they enter to prevent terrorist activity. Cloakrooms are provided to store coats and bags whilst visitors make their tour.

Access in visitor attractions

The following factors relating to access must be considered:

* mode of arrival by visitors
* provision of transport from rail and bus stations
* whether main access routes can cope with increased traffic
* access for supplier and maintenance vehicles
* car parking.

Where possible attractions will encourage their visitors to use public transport to lessen the impact of traffic on the local community.

Access for people with disabilities

The 1995 Disability Discrimination Act makes it a legal requirement to provide physical and intellectual access for people with disabilities. Part of the Act relates to rights of access to everyday services. By 2004, service providers, and that includes visitor attractions, should have made the necessary physical adjustments to their premises so that disabled people can access them. Most visitor attractions take this access issue very seriously and publish guides for disabled visitors.

Theory into practice

Choose a visitor attraction and find out what measures it takes to allow access to people with disabilities. Make notes on your findings for further discussion.

Visitor management

Visitor management techniques involve planning visitor access, the layout of the attraction and the route around it. A well-planned route and flow of visitors increases the capacity of the attraction and should enhance visitor enjoyment as they should not meet crowds of people and, in limited spaces, should not meet people coming the other way. At historic properties it is essential to manage visitor flow so that too many visitors or crowds of visitors in one place do not damage the fabric of the building.

As historic properties are becoming more popular, some owners, including the National Trust, are actually having to deter visitors because of the damage that too many visitors can cause to buildings. They manage the number of visitors by raising prices for entry and issuing timed tickets. This means visitors buy a ticket and can only enter the building at the time stated.

Timed tickets are used to reduce waiting times during peak periods at theme parks. Customers are entitled to collect a timed ticket for the popular rides and can get straight on at that time.

Remembering that attractions want to increase secondary spend, shops are carefully located within the attraction to sell merchandise. Where there is a tour, the shop will be located at the end of the tour so that the tour is not interrupted.

However, the shop is usually located in such a way that the visitor has to go through it in order to leave. This does not happen by chance. Flow management models have been developed by business consultants to maximise visitor flow to shopping areas.

CASE STUDY

Visit the website www.ropemakers.co.uk and find the interactive map and complete the following:

1. Comment on the layout of the attraction including position of toilets, shop and cafe.
2. How do you think visitors will arrive?
3. How long do you think visitors will stay?
4. What category of tourist attraction does Ropemakers fall into?

Customer care and services

Looking after customers is essential to the success of any business. Satisfied customers return and also tell their friends about their experience. There are many ways that a visitor attraction can look after its visitors.

Signage

We are surrounded by signs and there is a campaign to reduce them! However, signs are important at visitor attractions to show us the way to get to them and to help us round them. It is not only their information-giving quality that is important, signs need to fit in with the theme of the attraction. In one Area of Outstanding Natural Beauty (AONB) in Sussex, 16 different kinds of signs were found. It was decided to design a completely new system and replace them all. New designs were developed in conjunction with the Guild of Sussex Craftmen. These designs used local materials and built on the traditional style of Sussex countryside furniture. Then a new system of waymarking was developed which was designed to fit into the local landscape. The signs were made of rounded oak and give information such as designation, for example, footpath, and destinations or distances.

Languages

Providing information for tourists in their own language is part of making them feel welcome. It is usual to find leaflets in several languages at major tourist attractions and audio guides can also be produced in several languages. Guided tours can be carried out in other languages when it is known that there is sufficient demand, for example, when tours are pre-booked. Overseas tourists feel most welcome when personnel speak their language so staff should be encouraged to learn new languages.

Visitor satisfaction

Visitor attractions need to monitor the level of satisfaction of their customers. They can do this through surveys and requests for feedback. In addition they can receive recognition from their tourist board by being awarded an accreditation, 'Quality Assured Visitor Attraction'. This can be awarded following a satisfactory quality assessment. A visit takes place from an inspector who looks at the following:

* initial signage, car park and welcome
* the content and quality of the attraction
* toilets, their layout and cleanliness

* catering

* retailing.

A debrief follows the visit and provides feedback on the visitor experience and advises on future action.

Queue management

Queuing is the worst aspect of visiting a visitor attraction and can lead to customer dissatisfaction. We have already mentioned timed tickets as one effective way of dealing with customers. Theme parks have the worst problem with queues as the capacity of rides is limited and everyone wants to go on the newest, most thrilling rides. Because of this problem, theme parks have put a lot of effort into queue management. The time waiting in queues for rides or any other services is called the wait time and is a measure of customer satisfaction. Alton Towers suggest the following 'queue busting tips'.

Key concept

Wait time is the percentage of the total time spent in an attraction waiting for access to products or services.

To improve customer service, wait time has to be reduced. These are some of the measures taken:

* signs giving the wait time from a certain point

* information on entry, advising current wait times

* fast pass systems which allow a timed entry to a ride

* virtual queuing.

QUEUE BUSTING TIPS

Leave the most popular rides 'til last. It's the queue that shuts at the advertised time not the ride.

Take time to read this Gate Map and plan what you want to do.

Our guest Services team are here to help. You'll find them in Towers street, X-Sector and Forbidden valley.

Review queue times as you enter. They are displayed on a screen at the bottom of Towers Street and elsewhere around the park.

Remember to purchase your car parking token from selected areas in the park.

Avoid leaving bags on ride platforms. It's easier and safer to use the lockers at Guest services.

Parents take advantage of the parent Queue share passes from Guest Services and don't miss out on the extreme rides.

Mornings are usually quieter in X-Sector - Head there to beat the queues.

Get wet early - Water rides are generally quieter in the morning.

Take advantage of Fastrack on all Peak and Premium days.

Six Flags

Six Flags is a theme-park company with a total of 38 parks in North America, Europe and Latin America.

The company has introduced a virtual queue system to some of its parks. The system is called Lo-Q and is described as the 'ultimate line-management technology, giving guests maximum time and optimum flexibility to experience all the fun Six Flags has to offer' by the company's vice-president. This means that when visitors are queuing they are not spending money in shops or restaurants so the system boosts revenue by allowing the visitor to spend money and queue.

It works by means of a 'Q-bot' a pager-type messaging and locator device. One is needed for up to six visitors. There is a Lo-Q reservation point where the visitor points the Q-bot. The Q-bot beeps and displays a message with a ride time. The Q-bot beeps to remind visitors when it is their turn to ride and they join the Lo-Q entrance.

The system is not free, visitors have to rent the Q-bot, so it is an additional source of revenue for the parks. The benefits are higher guest satisfaction, efficient queue management and increased revenue.

Visit a theme park or think about the last time you went to one and note all the queue-management measures in place. Which measures make use of technology? Discuss your experiences with your group.

Consider this...

There are computer simulation models available for theme parks so that they can predict peak times and queue problems. You can try managing a theme park yourself. Have you seen 'Theme Park World', the computer game?

Dealing with complaints

In spite of best efforts there will be some complaints and a complaints policy must be in place with targets for response and clear lines of authority. It is best to try and resolve a complaint immediately. If not, the official complaints policy is implemented.

The complaints procedure will cover:

* recording the complaint
* passing to the appropriate member of staff
* a response within a specified length of time
* monitoring of the response to the complaint by the appropriate line manager
* compiling statistics on complaints for future action.

Data protection

Visitor attractions must comply with the Data Protection Act. There is a legal duty to protect any information collected from visitors. Data must be safeguarded and unauthorised access to data prevented. Customer details should not be passed on to any third parties unless permission is given to do so.

Staff and training

Staff are the face of the business attraction and must be welcoming and helpful to visitors to provide good customer service. Training is the best way to ensure staff provide good service. Most companies provide their own training but the local tourist boards will also provide the 'Welcome Guest' training programmes which attractions staff can join.

Having enough staff in the right place can enhance customer satisfaction. Many visitor attraction staff are part-time and can be brought in quickly as needed. Where no specialist knowledge is needed, staff can be cross-trained so that they can be deployed as needed. In historic properties, staff need to be knowledgeable about the property and artefacts and also provide security in the property.

Information

Part of the product and service offering by visitor attractions is information, particularly at educational and historic attractions. This information can be presented in many different ways from basic displays to interactive experiences. These techniques are explored later in this unit in 'Interpretation'.

All visitor attractions produce leaflets about their products and services. These can be displayed in Tourist Information Centres or in hotels, airports and so on, to get the attention of potential customers.

The Tate Gallery

The impact of visitor attractions

Socio-cultural

Broadening of culture

It is difficult to assess the socio-cultural impact of visitor attractions as there is debate about what culture is. You have heard the terms pop culture, youth culture, art and culture – these terms mean different things to different people but all can be considered worth studying and conserving. That is the role of our many galleries and museums – to conserve our culture so that it is there for future generations to see whether that includes 'Britart' or Victorian artefacts.

> **Key concept**
>
> **Britart** refers to a group of 'Young British Artists' formed in 1988. They were a group of 16 artists mostly from London's Goldsmiths and all participated in an exhibition put on by artist Damien Hirst. The exhibition was called 'Freeze' and was put on in a Docklands warehouse. Many of these artists are very famous today.

> The Tate Gallery first opened on Millbank in London in 1897. It operates as an independent institution under the terms of the Museums and Galleries Act 1992, and is one of the great public museums of the United Kingdom. In common with other museums it presents a perspective on history, but its particular responsibility is to collect objects of our time and places it in the privileged position of creating the frame through which future generations will judge our own culture.
>
> The Collection, as of 31 March 2004, consisted of a total of 64,765 works:
>
> - 4,607 paintings
> - 1,690 sculptures and reliefs
> - 160 installations and electronic media works
> - 37,463 works in the Turner Bequest
> - 3,734 works in the Oppé Collection
> - 12,525 prints
> - 610 miscellaneous items
>
> Source:www.tate.org.uk

There can be no doubt that our government supports the socio-cultural aspect of our public museums and galleries as they all receive funding via the Department of Culture, Media and Sport, to varying degrees and take on the responsibility of protecting our cultural heritage.

The following extract from the Tate website explains this role.

There is no point in having all these works of art unless the public goes to see them. Thus it is also the responsibility of our museums to attract different types of visitors and explain the exhibits to them, that is interpret them. The Tate does this via an extensive programme of activities and, of course, entry to the Tate and to other public museums is free. Our Natural History Museum welcomes 125,000 school children each year, successfully introducing children to exhibits and learning.

Revival of culture

Often visitor attractions offer a revival of culture and prevent it being lost. An example is the World Heritage Site, Holloko in Hungary. Holloko is a village which has traditional architecture and folklore heritage. It has become a living museum with craftsmen at work on wood carving, weaving, embroidery, candle making and pottery. Holloko is not only attractive to international tourists but allows domestic tourists to see these crafts and its conservation ensures that the crafts and skills do not die out.

Dilution of culture

Unfortunately, the reverse can also occur, where the visitor attraction is of poor quality and represents the culture in a poor way serving to dilute it or diminish it in some way. The intrusion of a successful visitor attraction into a locality can result in loss of identity for a small community and a lack of peace in their surroundings.

Home-based entertainment

There is often anxiety that home entertainment systems such as multi-channel television, playstations and computers will affect our appreciation of culture and deter us from visiting attractions. There is no evidence that this is the case as visits to attractions are steadily growing. The same anxiety was expressed about cinemas some years ago and yet multiplexes are now very successful and cinema-going has grown enormously.

Economic

Employment

Visitor attractions create jobs. Tate Britain, for example, employs about 800 people. In this kind of institution, many of these employees are highly skilled historians, conservationists, marketers and administrators. They also need fundraisers, building managers and educators.

However, in many visitor attractions there are few permanent staff. Staff may be employed on flexible contracts so that they can be called upon as needed, posts may be seasonal due to winter closures and pay is often low for unskilled work. Associations like the Association for Leading Visitor Attractions (ALVA) are aware of these problems and are lobbying the government for action and investment in training. In addition, there are a large number of volunteers working in historic properties.

Investment

Visitor attractions provide visitors to a local environment. The visitors generate wealth in the locality by spending their money in hotels, restaurants and amenities in the area as well as in the visitor attraction. The Natural History Museum attracts more than 3 million visitors a year. These visitors generate a lot of spending in London. It had a turnover of £52 million in 2002/2003 and claims to add £190 million to the economy each year (Treasurehouse and Powerhouse report 2004).

Development of new visitor attractions can attract investment from entrepreneurs or major companies.

Regeneration

A visitor attraction can be the means of regenerating a whole area. This was the case with Disneyland Paris which is situated in Marne la Valle outside Paris, an area which was largely agricultural prior to development. This site was chosen because of its close proximity to Paris, and also its central position within Europe. The area has several hotels which are not part of Disney but have benefited from its presence. At first, local people were opposed to the development especially as their land was subject to compulsory purchase by the French government. Today the park attracts many visitors from all over Europe and has undergone further development. The area is prosperous with a new railway station and many jobs available.

Disneyland Paris has brought prosperity to this area of northern France

Environmental

CASE STUDY

Proposal for a water park and snowcentre

The proposed site is located within 110.5 hectares of farmland and forestry at the extreme south west of Wales in the county of Pembrokeshire. The proposal is to develop:

- a holiday village of 400 dwellings with a central complex providing shops, restaurants and other services

- a water park available to residents and day visitors

- a snowcentre with skiing, snowboarding and sledging open to residents and day visitors.

Various bodies have been asked to comment on the proposal. This was the response of the Pembrokeshire Coast National Park:

'The position and design of the Snow centre will be prominent, incongruous and out of character with the standards of design and construction that would be expected on a site associated so closely with the National Park. The construction of the new roundabout at the access point will comprise major civil engineering work in close proximity to the actual park boundary, and will be particularly visible when lit at night. This will be severely detrimental to the conservation of the landscape quality, especially through light pollution during the hours of darkness.'

Source: www.wales.gov.uk

Comment on this response and develop a counter argument explaining the positive impacts of the development. If you have time, hold a debate within your group.

Congestion

Congestion arises from traffic, coach and car parking and crowds of people. Visitor attractions need to supply adequate facilities and access routes to minimise congestion and to manage the flow of visitors around their site to minimise crowds.

Sustainability

In some cases, visitor attractions actually suffer from their popularity. Historic buildings or sites can suffer deterioration and erosion. In these cases, measures must be taken to protect the building by restricting visits or closing for periods of time.

Stonehenge is a good example of sustainability. The site receives many visitors and the stones have suffered erosion and damage and so a means must be found to sustain it. It is one of the UK's most famous and oldest monuments and a World Heritage Site, but it has suffered from too many visitors over the years and is in need of protection whilst still maintaining access for the public who see it as part of their heritage. This is underway with the 'Stonehenge Project'. The project involves the building of a new visitor centre and the removal of roads from the site to restore the site to a peaceful location. There are several organisations involved in the project including the DCMS, English Heritage who manage the site and the Highways Agency because of the new roads.

In the visitor centre there will be exhibitions and audio-visual presentations to help visitors enjoy and understand Stonehenge. There will also be shops, catering facilities and an education area. Those who wish to visit the stones will walk from the centre. Perhaps less people will visit the stones and yet still get a flavour of what they are about from the visitor's centre by taking a 'virtual tour'. The central circle of stones is already roped off and visitors are not allowed to enter this area. This is not surprising when you hear that some visitors actually chip bits of stone off to take home as souvenirs.

Pollution

Pollution can occur through noise, litter/waste or chemicals. The nature of any potential pollution depends on the type of visitor attraction.

The Green Tourism Scheme helps tourism businesses to minimise the negative environmental impact of their business. Many of the members currently, are in the public sector, for example, tourist boards who are in a position to influence their members and encourage them to join. Businesses gain an award if they reach standards of environmental practice. These standards cover issues like efficient heating and lighting, education, interpretation, nature conservation and local crafts and produce. The scheme is most popular in Scotland where it was founded by VisitScotland. The scheme is now financed by membership fees.

Some visitor attractions are proud of their environmental policies and publicise them. This is an example provided by Woburn Safari Park.

An environmentally friendly business!

At Woburn Safari Park we are constantly examining our impact on the environment and looking for ways to improve. So far we have the following in place:

- re-using paper printed on one side for internal memos etc.
- re-using envelopes for internal mail
- use of email instead of memos where possible
- cardboard recycling skip
- office paper recycling collections (tree planted for every 50 sacks collected)
- printer cartridges recycled for Tommy's baby charity
- push button taps in public areas
- trial of water butts for animal drinking and cleaning
- sharing vehicles for movement around the Park
- public area lighting on timers/sensors
- using the 'power down' function on PCs
- member of Bedfordshire Green Business Network.

We are currently investigating:
- the use of bio-diesel
- becoming a carbon neutral business.

Source: www.woburnsafari.co.uk

Political

Visitor attractions can have a political impact on the community or even nationally. Collectively they can impact on government policy through joining relevant associations like ALVA. They can affect policy by working closely with VisitBritain or the local tourist authority. By working with People First, they can influence working conditions and training for employees.

There are several organisations which work to improve the sustainability of tourism. Visitor attractions are eligible to join these. An example is the Travel Foundation Forum. Members include some major tour operators. Membership gives the opportunity to share good practice, to influence areas of work and to put forward projects for funding.

Visitor attractions may attract funding from government sources such as the Heritage Lottery Fund for new developments which fit with government policy. The Victoria and Albert Museum has received a £3.5 million grant from this fund towards its £30 million renewal programme. The rest of the funding comes from private donations.

Visitor attractions can make sure they are represented at the annual National Conference of Visitor Attractions.

Government policy

'The Department of Culture, Media and Sport (DCMS) is responsible for Government policy on the arts, sport, the National Lottery, tourism, libraries, museums and galleries, broadcasting, film, the music industry, press freedom and regulation, licensing, gambling and the historic environment.'

Source: www.culture.gov.uk

This covers many of our visitor attractions. Historic buildings are listed and conservation areas protected through the DCMS. A publication, *The Historic Environment: A Force for our Future, 2001*, states government policy on the historic environment. The DCMS provides support and sponsorship to museums and galleries and has introduced free admission resulting in an increase in numbers of visitors.

Some visitor attractions may be eligible for EU funding for development. Applications are made to the European Regional Development Fund. The EU is committed to sustainable development and works with the European Community Network for Environmental Travel & Tourism (ECoNETT). This project brings together issues relating to tourism and the environment and provides guidance to tourism businesses.

Interpretation

Interpretation is part of the visitor experience and when it is done well, it makes visitors feel enthusiastic and involved with the attraction. They will enjoy themselves and want to come back or tell their friends about the attraction. Visitors will stay longer if they are enjoying themselves and spend more money.

Types of interpretation

Displays

Static displays are not very exciting but do have a place, particularly in museums and galleries where people sometimes want to stand and admire pieces. Even so, basic interpretation will include signage and labels and information about the artist or piece of work.

Interactive displays are more exciting for the visitor where they can participate and make something happen. Children particularly like interactive displays and learn more through them.

Animateurs

One way of communicating art to visitors is through the use of creative writing or storytelling workshops or performances. These techniques allow the visitor to become connected and emotionally involved with the exhibition rather than just looking at it. Galleries and museums use these techniques constantly and advertise them in their programmes.

Auditory interpretation

Audio guides are increasing in popularity in visitor attractions. They consist of taped information, available through an individual headset, in different languages.

They have many benefits:

* the individual can tour the attraction at their own pace

* they are cheaper than guides

* the individual can elect to hear extra pieces of information at the touch of a button

* special noise effects can be included.

However, it is difficult for the visitor to ask questions when they are plugged into the tape and it is a lonely experience being cut off from the other visitors.

Examples of visitor attractions using audio guides are Buckingham Palace, Althorp, the Churchill War Museum and Milestones' Museum in Hampshire.

The Milestones' Accoustiguide Programme for Primary Schools won an 'Interpret Britain' award for its interpretation of the county's history. Acoustiguides is a brand of audio guide using a listening device which combines narrative, music and sound effects. To encourage good interpretation in attractions, English Heritage holds an annual event 'The Interpret Britain and Ireland Awards Scheme'. The awards recognise outstanding practice in the provision of interpretive facilities at natural and cultural heritage sites throughout the United Kingdom and Ireland. The Award Scheme is open to organisations or individuals involved in interpreting a theme, place, site, collection, event or other facility for the benefit of the general public.

CASE STUDY

Science Museum

Here are some extracts from the education programme at the Science Museum in London. Note all the different interpretation techniques used to enhance learning and enjoyment. Note also special events for children with special needs. (The museum also has a new online resource for travel and tourism students. See www.sciencemuseum.org.uk/learning/leisureandtourism)

Unsung Heroes: Medical Marvels (KS2)
Celebration event – Black History Month

Gather round to hear the fascinating and inspirational tales of black doctors, nurses and surgeons who have made their mark in the field of medicine. To complement this event you could request to meet the Mary Seacole drama character.

Special Educational Needs Day (all ages)
This event for all ages takes place in *Pattern Pod*, a hands-on gallery, normally reserved for pupils aged 8 years and under. The gallery offers opportunities to explore visual, auditory and tactile patterns encouraging the use of skills such as repetition and prediction. The gallery also presents opportunities to improve language and social skills.

Drama characters (KS1, 2, 3, 4, post-16)

Meet one of our costumed actors bringing historical characters to life, enabling pupils to interact with people such as Mary Seacole, Amy Johnson, Isaac Newton, Michael Faraday, the world's first pregnant man or NASA astronaut, Gene Cernan. There's also a performance about the history of anaesthetics which is ideal for History of Medicine pupils.

Source: www.sciencemuseum.org.uk/learning

1. **Study the extracts and describe all the interpretation techniques used. Visit the Science Museum website and look for some current examples of use of interpretation techniques.**

Tourists at Buckingham Palace

Guides

Guides can be written in the form of books, leaflets or maps. All are useful for visitors but personal guides have the opportunity to bring an attraction to life. Guides are usually very knowledgeable and at their very best are performers connecting the visitor to the attraction.

The following features of good interpretation should be noted when producing written guides:

* it is targeted at the right audience
* each piece of interpretation communicates a clear message

* it is fun, not dull and boring
* it stimulates different senses
* it is interactive
* it doesn't have too much text
* it is updated and maintained as necessary
* it tries to be different.

Provision for special needs

There are many examples of good practice in provision for people of special needs at visitor attractions. In the Science Museum example above we saw how special events are put on for children with special needs. At the Tate Gallery in London many talks and events offer interpretation for hearing impaired or visually impaired people.

Almost all visitor attractions make provision for customers with special needs, as is now required under the Disability Discrimination Act of 1995. Purpose built attractions like the Eden Project have excellent provision and express their policy very clearly:

'The Eden Project welcomes people of all ages, backgrounds and disabilities. We are working to create equal opportunities for people to experience, learn and get involved in the Project.'

Source: The Eden Project

The government's Disability Unit has put forward recommendations to help visitor attractions ensure that they provide for the requirements of disabled customers. These include:

* think about the way you treat disabled customers – let them know how to request assistance and have a customer complaints procedure that is easy for them to use

* ensure you respect the dignity of a disabled person when providing them with services

* consider putting in place positive practices that will encourage disabled people and others to use your services

* make sure staff training includes your policy towards disabled people and their legal rights, as well as towards disability awareness and disability etiquette training

* regularly review whether your services are accessible to disabled people.

Source: www.disability.gov.uk

Appeal of visitor attractions

Type of attraction

Obviously different types of attraction appeal to different people. Visitor attractions have to be aware of their target audience and direct their marketing efforts at the right groups. Sometimes there are attempts to target a new audience in order to increase revenue. This could be done by working with VisitBritain to encourage inbound tourists to come to an attraction or by targeting different groups of domestic tourists.

The different types of attraction were described at the beginning of this unit. Now we will consider what types of visitors they try to appeal to and study the features of attractions that might affect people's choice of visit.

Types of visitor

Incoming tourists

Overseas visitors make an estimated 16 per cent of visits to UK visitor attractions according to the Visitor Attractions Survey.

Visitor attractions need to be aware of the country of origin of their incoming tourist visitors. This helps them to ensure that literature and interpretation is available in the relevant languages and that they know where to market their products and services. UK visitor attractions that depend on inbound tourists suffered a drop in visitors in the early years of the 21st century. Overseas tourists, particularly North Americans, were deterred from travelling after 11 September 2001 due to fear of terrorism and were also put off by a weak global economy meaning the UK was expensive for them and by foot and mouth disease. Happily, the number of visitors is once more on the increase.

Location

London attractions are most popular with our overseas visitors as London is the most popular destination. Other popular destinations include Scotland, Stratford, York, Oxford and Cambridge. Thus visitor attractions in these areas are likely to receive most overseas visitors.

Price

The price of entry to an overseas visitor varies according to the current exchange rate. In the early years of the 21st century the pound has been strong against both the euro and the dollar so that overseas visitors from Europe and the US find the UK expensive. Some attractions offer special prices for overseas visitors. At one time Asterix Park, near Paris, allowed all British children free entry, much to the chagrin of French people in the same queue who had to pay for their children!

Transport and access

Within London, overseas visitors are likely to depend on public transport and attractions must give clear directions and tube and bus stops on their literature.

Seasonality

Inbound tourists visit mainly in the summer.

Products and services

Those attractions with a world-wide reputation are likely to attract overseas visitors as they prefer to see things they have heard about.

Interpretation

Those visitors whose first language is not English will be looking for interpretation in their own language.

Consider this...

Without doing any research at all can you think about the attractions in New York which would appeal to you as a tourist there.

Educational

Educational visitors are usually in groups, although the groups and their needs are very diverse. They may be children from primary schools or university students doing specialist courses. Educational groups are a very important client group for many attractions from theme parks to museums to educational projects. The Eden Project welcomes about 250 children per day and some of them are from as far away as Scotland and France. As we saw earlier, Eden provides activities and learning materials for primary school children, GCSE and A-level course

students and special needs children. In addition they hold sessions for teachers.

Visitor attractions often employ education officers and hold events to attract students, providing case study and assignment material. At Disneyland Paris, a student convention for about 1,200 students from the UK is held every December. It brings in revenue when the park would otherwise be quiet and gives Disney a reputation for helping in education.

Location

Primary school children are usually taken to local attractions. For other student or pupil groups the nature of the attraction is more important than the location. Overseas trips will also incorporate visits to attractions.

Price

Price is an important factor for this group as schools and colleges do not fund student visits except in cases of extreme hardship. Parents are expected to pay, therefore prices must be reasonable as transport costs will also add to the price. All attractions offer group price concessions.

Transport and access

Most domestic school and college visits take place via coach transport. It is the easiest and safest way (in terms of keeping tabs on people) of transporting the group. Group leaders will expect attractions to have access for coaches and adequate parking facilities not too far from the attraction.

Seasonality

Educational visits take place mainly in term time. Alton Towers held an interesting campaign in October 2004. As their main target group of children and teenagers was back at school, they targeted adults who might like to avoid 'annoying kids'. They had an offer of £18 day tickets for people to take advantage of children being 'back at school, locked away in their classrooms, slaves to the bell and forced to eat school dinners'.

Products and services

Products and services depend on what is being studied but for school children, teachers look for attractions which provide products, activities and learning materials linked to the National

Curriculum. College students are taken to attractions which complement their A level or vocational courses.

Interpretation

Interpretation must be lively and interesting to attract and retain the attention of the educational groups.

Families

Families are often looking for a family day out when they visit an attraction. They may be domestic tourists or inbound tourists. Their interests will vary but they will require activities and facilities that occupy their children.

Location

The location could be anywhere as the visit might be part of a holiday or a day out.

Price

Price is very important if you are paying entry fees for a few people – families will look for a price structure that gives them a family rate.

Transport and access

Most families on day trips drive to attractions, therefore they want clear road directions, limited queues and close parking. Attractions which are close to major road routes will be more popular.

Seasonality

School holiday periods are the most popular times for visits.

Products and services

This type of customer requires many extra services – they need places to eat, toilets, baby-changing facilities, lost children centres.

Special interest

Visitor attractions which look for a niche market of a special interest type of customer are in the minority as they are not likely to attract visitors in huge numbers and make much money. However, some have an international reputation and do well by attracting visitors from all over the world. Car enthusiasts, for example, might travel to visit the National Motor Museum at Beaulieu. Many attractions make provision for special interest groups to attract extra custom outside the mainstream.

The following extract from Woburn's website shows how this is done.

> 'There are options for day visits or for short breaks for special interest groups at Woburn. Tailored packages or tours can be created for groups with special interests in art, furniture, silver or history at Woburn Abbey or conservation at Woburn Safari Park. The three championship courses at Woburn Golf and Country Club provide a tempting challenge for any golfer and the opportunity for a special golfing break.'
>
> Source: www.woburnsafari.co.uk

Location

Location is not really relevant if you are a dedicated enthusiast.

Price

Price depends on what the individual can afford, but enthusiasts might pay a premium or look for a package that includes visits to their special interest attractions.

Transport and access

There may be the possibility of inclusive packages so that the enthusiast doesn't have to consider transport and can meet others with a similar interest.

Products and services

This is the most important factor for this group – they only want to visit the attraction because it represents their interest and they will be in the market for guide books, souvenir picture books etc.

Interpretation

This depends on the nature of the attraction – it might allow the visitor to practise their hobby or interest.

Special needs

These range from groups from educational/care establishments to individuals with disabilities and other special needs.

Location

Location is not as important as the suitability of the attraction to the person's interest and its access.

Price

Price is an important factor for groups who will need to keep costs down – special group prices will be expected.

Transport and access

This is of vital importance for this type of customer. If there is no access for people with special needs, they will not visit the attraction. The Disability Discrimination Act now applies and should result in improved access and services for customers with special needs. New purpose-built attractions always have good access as it is factored into the design. Heritage attractions have greater problems. The extract opposite from a leaflet about Chatsworth illustrates this. Access for wheelchair users is limited and a video of the route is shown in the information kiosk so that wheelchair users don't have to try and get round the actual tour.

Products and services

These are an important factor when choosing an attraction, depending on personal interest.

Interpretation

Attractions should consider special needs customers when planning interpretation. There are many visual, audio and physical aids that can be included in interpretation.

Chatsworth House

Wheelchair access

'The structure of the oldest part of the house, which involves 160 steps, limits access to the visitor route. The rooms in the North Wing are accessible via the ramp outside the Orangery Shop; for your enjoyment and safety, we recommend that this area is visited when it is quieter at 11am. A video of the entire visitor route is shown all day in the information kiosk. The garden, farmyard, shops and restaurant are fully accessible – access plan and information on request. Accessible lavatories are available. There are three scooters and eight manual wheelchairs; please book to ensure availability.

Source: Extract from Chatsworth visitor information leaflet

Corporate customers

Corporate customers have different needs from other groups. They are interested in providing an experience for their customers or employees that is different, even unique. They will be using the visit to the attraction as an incentive for clients to buy their products or services or for loyalty and high regard from their employees.

Location

This depends on the nature of the corporate event. International companies will host events anywhere in the world if it is appropriate. Disneyland Paris is an important venue for corporate entertainment or conferences. Small companies will look for a local venue.

Price

Corporate packages are offered by attractions – price is dependent on facilities and services required and numbers. Corporate customers, whilst expecting value for money, do not usually base their choice of venue on price alone.

Transport and access

This is not so important for delegates who will be used to finding their way around although good directions should be provided. Access may be a factor if the corporate customer wants to use the attraction to display their products, for example, to display holiday homes. Not only would lots of space be needed but transporters would have to deliver them.

Seasonality

The corporate market is not really seasonal apart from a dip in the summer.

Products and services

These are very important for this group, although not in terms of the attraction itself. Catering, accommodation and possibly entertainment will be needed and should be of high quality. Visits to the attraction will be an added bonus for the delegates, not the main purpose of their visit.

Interpretation

The attraction may offer special tours or information in the language of the delegates.

Theory into practice

Match the visitor types to the attraction feature which is likely to be *most* important to them.

VISITOR TYPE	FEATURE OF ATTRACTION
Couple with twin toddlers	Lifts and wide passages
Japanese family visiting London	Quality accommodation and catering
Visitor in a wheelchair	Special working steam train day
Group of schoolchildren	Gallery holding Monet exhibition
Steam train enthusiasts	Activities based on the National Curriculum
Corporate customer wanting a 2-day conference	Interpretation in foreign languages
Student studying impressionist art	Family pricing, family friendly facilities

---

Assessment activity 18.3

Visit the following London attractions or their websites:

- Madame Tussauds
- Tate Modern
- London Eye.

Consider the following visitor types:

- a family of inbound tourists, with children of 12 and 14 years old, from Spain
- a corporate visitor who wants to organise a visit which incorporates entertainment and a meal for a group of 14 clients
- a wheelchair user who is visiting London for a couple of days with a friend.

1 Explain the appeal of each visitor attraction to each of these visitor types. You should think about the following features and indicate the importance of each to that visitor type:

- location
- price
- access
- products and services specific to their needs
- interpretation.

This task could provide evidence for P4.

2 Compare and contrast the appeal of each of the attractions to each of the visitor types given. You could produce this as a chart using the headings above with some conclusions supporting the chart.

This task could provide evidence for M3.

3 Suggest ways that each of the attractions could increase their appeal to the visitor types given. You must support your suggestions with good reasons.

This task could provide evidence for D2.

Knowledge check

1 Which are the most popular attractions in the UK?

2 What is meant by secondary spend?

3 What are timed tickets?

4 Why is secondary spend so important in museums?

5 How does the virtual queue system at Six Flags work?

6 What is Britart?

7 What economic benefits can visitor attractions bring to an area?

8 Why was Disneyland Paris situated in Marne la Valle?

9 Explain the Green Tourism scheme.

10 What is People First?

11 What do we mean by interpretation?

12 Describe three interpretation techniques.

13 What are the features of good interpretation?

14 Which 'appeal' factors are most important for school groups?

15 Which 'appeal' factors are most important for families?

UNIT 18 ASSESSMENT ASSIGNMENT

Your local newspaper has asked for your help in producing a supplement on local visitor attractions. They don't have the people power to assign a reporter to the supplement so they have invited students to do it. The aim of the supplement is to provide information about the visitor attractions in the area. The supplement will be attached to the evening paper and also to the free weekly edition so it will achieve very wide coverage of your area. The newspaper is read by local residents and also by visitors to the area. Your area attracts a lot of inbound tourists who are interested in learning about the visitor attractions available. Some local people worry about the numbers of tourists visiting your local attractions and about the impact on the environment and on their society, so these issues will be covered in the supplement.

Your responsibility is to research three local visitor attractions. Your work must be individual although colleagues might be researching other attractions for inclusion in the supplement. You must provide information for the supplement as follows:

1 The products and services provided by the three visitor attractions

Give a description of the products and services at each attraction.

This task provides evidence for P1

2 The impacts of the three visitor attractions

Explain the impacts of the attractions on the local environment and the community.

Consider the following impacts:

- both negative and positive
- socio-cutural
- economic
- environmental
- political.

This task provides evidence for P2.

Explain how each of your chosen visitor attractions had tried to minimise any negative impacts and how they have tried to maximise positive impacts on the local community and environment.

This task provides evidence for M2.

Suggest new ways that your three visitor attractions might minimise negative impacts and maximise positive impacts. Make sure you support your ideas with sound reasons.

This task provides evidence for D1.

3 The appeal of visitor attractions

Explain all the factors which lend appeal to your visitor attractions for a group of primary school children and a family of Japanese tourists.

Make sure you include all the following:

- location
- price – structure and examples
- transport and access
- seasonality – suitability of opening times
- relevant products and services
- interpretation – all techniques explained and why they appeal to these particular visitors.

This task provides evidence for P3 and P4.

Compare and contrast the appeal and range of interpretation techniques of your three chosen visitor attractions to the two types of visitors described above. Use the same list of factors. You could present this as a comparative chart to form part of the supplement. Make sure you draw some conclusions from your chart.

This task provides evidence for M2 and M3.

Make some suggestions on how your three chosen visitor attractions could increase their appeal to the two types of visitors described. Support your suggestions with sound reasons.

This task provides evidence for D2.

UNIT 19

Hospitality operations in travel and tourism

Introduction

Hospitality is central to the travel and tourism industry as it occurs both as a sector in its own right and as part of many other travel and tourism sectors, such as visitor attractions where hospitality is part of the overall visitor experience. In this unit we will be discussing trends and issues affecting the hospitality sector.

You will find out about the range of organisations in the hospitality sector and how they operate and what products and services they provide. In addition, you will examine the role of hospitality as a secondary function in other sectors.

You will study the different functions and departments within hospitality such as accommodation, food and beverage and administration, looking at examples of each.

You will develop an awareness of how customer needs and expectations affect the provision of hospitality and the level of service.

How you will be assessed

This unit is internally assessed by your tutor. A variety of exercises and activities is included in this unit to help you develop your knowledge and understanding of hospitality operations and prepare for the assessment. You will also have the opportunity to work on some case studies.

After completing this unit you should be able to achieve the following outcomes:

→ investigate the hospitality environment as a sector of travel and tourism
→ explore the range of hospitality providers in a travel and tourism context
→ examine hospitality functions in a travel and tourism context
→ explore how customer expectations influence hospitality service.

Hospitality environment

Travel and tourism and hospitality

Hospitality is the provision of accommodation, food and drink and other hospitality services. The main areas of the hospitality industry are hotels, restaurants, pubs, bars, nightclubs, youth hostels and holiday parks. Hospitality and travel and tourism are closely intertwined and interdependent. Some sectors, for example, holiday parks, fall across both industries. It is not possible to engage in travel and tourism without the provision of hospitality. An integral part of a holiday is the provision of a hotel room and restaurant meals. Similarly, a hotel relies on travel and tourism services to deliver its guests to its premises.

Areas of travel and tourism which focus on specific travel and tourism products and services still offer hospitality services. For example, customers visiting a theme park for the day will expect to buy lunch and other refreshments during their stay.

The size and scale of hospitality

The chart below illustrates the different types of establishments operating in the hospitality industry. You will note that the pubs, bars and nightclubs sector is the largest but the restaurant sector is almost as large. Both of these sectors are important to travel and tourism as they attract tourists to their establishments.

The nature of the hospitality business is that small, independent companies characterise the market. This is true in the areas of hotels, restaurants, bars and pubs. In contract food services and visitor attractions, the opposite is true and the market is dominated by a few large companies, for example, Compass, a food service provider, dominates contract food services.

Key concept

Contract food service companies provide food service for customers at a range of locations – offices, factories, railway stations, airports, universities, schools, retail stores and shopping centres. In travel and tourism their services may be contracted at airports, railway stations and in visitor attractions.

ESTABLISHMENTS ACROSS THE SECTOR BY INDUSTRY: 2002		
Industry	**Establishments**	**% Breakdown**
Hotels	12,488	6.9
Restaurants	58,262	32.2
Pubs, bars and nightclubs	59,219	32.7
Contract food service providers	20,315	11.2
Events	–	–
Travel and tourism services	12,665	7.0
Membership clubs	3,980	2.2
Gambling	9,957	5.5
Visitor attractions	740	0.4
Youth hostels	425	0.2
Holiday parks and self-catering accommodation	2,939	1.6
Hospitality services	–	–
Total	**180,990**	**100.0**

Source: Annual Business Inquiry from www.statistics.gov.uk

WORKFORCE ACROSS THE SECTOR BY INDUSTRY: 2002		
Industry	Workforce	
Hotels	292,954	17.7
Restaurants	536,447	32.4
Pubs, bars and nightclubs	320,262	19.3
Contract food service providers	201,303	12.2
Events	–	–
Travel and tourism services	133,960	8.1
Membership clubs	31,630	1.9
Gambling	71,620	4.3
Visitor attractions	16,056	1.0
Youth hostels	2,263	0.1
Holiday parks and self-catering accommodation	50,123	3.0
Hospitality services	–	–
Total	1,656,618	100.0

Source: Labour Source: Force Survey from www.statistics.gov.uk

Employment figures

Figures show how important hospitality is as a source of employment in the travel and tourism industry. Nearly a third of the workforce in all of travel and tourism is employed in restaurants as the table above indicates. Most of the workforce in travel and tourism is employed in hospitality of one kind or another.

National government tourism strategy

Policies for the hospitality industry are governed by the Department for Culture, Media and Sport (DCMS). In 2003 a new initiative known as Fitness for Purpose was introduced by the DCMS. The aim was to create a framework which provided customers with reassurance about the fitness for trading of hotels in England. It was part of the drive for better quality in tourism. A pilot scheme took place in 2003 and is now being implemented nationally.

'Fitness for Purpose is an initiative promoting better inspection and regulation of tourist accommodation as a way of tackling poor safety and trading standards and ensuring that minimum legal requirements are met. It is targeted at hotels, guest houses and bed and breakfasts which are failing to meet minimum legal requirements on health and safety, food hygiene, trading standards and fire safety, in order to help them improve. It aims to give those businesses the support they need to raise standards in those areas, whilst also taking a lighter regulatory enforcement touch to well-run businesses that are already complying with the necessary regulations.'

Source: www.culture.gov.uk

Theory into practice

Find out more about this initiative by looking at the DCMS website on www.culture.gov.uk. Note that the scheme is not a quality grading scheme so how does it work? Make some notes and discuss your opinions on the initiative with your group.

Trends and issues in hospitality

Nature of employment

Much of hospitality work is part-time, 42 per cent in hotels and 50 per cent in restaurants. This compares with only 25 per cent part-time work across all industries. This might be a good thing in terms of flexibility for employees but the work is also low paid and often seasonal. Employers are allowed to top up wages with tips so that the minimum wage is met, in spite of strong criticism from trade unions. The employers argue that food and accommodation are often provided for workers and that this should be taken into account when setting wages.

These factors cause recruitment difficulties and jobs are often taken by those who have difficulty finding work in other sectors, such as refugees and people with few basic skills or those for whom English is a second language. Having workers who have problems communicating in English or lack other basic skills impacts on customer service and hotels and restaurants often have to keep people lacking such skills away from customer-facing activities, giving them, for example, kitchen work. Even there a lack of English may cause other problems as instructions on catering and kitchen products can't easily be read.

Quality of training

The diversity and size of hospitality establishments mean that there are problems of communication and representation of the sector. Most establishments are small and employ few people. Many restaurants employ less than ten people. In addition, the restaurant sector comprises dining, fast food, coffee shops and brasseries and also comprises different ethnic groups, such as Oriental, Indian, Italian etc. So many small and diverse businesses make it hard to measure consistency of quality throughout the sector and to find out where and when good quality training is taking place.

A market assessment carried out by People 1st, the sector skills council for hospitality, found that there was generally a lack of training in management skills, information technology, basic skills, customer service skills and specifically in areas like food handling. According to a 2002 Food Standards Agency report more than a third of hospitality companies do not even train their staff in basic health and hygiene.

From this we can conclude that more training is needed across the sector. It is the role of People 1st to encourage and influence employers to provide this training.

As there is a high turnover of staff in this sector there is a need for constant training to cover existing and replacement staff. However, if good quality training were available it would be expected that staff retention would improve. Some businesses have understood this and managed to reduce staff turnover and recruitment costs.

Key concept

People 1st is the Sector Skills Council (SSC) for the Hospitality, Leisure, Travel and Tourism sector. It aims to represent the industry on skills matters, to optimise skills funding for the industry and to identify and endorse suitable training provision.

Other organisations encourage training, for example, the British Institute of Innkeeping has developed a qualification for pub tenants which will eventually become a requirement for new pub tenants.

Many organisations offer on the job training leading to NVQs. Relevant NVQs in hospitality include the NVQ in Hospitality and Catering levels 1 to 3. Chefs are often offered college day release to complete their NVQs but according to a recent Employers Skills Survey there is a shortage of chefs which has led to a tendency to deskill restaurant staff and provide a simple, standard menu which can be prepared by unskilled personnel.

The kind of training most often undertaken is that which enables organisations to meet their legislative requirements such as food safety training, health and safety and first aid training.

The best quality training is usually available in the large companies, such as hotel groups where investment has been made in training and in policies to retain staff.

Uncertainty of visitor numbers

Several issues over the early years of the 21st century affected tourist numbers and therefore hotels and restaurants. Firstly the events of 11 September 2001 led to a drastic reduction in the number of Americans prepared to travel. An outbreak of foot and mouth led to a decrease in tourism in countryside areas in the same year. The strength of sterling was another factor. This meant that tourists coming from either the US or Europe found that their currencies did not buy much sterling and the UK was a very expensive destination to visit. To enable survival in the face of such conditions, hotels and restaurants tried the following strategies:

* increased multi-skilling of staff so that they can be deployed where needed – for example, if a hotel has little need for silver service banqueting staff, it ceases to employ staff designated for that function but trains its housekeepers etc. in silver service and redeploys them when needed

* emphasis on high service levels to take advantage of the high spending customers

* joint promotions with VisitBritain to encourage inbound tourism.

These measures have had some degree of success and, in October 2004, figures showed that UK hoteliers outside the capital held occupancy and room rates at last year's levels, whilst those in the capital saw a reasonable rise in rooms yield. London hotels had average occupancy of 79.6 per cent in October 2004 which was a marked increase on October 2001 when it had fallen to 65.1 per cent.

> **Key concept**
>
> **Room yield** – Number of rooms occupied multiplied by the average achieved room rate.

ROOMS DEPARTMENT	2004	2003	% CHANGE
UK Regional hotels			
Average daily room rate per occupied room	£64.45	£62.20	3.6%
Average daily occupancy	75.6%	73%	3.5%
Average daily rooms yield per available room	£48.72	£45.43	7.2%

Source: PKF Regional UK Trends Survey

Licensing Bill 2003

New licensing laws were proposed in 2003 and are in the process of implementation. The law is

fairly detailed but one of the major changes is permitting bars and pubs to extend their opening hours. The government maintains that fixed and early closing times result in rapid binge drinking just before closing time and that disorder and disturbance occur on the streets when everyone has to leave a pub at the same time. Everyone then needs to find public transport or a taxi at the same time or goes to fast food outlets whose services are also put under pressure. A slower dispersal of people from pubs should result in less disorder. Hotels will also be affected where they have bars which allow non-residents.

Consider this...

What is your opinion about the new licensing laws? Will people be encouraged to drink more or less?

New technology

Large hotel groups are likely to have invested in new technology taking advantage of systems for ordering, communications and reservations. Small establishments are less likely to risk large sums on technology that might not exactly suit their requirements as they cannot afford to have it tailor made. Online reservations services have helped hotels worldwide, giving even small establishments access to international markets through the Internet. Distributors like lastminute.com offer a service to hotels, bringing hotels and customers together for a commission from the hotel group.

Hospitality management software systems are widely available and contain sections for all aspects of hotel and restaurant management. There are even systems that chefs can use to aid them in planning and budgeting their menus.

Assessment activity 19.1

Joshua Kintuck runs a pub in a small village in Suffolk. His partner is Spanish and a superb chef. She specialises in Catalan dishes, particularly fish dishes. Over the last ten years she has built up a reputation and people flock from far and wide to eat in the pub. On Friday and Saturday nights it is impossible to get a reservation without booking weeks ahead. Although the business is successful, it is not an easy life as the Kintucks take only one day off a week. Besides running the business and ordering and preparing the food, they have to hire and train staff. Their two children are grown up but have not chosen to work in the family business and work away from home. Because of the ties of the pub it is difficult for the Kintucks to find time to visit their children. To attract staff, Mrs Kintuck advertises in a London listing magazine. She has had some excellent young people whom she has trained as much as she has time for and she has been pleased with their performance. They are often young people who have come to the UK to learn English. Unfortunately, they do not always stay very long as there is a limit to the attractions of the countryside. This leads to a further round of recruitment and basic training.

At the very least the new recruits need food safety training. Some of the staff she recruits are from outside Europe and Mrs Kintuck has found it difficult to understand all the regulations regarding the employment of non-Europeans.

Another problem facing the Kintucks is the change in licensing laws. They close promptly at 11pm at present and do not wish to open longer. Although the new laws do not mean they are forced to open longer, they are concerned that they may be under pressure from customers to do so. They do not know how they would manage to work any more hours.

1 Describe the issues facing the Kintucks and the pub/restaurant business in general.
   This task may provide evidence for P1.

2 Choose two issues facing the Kintucks and explain them in detail.
   This task may provide evidence for M1.

3 Recommend appropriate courses of action for the Kintucks to deal with the issues facing them. Justify your recommendations.
   This task may provide evidence for D1.

Hospitality providers

Primary providers

By primary provider we mean that the main focus of the business is on hospitality, that is the provision of accommodation and food. These providers include hotels, guest houses, motels, holiday centres, self-catering establishments, camping and caravan parks, canal boats, cruise ships, restaurants and cafes. We will take a more detailed look at some of these types of business.

Hotels

A hotel is an establishment that offers accommodation, food and drink to anyone who is fit to receive and is willing to pay. Many hotels also provide leisure facilities, conference and banqueting facilities and business services.

There were 48,089 hotels in the UK in 2002 according to figures compiled by Horizon Foodservice Intelligence. These figures include all sizes of establishments so include guest houses. Most of these are independent establishments but there are several large groups as the following table of top 20 UK hotel brands illustrates. The table rates the hotels by size not by revenue or profit.

TOP 20 UK HOTEL BRANDS 2003–2004 (BY NUMBER OF BEDROOMS)			
Company	Number of hotels	Brands	Number of rooms
Whitbread Hotel Group	505	Courtyard by Marriott (11), Marriott (51), Premier Travel Inn (443)	37,148
InterContinental Hotels Group (as at 31/12/03)	204	InterContinental (2), Crowne Plaza*, Holiday Inn*, Express by Holiday Inn*	29,053
Hilton International	78		16,044
Travelodge (Permira)	255		13,300
Accor Hotels	84	Sofitel (1), Novotel (28), Mercure (1), Ibis (42), Etap (2), Formule 1 (10)	11,321
Thistle Hotels	54		10,122
Choice Hotels Europe	88	Quality (53), Comfort (27), Sleep (5), Clarion (3)	7,000
Jarvis Hotels	60	Ramada Jarvis (54), Jarvis (5), Travelodge (1)	6,745
Britannia Hotels	24		5,175
Macdonald Hotels	63		5,022
Queens Moat Houses	33	Moat House (32), Holiday Inn (1)	4,933
Corus Hotels	65		4,863
De Vere Hotels	35	De Vere Hotels (21), Village Leisure (14) Timeshare Lodges (132)	4,542
Millennium Copthorne Hotels	17	Millennium (6), Copthorne (11)	4,047
Jurys Doyle Hotel Group	15	Hotels (6), Inns (9)	3,401
Imperial London Hotels	6		2,944
London and Edinburgh Inns Group	64	Inns (36), Swallow (28)	2,916
Marriott International	10	Renaissance (5), Marriott (5)	2,953
Shearings Hotels	36		2,800
Warner Holidays (Bourne Leisure)	13	Historic (6), Character (3), Classic (4)	2,652

Source: *British Hospitality: Trends and Statistics 2004* (British Hospitality Association)

largest group with over 500 hotels. Just after the publication of these statistics, Whitbread announced the disposal of some of their Marriott hotels.

Approximately 22,000 hotels and guest houses are registered with the tourist boards as are 16,000 bed and breakfasts. The rest are unregistered. A lot of hotels are run by their owners and the average size of a hotel is 20 rooms. The major groups have a lot of influence on the hotel business.

The UK hotel industry turns over about £27 billion per year but is affected by economic issues including exchange rates which impact on tourist arrivals. When the pound is strong against the dollar and euro, tourists are less likely to visit the UK as they find it expensive. Fewer visitors results in rooms being let for lower rates and in lower room occupancy levels.

Although these figures were accurate at the time they were compiled, they change quickly as companies dispose of assets and buy different ones. It is evident from the table that Whitbread is the

Consider this...

What are the main hotel groups represented in your area? What local factors influence their bookings?

CASE STUDY

De Vere hotel group

De Vere used to be known as Greenalls and had a variety of different businesses in leisure, health and fitness, hotels and pubs. In 1999, the group decided to dispose of its pub divisions. They sold Greenalls to Scottish and Newcastle and sold their Inn Partnership to a Japanese company, Nomura.

Currently, the group has 21 hotels under the De Vere brand, the most famous of which is probably the Grand in Brighton. They also have 13 hotels under the Village brand. These are hotels and leisure clubs. The average room rate for the De Vere brand was £84.81 in 2004 whereas for Village it was £55.10. The De Vere Group also owns a chain of health and fitness clubs called Greens.

1. Why do you think De Vere decided to concentrate on the hotel business?

2. How does the health and fitness chain fit in with the core business?

3. What differences would you expect for a higher room rate in a De Vere branded hotel rather than a Village branded hotel?

4. Look at the De Vere website and see if you are right.

Many hotels are part of a franchise operation. This means that although they are independently owned they use the brand name, marketing and reservation services of a group. Of course, they have to pay for the benefits that they receive. This is usually a percentage of revenue.

CASE STUDY

Best Western is an example of a consortium. Best Western International claims to be the world's largest hotel chain with over 4,000 hotels worldwide. In Britain there are more than 300 member hotels. Best Western actively recruits hotels to join the group but carries out extensive quality inspections before accepting hotels.

The benefits of membership are outlined on their website and shown below:

- keep full independence, while being part of an international affiliation

- maintain quality standards by undergoing two independent assessments each year

- represented by the Best Western Great Britain central reservations service, open seven days a week and linked to our international reservations centres

- favoured by over 50,000 Gold Crown Club International members in the UK and over 1,000,000 members who are collecting points worldwide

- membership of Best Western gives independent hoteliers the strength to succeed in an increasingly competitive marketplace by maximising international marketing, sales, reservations and buying power.

Source: www.bestwestern.co.uk

1. **What do you think are the disadvantages of joining a group such as Best Western?**
2. **Explain how a loyalty scheme such as Gold Crown Club helps hotels.**

Budget hotels

A budget hotel is a type of hotel that caters for visitors on short stays and those who are travelling. This type of accommodation has more or less replaced the motel sector. Motels were one storey buildings where guests could park their car outside their room and go directly inside. They were built near major road routes so that they were convenient for travellers. Budget hotels are also often built near major routes but there is an increasing trend to build them in cities. These hotels have fewer facilities than other hotels, for example, there are few staff, perhaps just one person on reception and no room service. There are no luxuries and usually no catering facilities, although en suite bathrooms are provided.

This sector is growing because customers realise that the budget-hotel sector gives excellent value for money in convenient locations.

An article from *Caterer & Hotelkeeper* magazine explains:

'The number of branded budget hotel rooms is predicted to rise to 75,000 by the end of 2005 and to 87,000 in 2007, according to a new report from consultants Deloitte.

'This will mean adding between 6,000 and 6,300 new bedrooms each year and maintaining the level of growth seen in 2003, when more than 6,000 new budget bedrooms were opened. This represented a 10.6 per cent rise on the 4,500 new rooms that came on stream in 2002. Since then, the average size of budget hotels has grown from 61 to 64 bedrooms.

'Both owner-operated and franchised hotels will fuel the growth, which will be underpinned by an increase in room bookings via the Internet, said the report. (The number of online bookings doubled to 20 per cent in the two years to 2003.)'

Source: *Caterer & Hotelkeeper* magazine, 25 November 2004. www. caterer-online.com

There are several companies offering budget hotels. The chart below shows the number of budget hotels and their ownership in 2004.

BUDGET HOTELS IN THE UK 28 Oct 2004					
Brand	Company	Hotels 2003	Hotels 2002	Bedrooms 2003	Bedrooms 2002
Premier Travel Inn	Whitbread	443*	424*	26,319*	24,764*
Travelodge	Permira	255	234	15,000	14,271
Express by Holiday Inn	InterContinental Hotels	89	75	8,926	7,135
Ibis	Accor UK	42	39	5,398	4,522
Innkeeper's Lodge	Mitchells & Butlers	74	65	2,079	1,713
Comfort Inn	Choice Hotels	31	31	2,017	2,017
Campanile	Groupe Envergure	15	15	1,113	1,113
Days Inn	Cendant	17	14	1,043	874
City Inn	First Stop Hotels	4	3	1,029	569
Formule 1	Accor	10	10	749	753
Ramada Encore	Marriott International	3	1	353	104
Welcome Lodge	Welcome Break	5	8	319	531
Wetherlodges	JD Wetherspoon	11	10	314	213
Sleep Inn	Choice Hotels	4	4	310	310
Tulip Inn	Golden Tulip	2	2	235	235
Etap	Accor UK	2	2	150	150
Dolby	Dolby Hotels	1	1	65	65
Kyriad	Groupe Envergure	1	1	50	50
Total		**1,009**	**939**	**65,469**	**59,389**

Source: *British Hospitality: Trends and Statistics 2004* (British Hospitality Association)   *Including Premier Lodge

Budget hotels are such good value that they enjoy a 90 per cent plus occupancy rate. Travel Inn is the United Kingdom's leading budget hotel brand, totalling more than 230 hotels. There is a Travel Inn at County Hall, London, on the south bank of the Thames near Westminster and the London Eye.

Guest houses and bed and breakfast establishments

Usually the difference between a hotel and a guest house is one of size but also a guest house might not provide food and drink whereas a hotel usually does. Most guest houses are family run and only have a few rooms. They are often situated in large houses that would originally have been intended for families.

Years ago people often went to guest houses, or boarding houses as they were known, for their annual summer holiday. Families sometimes returned to their favourite houses year after year. They would expect to have a bedroom (a large room might be designated a family room), they would not expect to have a private bathroom but would share with all the other guests. Breakfast would be served at a set time and after that families had to go out, whether it was rain or shine, and not return until early evening. Dinner would be served at a set time in the early evening. Afterwards the family might go for a walk along the promenade or go to a show.

The British seaside was full of houses like this and of course there are still thousands. Today the facilities have mostly improved as people's expectations have grown. Many guest houses have rooms with private bathrooms and have lounges for guests to sit in if they wish.

The guest house in the photo below is an example of a typical British guest house.

Many guest houses have websites that give information about the accommodation provided and the location. The location of the guest house is often stressed to show that it is suitable for travellers. The websites also gives details of room rates and directions for getting there.

The websites are often linked to a national bed and breakfast website. Internet technology has made it much easier for customers and guest house owners to find each other. There are still many guest houses and bed and breakfast establishments who do not have website links and they rely on their local Tourist Information Centre to supply them with clients.

Holiday centres

These may be camping and caravan parks or purpose-built sites with accommodation, entertainment and leisure facilities. Examples include Pontins, Butlins and CenterParc.

Self-catering apartments and cottages

Many people prefer self-catering accommodation for the extra freedom it allows them in deciding when to eat and controlling the type of food on offer. Self-catering allows a greater level of informality on holidays. Many tour operators specialise in offering self-catering accommodation holidays. The accommodation may be quite basic, for example in tents on campsites, or it may be luxury villas.

Generally, self-catering properties are suitable for people who want to be independent and do not expect to have the services that would be provided in a hotel such as entertainment, bars and restaurants. However, many resorts have blocks of self-catering accommodation where all the facilities of a hotel are available and yet kitchens and cooking facilities are provided.

Camping and caravan parks

The UK Caravan Parks and Campsites Directory shows that there are an incredible 2,548 caravan sites, parks and campsites in the UK.

Camping and caravanning have become an important sector of the tourism industry both in the UK and throughout Europe. Camping has changed a lot over the years and campsites have become much more sophisticated and offer many more facilities than they used to.

Customers expect tents to be fixed rather than bring their own, but many prefer holiday homes to tents and in fact many campsites now prefer to be known as holiday centres and do not allow any campers to bring their own tents or touring caravans. This enables the campsite owners to exert much greater control over the layout and appearance of the site increasing its appeal to visitors. Campsite owners have also increased the level of services and hospitality on offer in line with increased customer expectations.

A wide range of accommodation and food services are on offer at some large camping and caravanning sites including a range of luxury accommodation, bars, restaurants, takeaways and supermarkets.

Water-borne holidays

Cruise holidays are rising in popularity (see Unit 9). Holidays are also available on canal barges or sea-going yachts.

Restaurants and fast-food outlets

Statistics on UK restaurant groups show that the largest group is McDonalds's with 1,235 restaurants. Many of the top fifteen would be better described as fast-food outlets rather than restaurants. More sophisticated establishments

that you might choose for a special occasion are classified as 'fine dining'.

The Restaurant Association looks after the interests of restaurateurs. It forms part of the British Hospitality Association and has over 10,500 members. According to the Association the restaurant sector has an annual turnover of approximately £21bn and employs over 500,000 full time and part time staff. 70 per cent of businesses are owner operated.

The restaurant sector is growing and there are several reasons for this:

* increased disposable income means people can afford to eat out

TOP 15 UK RESTAURANT GROUPS (BY NUMBER OF OUTLETS):		
Company	Number of restaurants	Brands inc
McDonald's	1,235	
Burger King	700 (2003)	

Whitbread
   Pizza Hut (578)
   TGI Fridays (41)
	619 (2003)	

TDI/Capricorn
   Pizza Express (340)
   Ask (170)
   Nando's (93)
	603	Cafe Pasta
		Zizzi

Wimpy	300	
The Restaurant Group	249	Garfunkels, Caffe Uno, Frankie & Benny's
Harry Ramsden's (Compass)	170	
Tragus	155	Cafe Rouge, Bella Italia, Abbaye
Out of Town Restaurant Group	127	Caffee Express, Bitz and Pizza, Potato & Bake
Giardino Group plc	56	Cafe Giardino, Pellini, Auberge, Aruzzo
Deep Pan Pizza	49	
La Tasca	42	
Conran	30	
Wagamama	26	
Loch Fyne	25	

Note: Pub-restaurants and take-away outlets not included

* greater interest in food due to cookery programmes and high-profile chefs

* increased travel has led to heightened interest in different foods

* greater choice of different kinds of restaurants.

Consider this...

What kinds of restaurants are available in your locality? Which ones do you think are fine dining rather than cafes or fast-food outlets?

Secondary providers of hospitality

Sometimes businesses offer hospitality to give added value to the range of products and services they provide but it is not the main focus of their business. The primary purpose of their business may be to transport passengers or to entertain. The revenue gained from customers spent on hospitality in these cases is known as secondary spend. We are going to look at some examples of organisations who offer hospitality as a secondary focus.

Airlines

It is evident that the primary business of an airline is to transport passengers from one place to another. Traditionally, airlines offer hospitality to their customers to enhance the customer experience on board the aircraft. The hospitality would take the form of meals and drinks. Today full-service airlines still offer this hospitality and it is included in the price of the ticket. Passengers on a cross-Atlantic flight from an airline such as Virgin or British Airways might expect a choice of meal, an afternoon tea or breakfast depending on time of day and free drinks including alcohol. The catering is provided by a contract food supplier and is specially packaged for airline use. Low-cost airlines such as Ryanair also offer hospitality in the form of snacks and drinks but passengers pay for whatever they choose and this is an important source of revenue for the airline. Thus the purpose of the hospitality for this type of airline is to make money as well as to offer a service.

Conference and exhibition centers

There are several purpose-built conference and exhibition centres in the UK. These include the NEC in Birmingham, Earls Court, Olympia and ExCeL in London. Visitors attending exhibitions will be there for a few hours and will expect to be able to buy food and drink. Hospitality is also essential for exhibitors as they may choose to entertain clients within the exhibition area. Again, the hospitality provision is a source of revenue for the exhibition centre.

Exhibition venues are also used for conferences and catering must be provided for delegates. A catering manager is available to advise conference organisers on menus and catering provision.

MENU

SALMON & VEGETABLE KEBABS
WITH SOY & GINGER

* * *

TANDOORI CHICKEN SPRING ROLLS
WITH CUCUMBER MINT YOGHURT

* * *

A SELECTION OF OPEN SANDWICHES
ON CIABATTA BREAD

* * *

BRIE CHEESE, LEEK & BUTTON
MUSHROOM TARTLETS

* * *

CHICKEN SATAYS BRUSHED
WITH ORIENTAL PLUM SAUCE

* * *

POTATO WEDGES FLAVOURED
WITH GARLIC & OREGANO,

* * *

SOUR CREAM & CHIVE DIP

* * *

BROCCOLI & BRIE PUFFS
WITH LEMON & HERB MAYONNAISE

Example of finger buffet for conference delegates

Menus may range from finger buffets to full dinners.

Rail and ferry companies

The range of hospitality offered by train and ferry companies is immense. It may be as simple as a drinks and snack cart on a train to a sophisticated dining car where the offering forms part of the overall experience, for example the Orient Express. Ferry companies may have their passengers on board for a few hours or a few days and they offer cabin accommodation, cafes and restaurants to provide hospitality for their passengers. As with airlines, the hospitality gives an opportunity to gain extra revenue from the passengers.

Theatres and visitor attractions

Restaurants, bars and cafeterias are usually provided in theatres and visitor attractions. They add appeal to the attraction and encourage visitors to stay longer and spend more money. They are an important source of secondary revenue. Theatres often sell pre-theatre dinners to their guests. They also sell pre- and post-performance drinks and have an interval drinks service.

Theme parks

Hospitality at theme parks helps keep guests in the theme park longer and the management hope that the longer they stay the more money they spend, not just on hospitality but in the shops and on photos etc. Some theme parks have extended their hospitality provision to the opening of hotels. Alton Towers has two hotels which are themed and help attract visitors to the park.

Corporate hospitality

The corporate hospitality market is very lucrative and many hospitality providers use their facilities to try and take advantage of the corporate hospitality market.

> **Key concept**
>
> **Corporate hospitality** is the provision of entertainment, dining and wining to business clients by another business. The purpose is to build good customer relations. Typically, a business will hold an executive box at a sporting or special event and invite special customers to be entertained on occasion.

Many events such as Ascot, Henley Regatta and Wimbledon benefit from corporate hospitality. If you were invited you would be entertained in a marquee and provided with free food and drink. You would also be able to watch the sport in a prime position. All the costs would be borne by the host company.

CASE STUDY

Newmarket Racecourse

The prime business of the racecourse is to provide a venue for racing with facilities for race-goers. You might be surprised to learn that races take place on only about 40 days per year. As there are two racecourses at Newmarket, this means that there are a lot of facilities whose use would not be maximised if they were not used for some other purpose. Newmarket racecourse is therefore offered for all sorts of hospitality use including conferences, weddings, parties and corporate events.

On race days a series of packages is available for corporate clients. A business can invite its customers to watch the races from an executive box where they will be able to eat, drink and place bets without leaving the box. Those with larger parties to entertain can hire their own marquee. An example of an executive package at Newmarket racecourse is given opposite. Note the prices are per person.

Executive Box Packages Rowley Mile – VIP Package
Morning Coffee & Pastries *
Premium Brand Champagne reception
Four course, four choice menu
Half bottle of Premier Wine per person
Full Afternoon Tea *
Full Complimentary Bar
Members' Enclosure admission badge
Car Parking Voucher (1 between 2)
Racecard
£5 Tote Betting Voucher
Executive Souvenir
Hostess
Floral Decorations
£285 per Raceday plus VAT
£450 on Premier Days plus VAT
£235 on Evenings plus VAT
* not included on Evening Meetings
Minimum of 12 persons.
All prices per person.

Source: www.newmarketraces.co.uk

Find an example of another corporate hospitality package. You might find an example at a venue in your own locality. Otherwise search on the Internet. Consider looking at theatres, visitor attractions and sporting venues.

Assessment activity 19.2

Catering facilities may be run as part of the overall business with dedicated employees or may be contracted out to a private catering company. An example is Compass. This is the world's largest food-service company with annual revenues of over £10bn and more than 375,000 employees in over 90 countries around the world. Compass Group is the parent company of a number of different brands. One of these is described below.

'Select Service Partner was developed as our international company providing top quality food and beverages for travel, retail and leisure outlets. It is particularly well known and respected in the airport and railway restaurant sectors, operating concessions in over 50 airports and 180 stations, as well as shopping malls throughout the world.

'Select Service combines owned and franchised brands such as Upper Crust, Caffè Ritazza and Burger King with innovative tailor-made concepts to create the appropriate mix for each location. At every operation, we aim to exceed the expectations of the travelling consumer by providing excellent choice, product quality and customer service and offering value to the consumer while delivering the kind of returns to our clients that they can expect from this unique trading environment.'

Source: Compass Group

1 Choose a local airport or railway station and visit it if you can. Find out what hospitality is provided and describe the providers. Are they owned, contracted concessions or franchises? You might have to ask or note the names and research them on the Internet.

This task may provide evidence for P2.

2 Choose three different hospitality providers in the same location and explain how their provision meets the needs of different types of customers.

This task may provide evidence for M2.

Hospitality functions

In this section of the unit we will explore all the different functions of hospitality that relate to travel and tourism.

Accommodation

As we saw there are many different kinds of establishments offering accommodation. They all have to offer the same services although on a different scale according to size. These include:

* reception

* reservations/front office

* housekeeping

* maintenance

* portering.

Large hotels usually have reception staff and reservations staff. In smaller guest houses these functions may be performed by the owner or manager.

Receptionists are the first people that the customer sees, therefore they must be totally customer focused. Their responsibilities are:

* welcoming guests on arrival and helping them register

* assisting guests during their stay as required

* operation of the switchboard, handling messages and passing them to guests

* making sure guest accounts are up to date

* selling hotel facilities such as room service

* securing guest valuables in safety boxes

* liaising with housekeeping and portering

* taking reservations as necessary.

You can see that this function is varied and there is a lot of contact with guests so it is very important in achieving customer satisfaction.

Receptionists have to have a lot of knowledge as they may be asked questions about the local area and directions as well as about the hotel. They have to be skilled at using the telephone and communicating with customers. Using the telephone is a constant activity for receptionists so they should be trained in its proper use and in

A good concierge can be an invaluable source of information

company policy. They may have minimum standards set for answering. They aim to answer the telephone in less than five rings and transfer callers efficiently to the right person.

In large city hotels, receptionists will direct requests for information to the concierge. Concierge is French for caretaker but in English the function is much greater. The concierge will know all about restaurants, theatres and places to go in a city and will be able to make reservations on behalf of a customer. A good concierge is well paid and can expect to earn a lot of tips.

Having a good concierge makes a hotel. They will arrange anything at all to improve your stay, including getting you a table at a top restaurant or booking tickets for a show. They may have contacts in top restaurants so it is worth guests asking for dinner reservations even if they think a restaurant is booked out. They will give customers maps with directions to bars and places of interest. They will arrange flowers and fruit in guest rooms.

Reservations

Reservations staff may take reservations by telephone, e-mail or by post. In addition, reservations may come through agencies or Internet hotel-reservation sites. People who arrive and wish to book a room immediately will be dealt with by reception. The responsibilities of reservations staff are:

* selling hotel rooms and maximising room occupancy

* making additional sales through upgrades or meal options

* updating and recording bookings

* answering correspondence

* liaising with other departments as necessary

* providing daily reports about occupancy levels

* overbooking rooms within guidelines.

Overbooking is common as sometimes guests book and don't arrive. If too many customers arrive they will be offered an alternative hotel.

Rooms need to be booked to make money. The normal room rates are known as rack rates and reservations staff may negotiate these rates in order to avoid empty rooms. When a guest is unwilling to book and seems put off by the rate, the receptionist should offer a special rate discounting by about £10. If the guest still doesn't book the reservationist may discount a little more.

Computer reservations systems

Guest houses and bed and breakfasts do not need a computer reservation system. Where there are only a few rooms a reservations book is suitable. Large hotels all have computerised systems. An example is Fidelio.

This system has two sections, profiles and reservations. Profiles are stores of information about guests, including name, address, telephone number etc. This information remains the same so can be found each time a guest makes a reservation. It also stores information on previous stays making up a guest history.

The reservation section has details of particular bookings, that is, dates, number of people, special requirements and payment method. The reservationist is able to see from the screen what rooms are available and what rates apply. When the guest has agreed the room and the price all the details are entered and the booking confirmed with a credit card number. Here is an example of the Fidelio reservations screen.

```
I ♥ Fidelio 6.11(3) CB              Bedford Moat House              29.02.00
                             ─── RESERVATION ───
  Name       Jones, David Mr    Group                   Last Rate          0
  Company                       VAP      0               Last Room
  Agent                         Country  GB  Lang.    E  Last Visit    .   .
  Source                        City     Doncaster, South  Pref.Room

  Arrival      23.11.00  Thursday     Conf./Share 46/
  Nights          1                   Created on  02.10.00    By CE
  Departure    24.11.00  Friday       CRS No.                  £   0.00
  Adult/Child     1    0              PO No:                Comps/House
  Number of Rooms 1                   Package
  Room Type    SSB                    Payment                          /
  Room No               0.00 Diff.    Release      :
  Rate Code    RACK          Reason   Deposit Reg.    0.00  Due on    .   .
  Rate            85.00               Deposit Paid    0.00  Date      .   .
  Resv. Type   1 Release              Specials
  Time  E.T.A.      :                 Extra Beds 0  Cots 0  Origin
  Block                               Booker
  Market       RAK   Rack Rat         Tel.No:
  Source of Bus.                      Telefax
  Confirmation              Notices
```

Source: Micros.com

The computer system is used for all hotel functions not only reservations. When messages arrive for guests they are entered into the system and can be sent directly to the TV screen in the guest's room. Of course, the message can also be printed and given to the guest.

The system includes a floor plan of the hotel so that at a glance it can be seen which rooms are occupied, which need housekeeping and so on. Even requests for maintenance can be made through the system. The receptionist or housekeeper enters in the details, for example, broken light, against the room number.

Maintenance checks the computer and collects requests.

As the reservation system is so sophisticated not much paperwork is required but the customer will be asked to complete a registration card on arrival. An example is given below from Moat House Hotels.

Theory into practice

Study the registration card and give examples of facilities mentioned on the card which enhance customer service.

Registration Card

Title   Initials   Surname

Name:

Home Address:

Postcode:

Telephone:

email:

Car Reg No:

What time would you like dinner? _____

What time would you like your early morning call?
_____

Which newspaper would you like in the morning?
_____

Arrival Date:

Departure Date:

No. of Nights: Room No:

No. of Guests: Room Rate:

I authorise this hotel to debit the credit/debit card presented on arrival for all charges incurred during my stay. Accommodation may be charged at the time of check-in and any extras not settled on departure may also be charged to this card.

Guest Signature:

Company Name:

How will the account be settled?

Cash   ☐

Cheque (with bankers card)   ☐

Credit Card   ☐

	All meals	DB&B	B&B	Room only
Account to company	☐	☐	☐	☐

Non E.U. Visitors

Nationality:

Passport No:

Issued at:

Next Destination:

Data Protection

Any data obtained from you may be used by us for our own administrative purposes and for the purpose of providing you with information relating to a range of services and products promoted by us or other members of the Queens Moat Houses Group of Companies ("the Group"). The data may be disclosed to other members of the Group for marketing purposes.

From time to time Moat House Hotels may wish to keep you up to date with products, services and developments by post or email. If you would like to receive this information please tick the relevant box/es:

By post: ☐   By email: ☐

Housekeeping

A large hotel will have a number of housekeepers, usually with responsibility for a floor. They will have cleaners or chambermaids working with them and part of their role is to allocate cleaning jobs to their team. Other responsibilities include:

* making sure high standards of cleanliness are adhered to

* organising and changing guest laundry

* issuing linen

* maintaining stores of cleaning products and bathroom products

* maintaining security procedures

* reporting of maintenance requirements.

Consider this...

What kind of skills does a hotel housekeeper require?

Maintenance

Very large hotels may employ their own electricians, plumbers etc. Most establishments employ general maintenance staff who can do most jobs and then experts are called in as needed. Guest houses and bed and breakfast would not employ maintenance staff but would have tradespeople to call on as needed.

Maintenance staff do not have to be very skilled as most of their tasks are minor but would impact on the level of customer service if left unattended.

Portering

Only large hotels have porters and bellboys. Their role is to help guests with luggage and to get taxis for guests. They will also show guests to their rooms. The pay is low and they expect to receive tips.

Food and beverage

Kitchen

In a hotel, the size of the kitchen and restaurant will depend on the size of the hotel and number of guests. Some accommodation providers do not provide food and beverages at all.

Restaurants employ chefs at different levels according to their skills and qualifications. They will also employ kitchen assistants. The responsibility of the chef is to plan menus, prepare budgets and run the kitchen efficiently, co-ordinating all the activities of the kitchen staff. In addition, the chef must order food from suppliers according to forecast levels of business and accommodating any special functions, for example weddings or parties. Stock must be controlled so that wastage is minimised.

The chef must ensure that all staff in the kitchen are aware of and adhere to relevant legislation. In the kitchen this includes the Food Safety Act and the Control of Substances Hazardous to Health (COSHH).

Bellboys are found only in large hotels

The Control of Substances Hazardous to Health Regulations 2002 requires employers to control exposures to hazardous substances to protect both employees and others who may be exposed from work activities. Examples of substances include cleaning agents.

Waiters

Waiting staff may be employed by hotels or restaurants or may be brought in from agencies as required for special functions. They are important to customer service as they have a customer-facing role. They have to serve guests, set and clear tables and help with cleaning the restaurant area. A good waiter will know the menu and be able to offer advice on food and wine. They need to adhere to health and safety and food hygiene regulations and they need to know about fire procedures as they would have to exit customers in the case of an emergency.

Banqueting

Hotels and restaurants cater for special occasions, such as weddings, parties or business functions. They provide a great deal of revenue and are important to the business. Gemma describes a typical wedding and the duties of the banqueting staff on the day. She reminds us that the bride has spent a year planning this day and it has to go well. All the staff understand how important the occasion is even if they have wedding functions every week.

Special functions are an important part of a hotel's business

The first thing we do in the morning is put the red carpet at the front of the hotel ready for the bride and groom's arrival. In the function room we lay out the tables according to the plan that the couple has agreed with our banqueting manager. We have menus and place cards to put on the tables. Sometimes we have little novelties or keepsakes provided by the bride to put on the tables.

When the guests arrive we serve welcome drinks in the function bar and they have photos taken outside in the gardens. Then it's time for the line up. This is where the happy couple welcome their guests in a line.

The meal is served when they are all at tables and we use silver service serving the top table first. We bring in agency staff when we are really busy but otherwise we use just about everyone in the hotel from cleaners to receptionists. They are all trained in silver service.

After the meal, we present the cake and the bride and groom cut it. Whilst they have speeches we take it away and cut it properly.

After the meal there may be an evening party. We clear the room and everyone goes away to their rooms or the bar for a while. We prepare the room for a disco and buffet. More guests will arrive in the evening. The bar closes about 11.30pm and we hope that we've made their wedding day special.

Bars

Bars may be found in hotels, restaurants or nightclubs or exist in their own right. Bars need cellar attendants to run the cellar and bar staff to serve the customers.

A cellar attendant is expected to be responsible for:

* ordering supplies
* taking deliveries and storing them according to health and safety regulations
* cleaning of cellar and stock
* practising stock rotation and control
* issuing stock to other departments if relevant
* logging of all goods received and issued.

A bar attendant is responsible for:

* selling drinks
* taking payments
* cleaning the bar area
* displaying bar stocks appropriately
* knowing licensing laws and acting in accordance with them
* observing health and safety and food hygiene regulations.

Room service

Hotels provide room service and sometimes provide it for 24 hours a day. Guests order from a room service menu in their rooms. Breakfast is often promoted as a room-service option. It means that all the guests do not descend on the dining room at the same time in the morning and portions can be carefully controlled. Usually room service incurs an extra charge for the guest.

Costing and budgeting

Food and beverage managers or chefs are responsible for costing menus and keeping to a strict budget. This is particularly difficult for new managers as it entails planning how many meals will be sold and what quantities of ingredients have to be ordered. In a good restaurant everything will be ordered fresh so there is more potential for waste. With experience, the process is easier. In a hotel, the food and beverage manager will submit revenue proposals and forecasts to general management. These will be reviewed by head office alongside the forecasts from other departments. Once agreed, each department tries to achieve the forecast and actual figures are then compared with the forecast to review performance.

Software is available to help chefs cost menus but they rely on food prices given by a specific supplier. The software is then regularly updated with new prices. The chef determines the retail price for a meal and profit margin required. The chef enters specific requirements, for example, hot starter, number of covers and the computer will give a number of options which meet the criteria entered.

This is an extract from a hotel's profit and loss account. It shows only the revenue section. Remember that costs have to be deducted from these figures to arrive at the trading profit figures. Costs for food and beverage would include, cost of the ingredients, laundry, staff, repairs and maintenance, administration and an allocation for sales and marketing.

PROFIT AND LOSS ACCOUNT

	Actual revenue	Budget	Variation to budget	% variation	Last year	Variation to last year	% variation to last year
Rooms	1,261,115	1,233,438	27,677	2.2	1,117,510	143,605	12.9
Food and beverage	620,499	573,947	46,552	8.1	548,167	72,332	13.2
Telephone	32,605	21,240	11,365	53.5	18,934	13,671	72.2
Leisure	133,467	139,517	(6050)	(4.3)	128,197	5,270	4.1
Other	45,652	49,425	(3773)	(7.6)	39,453	6,199	15.7
Total revenue	2,093,338	2,017,567	75,771	3.8	1,852,261	241,077	13

1. Did the hotel have a good year in terms of revenue? Give reasons for your answer based on the figures given.
2. The leisure department was up on last year but did not reach its budgeted figure. What do you think about the budgeted figure?
3. How might the leisure department cut costs if necessary?
4. Why was so much money made on the telephone?
5. What costs will have to be taken into account for the rooms figures?

Administration

Administrative departments are important to the success of a business. In a small business the owner or manager will carry out these functions themselves but a large hotel or holiday centre has dedicated departments, sometimes at head office.

Human resources

This department is responsible for recruitment, including selection and interviewing, as well as being responsible for the welfare of staff. HR personnel write job descriptions and draw up contracts of employment. They also have to deal with grievances from staff and disciplinary matters.

In some companies HR staff are also responsible for training. They should be aware of the latest legislation as it might mean setting up special training to ensure staff comply with the legislation or it might affect their recruitment. Examples include the Disability Discrimination Act which makes it unlawful for providers of goods, facilities or services to discriminate against members of the public on the grounds of disability. This also relates to employment.

As there are many job vacancies in the hospitality sector, many businesses in the UK are turning to workers from overseas to fill them. Human resources staff must be aware of the correct procedures to follow when employing immigrants.

Marketing and sales

You have studied marketing on your BTEC course and so you are aware of the complexity of marketing planning. The marketing function will be undertaken by head office in the case of a group but local marketing might be undertaken by local management with a set budget. Smaller establishments such as independent restaurants or guest houses undertake their own marketing and it is likely to consist of fairly simple activities such as promotion through the local tourist office or placing local advertising. Many establishments choose to have their own website and they may update and host this themselves or employ web managers, depending on their expertise.

Accounts

The accounts department in a hotel employs a large team ensuring that all accounts are accurate and up to date and also suitable for auditing. They look after revenue from sales and pay suppliers for purchases. Here are some examples of the functions the department carries out.

Credit control

The credit control section has overall responsibility for controlling all income from sales. This includes:

* setting up customer business accounts and ensuring credit worthiness (this doesn't apply to individuals who settle their bill on each visit)

* preparing bills and sending them out promptly

* preparing weekly and monthly reconciliation reports – these will show up outstanding bills

* dealing with guest queries and any under- or over-payments reconciled

* chasing outstanding debts.

Credit control is concerned with sales whilst purchase ledger assistants deal with hotel suppliers and purchases. These duties include:

* receiving delivery notes and reconciling with purchase orders

* marking invoices ready for payment and requesting payment

* liaising with suppliers as necessary

* preparing reports as requested by the financial controller.

All these staff will report to a financial controller who oversees their work and makes sure that all information from other departments is correctly processed. This staff member will carry out banking and control petty cash. There may also be a payroll clerk who sees that all staff in the hotel have their hours logged and are paid. Sometimes this is a head office function.

Customer expectations

Types of customer

Different types of hospitality are suited to different kinds of customers. Examples of customers are:

* families

* single people

* corporate

* special needs

* groups.

It is not enough to consider only the customer type when determining the type and level of service required. You must also think about the reason for that particular visit. For example, a single person on a walking holiday may look for comfortable bed and breakfast accommodation in an establishment that is big enough for them to meet other walkers. The same person on a city business visit may be looking for a top-class hotel, with many facilities in a central, safe location.

Try this simple activity as an introduction to customer types and their needs. Match up the customers on the table below to the most suitable form of hospitality and give the reason you think it is suitable.

CUSTOMER	TYPE OF HOSPITALITY	REASON FOR CHOICE
Jemima is a stockbroker – she is treating her boyfriend to a birthday dinner	A hotel belonging to a large chain situated at the edge of a city by a major road junction	
Joe is taking his twin 11-year-old boys away for a weekend for a summer treat	The Oxo restaurant, a smart expensive restaurant in London	
A property company wishing to put on a weekend exhibition about Spanish second homes	A city centre youth hostel	
A group of 200 doctors attending a conference about the latest research into airline passenger health	A university campus in the Easter period	
A group of students visiting Manchester for educational reasons	McDonald's	
A group of four young mothers who are taking a week away from their families for a rest and pampering	Splash Landings Hotel at Alton Towers	
Panday is six years old – her parents are taking her and six young friends out for tea	A spa resort in Majorca	

Establishments do not usually cater for just one type of customer. Large hotels in particular have to try to cater for different types of customer within one establishment. We will use the example of a Moat House Hotel to explain how they do this.

There are about 30 Moat Houses in the UK either in city centres or near motorway junctions. A typical Moat House hotel is either three or four star and caters for both leisure and corporate customers.

The Cambridgeshire Moat House has 134 bedrooms and 10 conference and meeting rooms with a maximum conference capacity of 200 people. The hotel has an 18-hole golf course, two bars and a restaurant. This Moat House prides itself on providing excellent service and has ongoing training for staff in customer service.

It is important for a hotel to fill its rooms all year round and not just in a particular season. Busy periods for the Cambridgeshire Moat House are tourist seasons like Easter and summer and student graduation periods when parents and guests attending graduation at Cambridge University need a hotel. Conferences occur all the year round but not often in the summer. This hotel has a maximum capacity for a conference of 200 delegates, limited by the size of the conference rooms.

To operate the hotel to full capacity, different groups of customers are identified and targeted by marketing activity.

Golfers

Golfers may be attracted by a 'Golf Break'. A two-night offer includes dinner, bed and breakfast and three rounds of golf. The hotel is able to offer this because it has its own golf course. The golf course is also open to local people who may hold annual membership and use the bars and facilities.

Corporate

Corporate customers may be individuals using the hotel as a base to attend meetings elsewhere. They expect to be offered secretarial services, Internet access, food at convenient times for their business needs as well as a comfortable room. They also expect a good restaurant and bar where clients can be entertained. Many hotels now recognise that business customers often require leisure facilities and provide a gym or fitness centre and sometimes a pool. The Moat House has these and they are free for all residents to use.

Typical room facilities for all customers include:

* tea and coffee making
* trouser press
* hairdryer
* television and movies
* toiletries.

Most hotels also offer superior rooms At the Moat House some rooms are more luxurious and offer better toiletries, bathrobes, juices and free newspaper. Of course, all this costs more.

Corporate customers may be attending a conference. This will be organised by the hotel's conference and banqueting manager. The conference business is very lucrative and the conference manager has targets to meet and must encourage conference business.

The hotel produces sales literature aimed at the conference market and offers delegate packages per day or per number of days. The day-delegate package is shown here:

Weddings

Weddings can take place almost anywhere these days and hotels try to use their facilities for wedding receptions. This dovetails very well with conferences as most weddings are at weekends and most conferences are during the week. Wedding customers can have the services of a wedding co-ordinator. Some weddings are booked and planned a year in advance and the wedding coordinator will offer a range of packages including menus and drinks, evening buffet, master of ceremonies and even advice on wedding etiquette.

Targeting age groups

A hotel which has a leisure club usually offers membership to local residents to achieve as much revenue as possible from the facility. Moat House Hotels operate a special membership for over 50s. The club is free to join and members get discounts off leisure club membership and also off meals and rooms in the hotel.

Special needs customers

Hotels are aware of their obligations under the Disability Discrimination Act and most extend a welcome to guests with special requirements. A series of symbols is used to illustrate the extent of wheelchair access and some hotels provide rooms adapted for disabled users.

A charity called Holiday Care is concerned with accessible tourism enquiries. It works with tourism boards and is accredited to inspect accommodation in the UK against 'Tourism for All' National Accessible Scheme Standards. These standards were revised in 2002.

Families

Hotels, including the Moat House, offer special deals for families. Examples are free accommodation for children sharing a parents' room and meal offers for children. A swimming pool and children's play room is appealing to families.

Moat House Day-delegate package

To help you choose the right venue at the right price, we have arranged our hotels in regional bands. We also offer a number of delegate packages to suit your exact needs and budget. The Day-delegate package includes the hire of the main meeting room, flipchart, marker pens, ice cool water coolers, a Meeting Centre Toolkit (containing a range of stationery items), morning and afternoon tea/coffee, biscuits and a conference lunch.

Source: Moat House Hotels conference and meeting facilities brochure.

You have seen some examples of what a hotel chain offers its customers. You should acknowledge that more discerning customers may opt for more upmarket hotels and the budget conscious will look for a budget hotel or guest house.

Customer needs and expectations

Hotel groups are very aware that one brand does not suit all and they offer branded hotels which may offer similar facilities but at different levels of luxury and service. One such hotel group is the Accor group and it serves as a good example of branding in the hotel business.

The group operates worldwide with nearly 4,000 hotels and claims to cover all market segments from economy to upscale. It also has restaurants and casinos. Accor offers several brands but the extent of the range is exemplified by the brands of Sofitel, Novotel and Ibis. Sofitel is extremely luxurious, Novotel is a mid-range contemporary hotel and Ibis is a budget hotel.

The brands are described by Accor on its website as follows:

Sofitel

Sofitel is the premium hotel brand of Accor. To establish a top-tier position in the highly competitive deluxe hotel industry, Accor works with leading specialists, from world-renowned architects and top interior designers, to award-winning chefs. In prime business and leisure destinations the world over, discerning international travellers with a penchant for art, culture and luxury know that Sofitel quality will always meet their expectations.

Novotel

Every day, in city centres or just at the outskirts, near major motorways, airports or at the seaside, Novotel hotels throughout the world welcome guests. Novotel is a relaxing spot for people travelling on business as well as for families on weekends or holidays.

Ibis

Ibis hotels offer excellent service and quality at the best possible prices: comfortable rooms with bathrooms, a 24-hour reception desk, a cosy bar area, snack service at any time day or night and usually a varied choice of restaurants. Ibis hotels stand out in their category by their strong concentration in city centres and easy access.

Source: Accor website

It is difficult to understand the difference in service and quality between different classes of hotel without experiencing it. A budget hotel such as an Ibis still aims to offer good customer service and a wide range of services but is by no means as luxurious as a Sofitel or similar class of hotel. Read Tamara's accounts of staying in a Sofitel and an Ibis to see the difference.

Staying in a Sofitel

'When I arrived at the revolving entrance door of the hotel I was met by a uniformed porter who took my bags for me. The lobby was magnificent and spacious with chandeliers, plush sofas and coffee tables. There were three receptionists in smart navy suits, one of whom greeted me and found my reservation. I was directed to my room and the porter arrived with my bags within five minutes. The room was gorgeous. There was a huge bed with soft quilt and pillows. In one corner was an easy chair. The furniture was dark wood and there were two large and heavy wardrobes. In one hung a fluffy white bathrobe and there were little white slippers by the bed. A television was revealed on opening a cabinet. The two windows had heavy, draped curtains which were fastened back to the wall. The bathroom was equally luxurious – a huge bath and a separate shower. I spent ages looking at the little bottles of toiletries, all of an expensive brand. There was even a sewing kit and shoe shiner. A hairdryer was provided. There were piles of huge white towels. I noticed that there was stationery in the drawers with headed paper and menus available for room service or breakfast in my room.

'Back in the lobby I looked around to find the bar. There was a smart cocktail bar as well as a lounge area for guests to sit and read. Newspapers were provided. There was also a lovely French restaurant on the ground floor – it was very expensive but looked good. I wanted to go out that night and went to reception to get some advice. I was directed to the concierge who answered my questions and made a reservation for me.'

Staying in an Ibis

'When I arrived, I walked up to reception. This was situated on the ground floor with a bar and cafe area next to it. This was also the area where breakfast was served. The area was functional and bright but not luxurious. The receptionist was dressed in a dark skirt and a white shirt. She found my reservation and gave me my room key. I made my way to my room with my bags. My room was clean and pleasant. There was a bed, a built-in hanging and shelf area and bedside tables. There was a television and a telephone. I decided to write a note to a friend but couldn't find any paper.

'The bathroom was a 'pod'. I mean it was pre-fabricated and built in one unit with a toilet and shower built in. There was a little bar of soap and shampoo/shower gel in a dispenser on the wall of the shower. There were two clean but smallish towels. The shower was lovely and hot and I washed my hair. There was no hairdryer but I phoned reception and one was brought to my room. I also needed more pillows and these were brought.

'I went downstairs for a drink. The receptionist came to serve me at the bar. I noticed that breakfast was available here for less than £4. Also snacks and light meals were available. When I asked for directions the manager was called and advised me in a very helpful way.'

What we see from Tamara's accounts is that good service can be offered even in a less luxurious environment and that a basic hotel can be sufficient for the customer's needs, depending on the occasion and budget.

Theory into practice

Think about your own experience of staying in a hotel. If you have never stayed in a hotel, interview someone who has. Write notes on the services and quality at the hotel. Are there any improvements that can be made without increasing the prices at the hotel? Write up your findings as a chart with explanatory notes and discuss your work with your tutor.

Ultra-luxurious hotels

You saw earlier that budget hotels are becoming increasingly popular. At the other end of the scale, ultra-luxurious hotels are being built. The Emirates Palace is a 394-room hotel recently built in Abu Dhabi (United Arab Emirates). The hotel has 114 domes covered in mosaic glass and topped with gold. Inside there is gold and silver everywhere and over 1,000 chandeliers made from crystals. There are 2,000 staff to look after you including your own butler. There is even a bath concierge whose job is to draw a bath using your choice of perfumes and petals.

The Emirates Palace hotel in Abu Dhabi

Visit the Accor hotels website at
www.accor.com.

1 Find out what products and services are
offered at a Sofitel and an Ibis and describe
them. Explain how the products and services
offered are influenced by the different
expectations of customers at each of the
brands, that is, Sofitel, Novotel and Ibis. Write
up your findings as an information sheet.

This task may provide evidence for P4 and M2.

2 Draw up profiles of three different customer
types who might use one of the Accor hotel
brands. Analyse how the needs and
expectations of these types of customers help
Accor determine what products and services
to offer in their hotels.

This task may provide evidence for D2.

Use of grading schemes

VisitBritain has created quality standards for a
wide sector of accommodation in England.
Scotland, Wales and Northern Ireland have their
own schemes. Trained assessors determine the
gradings.

Star ratings

Hotels are given a rating from one to five stars,
the more stars, the higher the quality and the
greater the range of facilities and level of service
provided.

Self-catering accommodation is also star-rated
from one to five. The more stars awarded to an
establishment, the higher the level of quality.
Establishments at higher rating levels also have
to meet some additional requirement for
facilities.

Holiday parks and campsites are also assessed
using stars. One star denotes acceptable quality.
Five stars denotes exceptional quality.

Diamond ratings

Guest accommodation is rated from one to five
diamonds. The more diamonds, the higher the
overall quality in areas such as cleanliness, service
and hospitality, bedrooms, bathrooms and food
quality.

Ratings in other countries

The aim of the grading system is to make it easier
for tourists to compare the quality of visitor
accommodation offered around the country.
However, as the Scottish and Welsh tourist boards
use different systems and the English system uses
a diamond system and a star system, it is still
confusing.

When you travel abroad, you will find that
there is no standard system. The star grading
system is more or less accepted in Europe but
cannot wholly be relied on. Tour operators tend to
use their own grading standards so that they can
indicate a level of quality to their customers. An
example is the 'T' system adopted by Thomson.

Restaurant ratings

There are different schemes for rating restaurants.
The Michelin guide is probably the best reputed.
Inspectors from the guide visit restaurants, often
on the recommendation of satisfied customers.
The rated restaurants are mentioned in the
Michelin guides for each country and it is quite an
achievement just to be mentioned. If stars are
awarded then this means the restaurant is of a
high quality.

These are the ratings as described by Michelin:

3 Stars: Exceptional cuisine, worth a special
journey. One always eats here extremely well,
sometimes superbly. Fine wines, faultless
service, elegant surroundings. One will pay
accordingly!

2 Stars: Excellent cooking, worth a detour.
Specialities and wines of first class quality. This
will be reflected in the price.

1 Star: A very good restaurant in this category.
The star indicates a good place to stop on your
journey. But beware of comparing the star given
to an expensive 'de luxe' establishment with that
of a simple restaurant where you can appreciate
fine cooking at a reasonable price.

Source: *The Michelin Guide*

1 Describe the nature of employment in the hospitality sector.

2 Which government department determines policies which concern the hospitality sector?

3 Explain why hospitality is an important part of travel and tourism.

4 Which sector of hospitality employs most people?

5 What are the benefits of good training in hospitality?

6 Discuss three issues currently impacting on hospitality businesses.

7 Define a hotel.

8 What is a budget hotel?

9 What are the duties of a concierge?

10 Outline the Food Safety Act.

11 Describe the functions of the front desk in a hotel.

12 What is the function of the accounts department in a hotel?

13 Describe three different target groups for hotels.

14 How does budgeting and costing take place in a restaurant?

15 What extra luxuries can make a hotel room special?

UNIT 19 ASSESSMENT ASSIGNMENT

When you left college with a BTEC National qualification you found a job at a hotel in London belonging to a major chain. You were accepted onto their management trainee programme and have so far worked in two of their hotels. You are currently working in the marketing department where it has been decided to produce a monthly newsletter to be distributed to hotel staff throughout the group. The aim is to improve communication between management and staff and use the newsletter to inform staff of company policy and educate them about industry issues. The newsletter has to be of interest to staff at all levels from cleaning and waiting staff to managers.

The first edition will introduce some issues relating to the hospitality business.

You are to produce three articles for the first edition of the newsletter. You should consider the layout of the articles and how they might be illustrated.

1 The first article will describe the range of hospitality providers in travel and tourism. Ensure you include both primary and secondary providers. You should also describe the environment in which they operate including any current trends and issues.

   This task provides evidence for P1 and P2.

   Choose two issues which currently affect hospitality providers, and your hotel group in particular, and discuss them in greater detail. You could write a column on each.

   This task provides evidence for M1.

   Analyse the impact of current issues and trends in the hospitality environment and recommend courses of action for your hotel group.

   This task provides evidence for D1.

2 The second article concerns the functions of hospitality. Firstly, describe the different functions of hospitality in different areas of travel and tourism. You might consider the functions of hospitality in a hotel, in a restaurant and in a theme park.

   This task provides evidence for P3.

Make a comparative chart of the information you found above and compare and contrast the hospitality functions. You should consider different parts of the travel and tourism industry.

This task provides evidence for M3.

3   The third article is about customer expectations and how they affect the products and services offered. You should choose three different hospitality providers and explain how they develop their products and services to meet the needs of their different customer types. You should consider different parts of the travel and tourism industry.

You will achieve a pass in this task if you give a basic explanation of how customer expectations influence hospitality provision.

This task provides evidence for P4.

You will achieve a merit if your article details how the three providers have adapted their products and services for different customer types.

This task provides evidence for M3.

You will achieve a distinction for this task if your article shows that you have analysed how specific customer needs and expectations have led to changes in the products and services offered by the industry.

This task provides evidence for D2.

UNIT

Handling air passengers

Introduction

Air transport is a fast-growing sector of travel and tourism. The advent of low-cost airlines and competitive fares has led to an increase in the numbers of passengers flying and to further development and improvements in our airports, particularly in the regions.

In this unit you will learn about the options available to passengers when arranging a journey, including a flight, and determine the essential and desirable information a customer needs when arranging their air travel. We will also look at the factors that influence different types of customers when they are booking.

You will learn about the functions of the many different organisations which operate at airports and the services they provide. You will look at the complete process that passengers go through from arriving at the departure airport to leaving the arrival airport.

We will examine the in-flight facilities and services offered by airlines for passengers, including the facilities provided for those passengers with special needs. Health, safety and security procedures are very important to air travel and you will look at the procedures used at airports and on airlines to mitigate health, safety and security risks.

During your studies for this unit you should visit at least one airport so that you have first-hand experience of what is provided for passengers.

How you will be assessed

This unit is internally assessed by your tutor. A variety of exercises and activities is included in this chapter to help you develop your knowledge and understanding of handling air passengers and prepare for the assessment. You will also have the opportunity to work on some case studies.

After completing this unit you should be able to achieve the following outcomes:

→ explore the options available to customers when arranging a journey and making a booking

→ examine airport facilities and identify airport and airline personnel

→ examine the procedures for processing passengers for a flight

→ investigate the in-flight customer service and on-board facilities offered by airlines.

Arranging a journey and making a booking

Where to book your journey

There are many options available to passengers wishing to book a flight. Most of them provide many different services not just flight booking. We will examine all the outlets which sell flight tickets.

Airline direct

If a passenger knows which airline they want to use for a journey then it is straightforward to contact the airline online or by telephone to make the booking. All airlines offer an online-booking system although the ease of use and speed on the websites is variable. Low-cost airlines such as Ryanair and easyJet were the pioneers of online

A ticket desk at an airport

booking. They wanted to encourage online booking as selling in this way reduces their distribution costs. A discount is offered as an incentive to customers to book online. When a passenger books online there is no commission payable to an agent so this is another saving for the airline. However, Ryanair and easyJet do not pay commission to agents anyway.

Airlines have ticket desks at airports so it is possible for passengers to turn up and pay for a flight. Such tickets are sold at the highest price and there may not be seats available for last minute customers.

Travel consolidators or bucket shops

These distributors sell on behalf of a large range of carriers and take commission from the carriers on each sale. For this reason, flights from airlines that do not pay commission will not be available through consolidators. Well known examples in the UK include Trailfinders, Expedia and Bridge the World. You will find their advertisements and telephone numbers in travel sections of newspapers although most also sell online. Specialist websites include telme.com, traveljungle.com and travelsupermarket.com. The drawback of many of these sites is that it is difficult to book flights which originate outside the UK and low-cost airlines are not usually represented.

Tour operators

Key reminder

A **tour operator** is an organisation which puts together and sells a package holiday including transport, transfer and accommodation.

As you know, a flight is often part of a package holiday sold by a tour operator. A customer booking a package will be given flight information along with hotel and transfer details.

Sometimes tour operators do not fill their flights to capacity and are keen to sell spare seats. They do this directly through their websites and call centres or through travel agents. These seats are known as 'flight only' sales and the seats are on charter flights which are owned or leased by the tour operators.

Travel agents

Travel agents sell a range of products including flights. A travel agent may belong to a major travel group like Thomson. Where it does, staff usually give priority to selling their own products thus a Thomson travel agent should try to sell Thomson holidays and flights. For a customer booking a flight, the destination and departure airport carry more influence on the booking than choosing a specific airline. A customer calling into Thomson looking for a flight to Malaga will be offered whatever is available on their chosen departure date and at their chosen departure airport and it would be coincidental if this were a Thomson charter flight.

Some customers go round all the travel agents in town when looking for a flight. Their aim is to compare prices and see where they can get the best deal. This is pointless as each agent has access to the same global distribution data and there is little variation in price between agents unless they cut their commission.

Specialist travel agency knowledge is useful when booking complex flight arrangements, for example, a business trip to Asia, with several stops. A good agent will find the most convenient connections and best prices. Business travel agents have greater expertise in this.

Airline alliances

One World is an example of an airline alliance. Its partners are Aer Lingus, American Airlines, British Airways, Cathay Pacific, Finnair, Iberia, Lann and Quantas.

The network covers over 550 destinations. When customers are members of one of the airlines loyalty or frequent-flyer programmes then they can earn benefits when they travel with any of the partners.

Passengers should find that luggage is checked through to final destination and that transfers from one airline to another are smoother when travelling with partner airlines. Frequent flyers also have access to the airport lounges of all the partners.

Services, information and documentation offered by outlets

Most outlets offer a similar range of products and services with some minor variations. Here we will examine the range of services and information that can be expected and find out who offers what.

Booking terms and conditions

These must be given to the customer as they form part of the contract. As they can be very lengthy, the customer may be given an overview of the booking conditions with a reference to the source of the full conditions. When booking online a passenger receives an eticket or reference number which has with it a resume of the booking conditions. The information with an easyJet eticket runs to many pages. Much of the information concerns the Warsaw and Montreal Conventions which cover air travel. The information is complex and it is unlikely that passengers read it unless they have a problem. An extract from the booking conditions is shown here.

3.1. Ticket Prima Facie Evidence of Contract

The evidence of the contract of carriage is the Ticket. The Ticket, these Conditions of Carriage and our Carrier's Regulations (incuding applicable Tariffs) together constitute the terms and conditions of the contract of carriage between you and us.

These Conditions of Carriage and our Carrier's Regulations are accessible in full on the Website and copies may be obtained from our offices at the addresses stated at the end of these Conditions of Carriage and at check-in.

3.2. Changes to your Ticket

If you wish to change your flight or the Passenger to be carried you may do so in the circumstances provided in Article 6.2 and our Carrier's Regulations. Otherwise, your contract of carriage with us is not transferable. We shall not be liable to any person entitled to be carried by us or for any refund in connection with a proposed flight if, in good faith, we provide carriage to a person purporting to be entitled to carriage or make any refund to the person entitled in accordance with Article 11.

3.3. Validity

A Ticket is only valid for the Passenger named and the flight specified being the person and flight for which the reservation was originally made or as subsequently changed and accepted by us in accordance with Article 3.2 above.

3.4. Name and Address of the Carrier

Our name and address may be abbreviated on any of our documents of carriage or on the Website. The address of our registered offices can be found at the end of these Conditions of Carriage.

Source: easyjet.com

The full booking conditions are usually found on an airline's website. However airline websites contain so much information that it would be surprising if a passenger read it all. Passengers should be able to find what they need to know quickly and the essential pieces of information should be with their ticket. Tour operators publish their booking conditions in their brochures so these are easily accessible to the customer. Travel agents are usually taking bookings on behalf of a principal such as an airline so they pass on the booking conditions to the customer.

Other important information

Some tour operators and travel agents give out lots of information to customers. Examples include leaflets or guide books about the destination, maps, directions, information about car parking and health information.

Airlines may also give out information prior to travel. Virgin Atlantic issues several leaflets. One comes with the ticket and covers issues such as baggage, dangerous goods in baggage, denied boarding compensation and conditions of contract. Another concerns in-flight health.

CASE STUDY

Notice of Cancellation

3. **If your flight is cancelled other than as a result of extraordinary circumstances which could not have been avoided even if all reasonable steps had been taken**

You would be entitled to the above. In addition, you may be entitled to compensation in the sum of €250 if your flight is 1500km or less and €400 if your flight is over 1500km ('Compensation'). Please note that if you are offered re-routing under options 1 or 2 above, this sum will be reduced by 50% where your arrival time does not exceed the scheduled arrival time of your booked flight by 2 hours (flights of less than 1500kms) and 3 hours (flights of more than 1500km).

You will not be entitled to Compensation in the following circumstances:

a) If you are informed of the cancellation at least 2 weeks before the scheduled time of departure; or

b) If you are informed of the cancellation between 2 weeks and 7 days before the scheduled time of departure and are offered re-routing, allowing you to depart no more than 2 hours before the scheduled time of departure and to reach your final destination less than 4 hours after the scheduled time of arrival; or

c) If you are informed of the cancellation less than 7 days before the scheduled time of departure and are offered re-routing, allowing you to depart no more than 1 hour before the scheduled time of departure and to reach your final destination less than 2 hours after the scheduled time of arrival.

Source: www.easyjet.com

1. **Read the extract shown about cancellation. Why might cancellations occur?**

2. **Look up the regulations on denied boarding and find out what you are entitled to if a flight is cancellled.**

CASE STUDY

This is an extract from a booking confirmation from easyJet. Note the information deemed important enough to send to passengers. Other information is available on their website.

EasyJet does not issue tickets, so please make a note of these details. All you need to check-in is your passport (or other approved photographic ID) and booking reference.

Important information

1. No tickets. EasyJet is a ticketless airline, and your booking is now confirmed. You do not need to contact us before flying to re-confirm your travel arrangements.

2. Check-in information. Check-in desks open two hours ahead of the flight's scheduled departure, and close promptly 30 minutes before the flight is scheduled to leave. If you're late, you will forfeit your seat and no refund will be offered.

3. Passports and ID. Approved photographic ID is required on all flights, including domestic services.

4. Pack safely. Take care when you pack your bags! You cannot take any dangerous goods in your luggage, and some other items (e.g. cigarette lighters and matches) can only be carried in certain parts of the aircraft.

5. Baggage allowance. Each paying passenger may take one standard piece of hand luggage, dimensions 55x40x20cm and one piece of standard checked-in hold baggage weighing no more than 20kg. Passengers are also allowed a free allowance of 10kg of sporting equipment as hold luggage, provided it is packed separately, and subject to space availability on the aircraft (and to an additional fee where manual handling is required). Additional charges apply if you exceed this allowance.

6. Free seating. EasyJet does not allocate seats, and you can choose where to sit when you board the aircraft. The aircraft is boarded in priority order, however, so the earlier you check-in, the more choice you will have!

7. Special requirements. Passengers with special requirements (e.g. carrying unusual items or needing assistance at the airport) should check-in no later than 90 minutes before the scheduled departure time. Passengers may also need to contact our call centre in advance to make the necessary arrangements.

1 Find out what is meant by approved photographic ID on domestic flights and on international flights.
2 Find out what the excess luggage charge is.
3 Explain what would happen if a passenger missed the 30 minute check-in deadline.

Passport and visa requirements

Travel agents will give passport and visa information to customers and tour operators will mention what is required in their brochures. Airlines include information on their websites. However, in all cases the onus is on the passenger to ensure they travel with the correct documentation. If they arrive at the airport without it they will not be allowed to travel.

Consider this...

The UK Passport Office website tells you how to apply for a passport. Forms are available from the Post Office. To find out about specific country requirements you have to ask the Embassy or Consulate of that country. Details can be found on websites. It is always a good idea to check because there are sometimes surprising requirements. For example, if you are British and visit the island of Grenada you should make sure your passport is valid for at least 6 months from the date of departure and if you go to Australia you need a visa.

Find out the requirements for:

- an EU resident travelling to Nepal
- an EU resident visiting the UK
- an Australian visiting the UK
- an American visiting Australia.

Health advice

Specific health advice for countries is often mentioned in brochures by tour operators.

In Airtours Far & Away 2004–05 brochure they recommend the following vaccinations when visiting India: vaccinations against hepatitis A, polio, tetanus and typhoid. Malaria tablets and a mosquito repellent are also recommended and to check with your doctor.

Sometimes vaccinations or precautions against malaria are required or recommended. Travel agents are able to advise on these. Airlines do not usually give this kind of information but concern themselves with issues regarding in-flight health. Travellers going to places with a large population of HIV positive residents may be warned about sexual health in travel literature. The UK government issues a leaflet called 'Health Advice for Travelling Abroad', which contains lots of advice.

Travellers should ensure that they have adequate travel insurance to cover medical problems or accidents whilst they are abroad. Within the EU there is a reciprocal agreement that EU residents may be treated as long as they have a form E111. This form is free but must be completed at a Post Office and stamped.

The benefits of the E111 are that travellers are entitled to medical and hospital services of the country's national health system.

Travel insurance

Travel insurance is available from all outlets selling flights including tour operators, travel agents and airlines as it is an extra source of revenue. The prices are very expensive. It is much cheaper to buy travel insurance from an insurance broker. Anyone who travels more than a couple of times a year should buy an annual policy. These represent good value for money.

Travel insurance policies generally cover medical issues, accidents, delayed and missed departures and loss of passport. The amount payable varies according to the policy and fee paid. An extract from Direct Travel Insurance giving descriptions of cover and amounts payable is shown opposite.

It is important for travellers to check exclusions from their travel policies. They do not usually cover acts of war or terrorism. In case of emergency or disaster, like the tsunami of December 2004, tourists travelling on package holidays with tour operators are looked after and repatriated if necessary as the tour operators are bonded, for example by ABTA, as well as having a moral obligation to their customers. However, independent travellers have to fend for themselves in such circumstances until government and aid workers step in. They may have entitlements from insurance but this depends on the cover of the policy.

Another area of contention is the collapse of holiday companies or airlines. Several have collapsed in recent years. Passengers who hold bookings with bonded agents get their money refunded but those who have booked independently with airlines do not unless they are covered by insurance or have paid more than £100 on a credit card. In this case, the credit card company pays the refund.

Find out details of three different travel insurance policies covering a two-week holiday in January in Goa. Compare the prices and what is covered. Check whether the policies cover natural disasters and collapse of companies. Report back to your colleagues on your findings.

You can find this information on the Internet on travel agency, tour operator, airline or insurance company websites.

Summary of Cover – per person – FORM 1

Section	Standard Annual Multi Trip & Single Trip	Premier Annual Multi Trip only	Premier Plus Annual Multi Trip & Single Trip	Description of Cover
Medical Emergency, Repatriation and Associated Expenses *	£10,000,000	£10,000,000	£10,000,000	24-hour emergency assistance, search & mountain rescue, direct payment of hospital bills and repatriation when necessary
Hospital Benefit	£1,000 £10 per day	£1,000 £15 per day	£2,000 £20 per day	Cash benefit for each 24-hour period that you are in hospital as an in-patient
Emergency Dental Treatment *	£200	£200	£200	For emergency dental treatment to relieve sudden pain
Personal Accident Death Benefit	£15,000 £5,000	£30,000 £10,00	£75,000 £25,000	Compensation for loss of limbs, sight, permanent disablement, or death following an accident
Personal Liability *	£2,000,000	£2,000,000	£2,000,000	If you accidentally injure someone or damage their property cover is provided for costs you are legally liable for. (This cover does not apply if you are driving a motor vehicle.)
Legal Advice	£50,000	£50,000	£50,000	Legal assistance to pursue legal action as a result of death, illness or injury during the period of insurance
Cancellation/Curtailment *	£3,000	£4,000	£6,000	If you have to cancel or cut short your holiday due to illness, bereavement or other circumstances detailed in the policy wording
Abandonment *	£3,000	£4,000	£6,000	After a delay of 12 hours if you decide to abandon your holiday before you leave the United Kingdom
Delayed Departure	£100 £10 after 12 hrs	£100 £20 after 12 hrs	£300 £30 after 12 hrs	If the aircraft, sea vessel, train or coach on which you are booked to travel is delayed at its departure point by more than 12 hours
Missed Departure	£600	£600	£1,000	If you do not get to your departure point because public transport does not run to its timetable or the vehicle you are travelling in has an accident or breaks down
Personal Possessions Single Article, Pair or Set/Valuables Limit	£1,500 £200/£200	£1,500 £200/£300	£2,000 £300/£300	If your baggage is damaged, stolen, lost or destroyed

Source: Direct Travel Insurance

Individual needs

Booking online is convenient but does not allow a passenger to ask any individual questions relating to their journey. Frequently asked question (FAQ) sections are included to try to help and customer service numbers may be given. Some low-cost airlines positively discourage passengers from telephoning and do not give a contact number. Travel agents are the best source of information for those passengers who lack confidence in making a booking and have lots of information needs.

Foreign currency facilities

Many booking outlets offer currency exchange facilities to customers when they book. The commission on the exchange provides an extra source of revenue to the booking outlet as well as providing another customer service.

Customer profiles

> **Key reminder**
>
> **Types of travellers** – categories used for statistical purposes are business, leisure and visiting friends and relatives (VFR).

Airlines are keen to attract business customers. Business customers' travel is paid for by their companies and business people depend on reaching destinations at specific times. This means price is less of a factor in choosing a flight. Policy on class of travel differs from company to company often depending on their financial situation. Some companies have a policy of flying economy class whilst others allow their staff to take advantage of the extra comfort of business and first class. Much of the marketing for first and business class is targeted at business travellers.

The benefits of travelling first or business class start even before travel and may include spa treatments at the airport, use of VIP lounges at the airport and a meal before embarking. Virgin Atlantic even offers a limousine service to its first-class passengers. They can be collected from home and driven to the airport.

In addition, airlines operate frequent-flyer programmes to encourage loyalty to their airline. The best known of these is the AirMiles scheme which has been extended beyond British Airways to other partners including retailers like Tesco. Virgin Atlantic has its own loyalty scheme called 'Flying Club'. It is free for passengers to register and the benefits are outlined here:

* passengers earn at least one mile for each mile flown on qualifying flights.

* there are different tiers of membership with increasing benefits.

* Flying Club miles can be spent on a wide range of rewards including flights and upgrades.

* passengers can talk to each other in the 'Flying Club Members Forum'.

Factors influencing customers when booking

Type of airline

Most passengers are unaware of the differences in types of airline. When they travel, however, they will notice differences in service levels between a full service scheduled and a low-cost airline. Business passengers are unlikely to use charters as the flight times and departure days are inflexible and may require a stay of one or two full weeks at the destination.

Travel times

Travelling late at night or in the early hours of the morning is inconvenient. But some people will choose these times as the flights will be cheaper.

Convenience of departure airport

Research has shown that convenience of departure airport is the first priority in booking a flight. No one wants to travel a long way to reach the airport. A passenger looks for an airport near to home that serves their desired destination. The growth in use of regional airports satisfies this consumer need.

Cost and payment arrangements

The cost must represent good value for money to the customer. Premium fares are most likely to be paid by business travellers flying with little notice and with deadlines to meet. This applies to low-cost airlines also. A business traveller booking a flight from London to Edinburgh the day before a meeting, will pay a high fare. Business passengers will also expect corporate account payments rather than have to pay out themselves. People without a credit or debit card cannot make online payments so must choose another method of booking.

Consider this...

Most airlines make a charge for processing a credit card. This could add a few pounds to the price of a flight.

Individual needs

Some people prefer the security of booking with a travel agent or tour operator rather than independently. We have seen the advantages of greater protection if things go wrong on the journey and the provision of more information. Individuals booking in this way are able to ask all the questions they need to and feel that someone is responsible for them and their journey. Remember, too, that not everyone has access to the Internet.

Theory into practice

Match up these passengers with the booking outlets or products.

PASSENGER	OUTLET
Mr Fraser, travels frequently between New York and London on business – works for a large corporation	Low-cost airline website
The Sanjeros – elderly couple without Internet access – want to visit family in Spain	Tour operator website and call centre
Sally – visiting a friend in Holland from Liverpool – does this trip several times a year	Company-based business travel agency
Kate and Gustavo looking for a flight to Australia for a three-week holiday	Consolidator call centre (e.g. Trailfinders)
Juan misses his flight to Barcelona but notes that there is another one in an hour with a different airline from the same airport	Travel agency
Christine and Martin have a timeshare in Malta – they are looking for a flight-only deal	Airline ticket desk

---

Assessment activity 25.1

Maria Hatzebruch wants a flight to Geneva to go skiing at half term for a week. She is travelling alone and has accommodation in a friend's chalet. Describe all the options available to Maria for booking a suitable flight to Geneva from Manchester. Give the advantages and disadvantages of each option. You might present this information as a chart.

This task might provide evidence for P1.

Airport facilities and airport and airline personnel

Airport infrastructure

There are several features which are essential for an airport to function. Here we will examine these and consider some examples of particular airports.

Accessibility

Firstly, the airport must be accessible to passengers. They may choose to arrive at the airport by public transport or by car. Public transport links include road and rail links. Often airport access roads and railways are built especially for airport access. Recently a new exit and road was built from the M11 in Essex to provide improved access to Stansted Airport.

Within the airport complex there must be provision for bus stations, taxi ranks and rail stations. These are an integral part of the development of an airport, particularly as passengers should be encouraged to come to an airport by public transport so that access roads are not congested and land is not overused for car parking.

At London airports public transport links are of even greater importance to avoid congestion. Dedicated trains are provided for passengers, for example the Gatwick Express. Three million passengers a year use this service which runs between Gatwick and Victoria station in central London. Heathrow is accessible by tube as well as the Paddington Rail link.

Car parking

Car parks are located as near to the airport as possible to allow passengers quick access. Those nearest to the terminal are deemed short term and people are deterred from parking there for long periods by the price. Long-stay car parks are further away and passengers are transported in to the airport by shuttle bus. Some airports now have 'mid-term' car parks. This simply means that the car park is midway between the long term and the short term and so is the price.

Check-in areas

Situated landside, the check-in area of the airport is a series of desks with room for passengers to queue and little else. Screens provide information about departures. Nearby, airline ticket desks are situated and any special baggage dropping areas, for example fragile baggage.

Departure lounge

Passengers enter the departure lounge once they have passed through passport control and they are now airside. In a large airport this area is very interesting as it has many shops and eating places. Toilets are provided as well as screens giving departure information.

From the departure lounge passengers go to gates. The gates are the point where the passenger actually boards the aircraft by airbridge or steps. The gates may be located in a satellite which is an extra building like a small terminal, built to accommodate more passengers and planes. In a small airport not many facilities are provided in the departure lounge, which is disappointing if there is a delay.

HM Customs and Excise offices

These offices are situated next to the baggage reclaim area in arrivals as passengers must pass through customs as soon as they collect their bags.

Police and emergency services

Each airport has its own emergency services located on the airport site. A passenger might not know of their presence unless an emergency occurs. Police presence is more obvious currently to emphasise security.

Baggage reclaim

The belts for reclaiming baggage can take up a lot of space in a large airport. Also there is a large area devoted to moving baggage on a conveyor system underneath many large airports. The

CASE STUDY

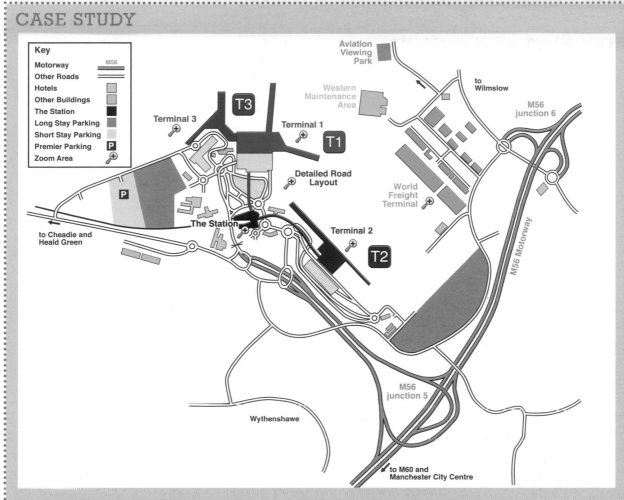

The map above shows an overview of Manchester Airport. Study the map and comment on or explain the following:

- road access
- maintenance area
- location of aviation-viewing park
- location of the station
- location of car parks
- location of freight terminal.

If you want more information to help you go to the Manchester Airport website. Discuss your comments with your group.

passenger doesn't see this although they may sometimes wonder where their bag goes before it reaches the aircraft.

Other areas

Some airports provide a children's play area in the departure lounge and most airports will provide an aviation-viewing area for those plane-spotting enthusiasts. Although all airports are no smoking, there will usually be a specific smoking area where smoking is permitted.

Theory into practice

Put these areas of an airport into the relevant landside and airside areas:

- departure lounge
- check-in area
- arrivals meeting hall
- baggage reclaim
- gate
- Customs and Excise
- car park
- runway
- airbridge
- transport to satellite.

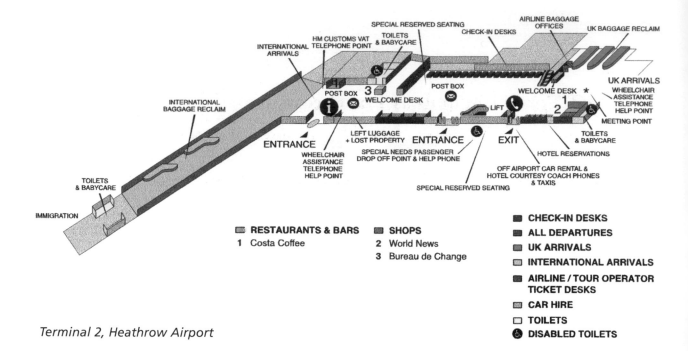

RESTAURANTS & BARS
1 Costa Coffee

SHOPS
2 World News
3 Bureau de Change

- ■ CHECK-IN DESKS
- ■ ALL DEPARTURES
- ■ UK ARRIVALS
- □ INTERNATIONAL ARRIVALS
- ■ AIRLINE / TOUR OPERATOR TICKET DESKS
- ■ CAR HIRE
- □ TOILETS
- ⚫ DISABLED TOILETS

Terminal 2, Heathrow Airport

It is important to recognise that airports vary enormously in size. They will all have the infrastructure described but large airports may have it repeated for different terminals. At Heathrow, for example, there are four large terminals serving 63 million passengers a year.

The map above shows the ground floor of terminal 2 at Heathrow. Note the positions of immigration and customs. An arriving passenger first goes through immigration, claims their bag and then goes through customs.

Facilities at the airport

Airport owners and management determine what facilities should be offered at airports. Some are essential, for example, washrooms must be provided and there needs to be some kind of information system to allow passengers to reach the right aircraft on time. Many are, however, discretionary and also surprising in terms of service offered to passengers.

Here are some travellers' views on various airports.

'I was very disappointed with Newark airport in New York. There was a coffee cart, a newsagent shop with a few souvenirs on sale and a duty free shop which was closed. Apparently, the manager hadn't turned in that day.'

'We had to spend 5 hours at El Prat airport in Barcelona. There were loads of reasonably priced places to eat and lots of fashion shops including high street brands, not just the expensive designer names. There was a bookshop with lots of magazines and papers in English too. I wanted to buy some tissues and paracetamol as I had a cold but these couldn't be found. Nothing like Boots! Also it would have been good to have Internet access as I was bored with the delay.'

'Tobago airport was amazing – we had to queue 3 times before we got to departures: at check-in, to pay departure tax and ages for security (only one x-ray machine). In the departure lounge there was a little bar and a few basic shops. There were toilets and far too few seats for two large plane loads of passengers waiting.'

'I had a delay at Carcassonne airport in France. There is one duty free shop in departures. Landside, there is a fairly good restaurant and some toilets and tourist information. Luckily it was a hot sunny day so I just sat outside on the grass and enjoyed the sun.'

What we can learn from these experiences is that it is the larger, more sophisticated airports which offer most facilities. Those airports in developing areas offer less. There are good reasons for this – experienced airport owners like the British Airports Authority (BAA) realise that offering facilities to passengers alongside airline customers gives an excellent source of revenue. BAA makes a great deal of money as a landlord offering space to rent to retailers and other companies in its airports. Here we look at some of the organisations who operate in the airport environment and why.

Car hire

It makes sense for car-hire companies to be located at airports. Passengers used to have to be shuttled by bus to the car-hire depots from the airport and this was time consuming. Now you expect to collect your car immediately you disembark. This provides better service for the customer, the car-hire company gets more business and the airport authority can charge the car-hire company for office space and for the large amounts of car park it requires.

Car parks

We have already noted the types of car park. The car parks are not usually run by the airport but by specialist companies like NCP or Pink Elephant. They are able to charge very large sums for passengers to have the privilege of parking at the airport. The airport in turn charges the car-parking company for their land. In some small regional airports it is still possible to park for next-to-nothing. The car-park companies also run a courtesy bus service (it's included in the price of parking).

Shopping

BAA is one of the UK's most successful retail landlords. The shopping is so good at some airports, like Gatwick, that people go to shop who are not even travelling. Shops are located both landside and airside. Airside shops are only available to travellers. When there are delays, these shops have a captive audience with little else to do but go shopping. Also, as people are often travelling because they are beginning their holiday, they are in holiday-spending mode which is a recipe for success for retailers and for the airport. Some airports have negotiated a deal with retailers where they take a percentage of takings rather than rent.

Financial services

Passengers expect to find cash point machines and also facilities to change currency. All UK airports have these facilities but they are not always available globally.

Executive/VIP lounge

Such lounges are provided by airlines to give extra services to first- or business-class passengers. Economy-class passengers are allowed to go in for a fee of around £20. Business services will be on offer, for example Internet access, faxing and telephone.

Airport chapel

Some airports provide a chapel – this is a service that does not make much money. It is for the benefit of passengers, airport personnel and crew.

Restaurants and bars

Like the shops, these are a good source of revenue for the airport and provide a useful service for passengers.

Baggage trolleys

Customers expect to find baggage trolleys available for their use. Some airports charge for their use with the necessary insertion of a pound coin or a euro. This is irritating to passengers if they have no change. Less sophisticated airports still rely on porters rather than trolleys. Porters should always be tipped.

Left luggage and lost property

A left-luggage facility can be provided for passengers at a charge. Lost property is common at an airport so there is a point of contact for passengers looking for lost items.

Medical facilities

Like any other public area, passengers can expect to find first-aid facilities at an airport. Some airports also have defibrillators in case of emergency. At Manchester airport there is even an NHS walk-in centre where medical advice is offered to passengers.

Meeting areas

Situated right next to arrivals, this area is the scene of many happy reunions in the airport. In addition, information points are the location for passengers to leave messages or reunite with lost friends and family.

Information for tourists

The extent of provision depends on how busy the airport is. In London, there are manned information desks and hotel booking services. In smaller airports there may be just a display of leaflets.

Facilities for those with special needs

Help points and phones are provided by some airports where people with special needs can easily request assistance. Once the passenger has been assisted to check-in, the airline takes over responsibility for helping the passenger.

The following extract from the BAA Stansted website explains the facilities available at Stansted.

Facilities for the hard of hearing

Induction loops are fitted in many areas of the terminal and satellites and are identified by the sympathetic ear sign.

- All telephones throughout the airport are fitted with induction couplers.
- Public text phones are situated in the internal arrivals area and in the satellite two departure lounge.
- The main airport call centre for general enquiries has a minicom number 01279 663725.
- A number of airport staff are proficient in BSL stage one and the majority have been trained in deaf awareness.
- Many of the staff are able to finger spell.

Facilities for the blind and partially sighted

Guide and hearing dogs are the only dogs allowed in the terminal buildings.

- The airport directional signage is black on yellow to provide optimum contrast to assist all users.

- Reserved seating areas aim to provide low level flight information screens, but if you have difficulty seeing the monitors generally, please advise your airline or handling agent at check-in.
- Your airline will provide you with assistance on request.

Toilet facilities

Unisex accessible toilets are provided on the main concourse and within the departures lounge. Parents travelling with children are welcome to use the unisex accessible toilets.

Reserved seating areas

Reserved seating areas, clearly identified by the use of special needs pictograms, are available for special needs passengers and are located throughout the airport in the general seating areas. These areas aim to provide the following features:

- induction loop
- arms on both sides of seats
- space for wheelchair users
- low-level flight information monitors.

Security checks

All passengers must pass through the security check before they enter the departure lounge. Should you have to be searched at the security check this will be carried out by hand following set procedures. You can ask to be searched in a private area away from the main security search if you prefer.

Getting to your gate

Certain gates are accessed from the departure lounge via the airport transit system which operates every two minutes. All trains are fully wheelchair accessible with help points either end of the car. Routes to other gates are serviced by lifts, escalators and travelators. If your aircraft is not linked to a satellite, your airline or their handling agent will arrange your transfer. Please advise them of your requirements at the time of check in and ask if there is a charge for the service.

Helpful staff make processes such as check-in much smoother for passengers

Airport and airline personnel

Airports are major employers in the regions they serve. There are many departments in an airport and passengers will be unaware of most of them. They will however meet some personnel on their journey through the airport. All these personnel are part of one team at the airport and must work together in order to make sure that the passengers are processed efficiently throughout the airport and their journey.

Ground handling agencies

Many personnel are employed by ground handling agencies who support airlines at the airport, although some airlines prefer to employ all their own staff. An example of a ground handling agency is Servisair/Globeground. They offer many support services to airlines besides passenger services. Their passenger services cover:

* check-in – working at the check-in desk ensuring passengers are checked in according to the airline's procedures

* customer service – deals with any specific problems that occur, looks after VIP departures and arrivals

* baggage handling – very physical work, loading and unloading baggage onto and from aircraft

* security screening – checking passenger baggage on x-ray and randomly searching bags or people

* special services – looking after passengers with special needs on behalf of the airline and guiding them through the airport.

Customs and Excise Officers

Passengers will also meet Customs and Excise Officers. These people work at the airport but are employed by the government and could be working at any port of entry including sea ports. Their role is to make sure that entering passengers comply with Customs regulations and they try to apprehend smugglers. People with forbidden goods may be fined or arrested.

Immigration officers

Passengers meet immigration officers on entry to the UK. There are separate channels for EU residents and for others. Immigration officers are also employed by the government and they are

Customs and Excise Officers check for smuggled goods

checking passports and visas to make sure that only those who have a right to enter the country do so.

Air cabin crew and flight deck crew

The passenger meets the cabin crew as they board the plane. They probably will not meet the flight crew but they might hear them say a few words on the flight. The role of both sets of crew is to look after the safety of the passengers and deliver them to their destination. Cabin crew and flight crew are employed by the airline.

The cabin crew ensure that the journey is safe and comfortable for passengers

Make a visit to an airport and arrange for a member of management or the customer service team to give a tour and talk to your group. You may not be able to go airside but you will gather enough information landside.

Make notes on your tour of the airport so that you are able to write a newspaper article on return. Take photos if permitted.

Your article should:

- describe the infrastructure of the airport, the facilities provided and the role and responsibilities of the staff that customers come into contact with

  This task may provide evidence for P3.

- explain how the different departments in the airport work together to ensure the process of making a journey is safe, swift and convenient

  This task may provide evidence for M1.

- evaluate the development of the airport in terms of how it has improved the passenger experience through the airport.

  This task may provide evidence for D1.

Processing passengers

Check-in procedures

Those of you who are seasoned travellers will find checking in a simple process but for new travellers the process can be quite daunting. Getting to the airport on time can be stressful and then the passenger has to find the right place to check in and often has to queue.

Check-in desks open two or three hours before the flight is due to depart but the passenger must be aware of the latest time they can check in. This varies between airlines and can be as little as 30 minutes for a short-haul flight or as much as two hours for a long-haul flight. The airline informs passengers of the check-in time when they book with other important information (see page 213)

Passengers arriving after the check-in has closed miss the flight even if it is delayed. Airlines are very strict about this and if they were not then passengers would be less careful about arriving in time but this issue does give rise to many passenger complaints.

When the passenger enters the airport they will find screens advising them of the numbers of the check-in desks assigned to their flight. They then make their way to the check-in desk. Some airlines assign a separate desk for each destination, others have one queue for all passengers checking in. The latter system is more stressful for passengers as they may be in a long queue with people ahead of them who are taking later flights. Airline personnel are supposed to comb the queue and pull out those people who need to check in for flights leaving soon.

Documentation requirements

At check-in the passenger must produce their ticket or e-reference number and their passport if travelling on an international flight. Photo ID is also required by most airlines for domestic flights. It is best for passengers travelling on domestic flights to carry their passport if they have one as there can be disagreements about what constitutes a photo ID. For example, Ryanair only accepts a driving licence with a photo or a National Identity Card. An elderly person with a photo bus pass would not be allowed to travel.

Check-in staff are very careful about checking documents as any passengers who arrive in a European country without the proper documentation can be refused entry. The airline is responsible for ensuring passengers board with the correct passport/visa. Authorities fine airlines who make mistakes and the airline also has the problem of removing the passenger from the country.

Key concept

A **National Identity Card** is issued to residents of some countries and is valid for international travel. In the UK we do not have identity cards so a passport is required for international travel.

Security questions

The check-in person must ask the passenger questions about their baggage. These will be:

'Did you pack your bags yourself?'

'Could anyone have interfered with your baggage at any time?'

'Do you have any of these items in your luggage?' – A list of the items will be on the desk.

A passenger giving a positive response to any of these questions will invite further investigation from security.

Suspicious passengers

Check-in staff are expected to watch out for passengers behaving in a suspicious manner, for example, carrying empty bags or bags for someone else. They would refer such passengers to security.

There is a given profile of passengers who might be trying to travel without the correct documents. The check-in staff might be wary if the following profile fits a passenger:

* young single male

* checks in late

* has little baggage

* seems nervous

* language does not match country of origin e.g. has a British passport but does not speak English.

Dangerous and restrictive goods regulations

These regulations are regularly updated and amendments were made in January 2005.

Certain items are not allowed in hand baggage. These are:

* toy or replica guns
* catapults
* household cutlery
* knives
* paper knives
* tradesmen's tools
* darts
* sporting bats
* razor blades
* hypodermic syringes.

There are also items which cannot be taken in any baggage as they are regarded as dangerous. These include:

* compressed gases
* flammable liquids
* weapons
* briefcases with alarm devices
* corrosives
* radioactive materials
* oxidising materials
* poisons and infectious substances.

Consider this...

Why do you think the regulations need to be regularly updated? What would happen if you were carrying a knife in your hand baggage?

Baggage allowances

Allowances are given for hold and cabin baggage. These differ between airlines and between classes of travel, thus a first-class traveller gets a bigger allowance than an economy-class passenger. The lowest allowance for hold baggage is 15kg on a low-cost flight and yet in first class on some Virgin routes, passengers can take three pieces of up to 32kg each. The 32kg limit per piece is set for the health and safety of baggage handlers. Some airlines set restrictions by number of pieces rather than weight.

Restrictions on cabin baggage depend on how much space is available in the aircraft. Generally, passengers are allowed one piece of cabin baggage which must be within certain dimensions. A measuring device is provided at check-in.

Boarding cards

betterairlines

FLIGHT	DESTINATION

Please board the aircraft by

FRONT Entrance	REAR Entrance	**BOARDING CARD** Passengers are permitted only one piece of hand luggage each in the aircraft cabin
		Seq no.
Your seat No.	Your seat No.	

An example of a boarding card

Once the baggage has been checked in and tagged, the check-in assistant hands a boarding card to the passenger. This card this gives details of seat number, if applicable, gate number and time of boarding. This is a vital document as the passenger cannot go through to departures or board the flight without it. It will also be required if the passenger wants to purchase anything in the duty free shops.

Passport control

After check-in the passenger proceeds to departures. There are separate departure points for international and domestic flights. If the flight is international the passenger will show their passport and boarding card before being allowed through. This is straightforward on departure although sometimes passport control are looking out for wanted people who may be trying to leave the country.

Security screening

The next step of the process is security screening. In the UK and in the US the procedures are very thorough and may take some time. The passenger puts all their hand baggage and coat onto a conveyor belt which passes through an x-ray. In the UK, passengers must sometimes remove their shoes. The baggage is examined on screen by a member of security staff. If anything untoward is noted, for example a knife in a bag, the bag is searched. Passengers are also screened. If anything metal is detected an alarm sounds and the passenger is searched. Random searches also take place.

This whole process must be taken very seriously; passengers who have made foolish jokes about bombs etc. have been arrested and imprisoned.

Hold baggage also goes through a screening process. Sophisticated baggage identification systems are used at some airports, e.g. Stansted. Baggage has a bar code attached at check-in which allows it to be identified at any stage of the process to arriving at the aircraft. The baggage is x-rayed as it is goes along the conveyor system and if it needs to be searched, the passenger is alerted and the bag is searched in front of the passenger.

Passengers and their baggage are screened

Aviation Security Act 1982 and Aviation and Maritime Security Act 1990

These acts cover safety and security at airports and on aircraft. It is an offence to endanger safety at airports or on an aircraft. It is also an offence for an unauthorised person to enter the restricted zone of an airport or an aircraft and to remain there after being asked to leave. The Anti-Terrorism, Crime and Security bill of 2001 extends the Aviation Security Act and gives power of removal of unauthorised persons.

If a passenger gives a false statement when asked questions, for example about their baggage, they can be prosecuted under the Aviation and Maritime Security Act.

Passengers with special requirements

Wheelchair passengers

The International Air Transport Association (IATA) provides definitions of wheelchair passengers:

* WCHR – cannot walk long distances, can manage stairs

* WCHS – cannot walk upstairs, cannot manage to board without a jetbridge or wheelchair from gate

* WCHC – immobile: relies on others for mobility.

It is important for check-in staff to know which category a wheelchair passenger falls into, as they will arrange the necessary assistance for them. There is some dispute about who should provide wheelchair assistance – the airport or the airline.

Infants

An infant is a child under two years old. They travel free but have to sit on an adult's lap with a special seat belt.

Young person or unaccompanied minor

An unaccompanied minor is a child travelling alone. Some airlines accept young people (aged 12–15) travelling alone. They may be given assistance depending on airline policy. Again airline policy on taking them differs.

Expectant mothers

They do not require any special treatment on board the aircraft but are only allowed to fly until they are 36 weeks pregnant. Individual airlines' policies may differ however.

Seat allocation

Most airlines will offer passengers with special requirements the ability to pre-book their seat allocation as well as any special dietary requests.

When check-in staff allocate seats, they have to make sure that able bodied people are seated at the emergency exits. They remember who should not sit in the exit row by the pneumonic CODPIE:

Children, obese, disabled, pregnant, infants, elderly.

Non-English-speaking passengers

Non-English-speaking people boarding an aircraft may be at a disadvantage on a British flight as it is not always the case that cabin crew have a second language and even when they do there is no guarantee it is the needed language. The main problem is that they may not understand safety announcements. Safety cards are provided with illustrations so that everyone can understand them.

Purchasing goods

Once through into the international departures area passengers have the opportunity to shop in the duty free shops. Some airports have major shopping areas, like Gatwick or Heathrow. At these airports it would be quite easy to spend a whole day shopping. At Heathrow, there are numerous designer shops as well as gift and chocolate shops. Most airports have at least one shop where passengers can buy duty free goods. These shops stock perfumes, cosmetics, all kinds of alcohol and tobacco.

A two-tier price system is in place for alcohol and tobacco and that is because the duty free allowances only apply to passengers travelling outside the European Union. Passengers travelling within Europe can buy alcohol and tobacco but they will have to pay the duty. Passengers travelling into the UK from outside Europe must be careful that they do not exceed their duty free allowances. Customs issue leaflets with these on and they are displayed in the shops.

The following extract is taken from a HM Customs and Excise leaflet entitled A Customs guide for travellers entering the UK:

For travellers arriving from outside the EU (including the Canary Islands, the Channel Islands and Gibraltar).

- 200 cigarettes or 50 cigars or 250gms of tobacco
- two litres of still table wine
- one litre of spirits or strong liqueurs over 22% volume; or two litres of fortified wine, sparkling wine or other liqueurs
- 60cc/ml of perfume
- 250cc/ml of toilet water
- £145 worth of other goods including gifts and souvenirs.

Boarding the aircraft

Passengers make their way through departures to the gate for boarding. Once passengers reach the gate they will wait in a seated area until their flight is called. The people looking after the passengers and boarding them are ground crew. They may be employed by the airline or they may be employed by a ground handling company like Servisair. In either case they will wear the airline's uniform.

Key concept

Despatcher – The despatcher is a member of ground crew and has particular responsibility for making sure that all passengers are on board and paperwork completed so that the aircraft can depart on time.

The air crew at this time are preparing the aircraft and doing their pre-flight safety checks.

Wheelchair passengers and people with small children are always asked to board first and then the ground crew will call other passengers forward in turn according to seat numbers. On some flights seats are not pre-allocated and this leads to anxiety amongst passengers who try to get on first to make sure they can sit with their friends and families. Passports have been checked at check-in but are checked again at the gate and against the boarding card so that the boarding card cannot be handed to another person after check-in. Staff also check the destination on the card to ensure the passenger is getting on the right flight.

Announcements are made to find late passengers and get them to the gate. If there are still people missing their bags are off loaded and they miss the flight. For security reasons the bags do not go without their owners.

At the gate staff will once again be on the alert for suspicious behaviour and are able to bar passengers from boarding the flight if necessary. Drunken passengers or those who threaten the safety of others will not be allowed to board. This is covered by the Air Navigation Order of 1995. The Order also covers smoking on board an aircraft.

Consider this...

It is not only the passengers who must be sober! In 2004 a pilot was due to fly 225 passengers from Manchester airport to Turkey. He was arrested minutes before take-off and breathalysed. Police have had the power to breathalyse crew since March 2004 if there is a suspicion that they are drunk. We don't know who reported him – maybe one of the crew – but he got six months in jail.

Facilities and restrictions for stowing hand baggage

Once on board, passengers must stow their hand baggage. Overhead lockers are provided for this use. If these are full, passengers can put bags under their seats but exits and aisles must be kept clear in case of emergency.

Landing, disembarkation and arrival procedures

When a flight arrives at an airport, passengers disembark once the plane has come to a complete stop. Depending on facilities available and on how much the airline chooses to spend, the passengers get off by means of an airbridge or steps. The advantage of the airbridge is that passengers are protected from the elements.

Passengers with mobility problems get off last when assistance arrives for them.

Immigration procedures

Before retrieving their baggage, passengers go through immigration. This is fairly rapid if you are a European travelling within Europe or you are British returning to the UK. Non-EU passengers enter through a different immigration channel and are subject to more stringent checks.

If passengers are travelling from the UK to another non-European country they may have to fill in a landing card which can require a lot of detail.

The US have introduced very strict immigration procedures. Besides completing the landing card, visitors have to have their finger prints taken and be photographed on entry.

Baggage reclaim

The baggage reclaim hall is situated after immigration in an airport. There are screens informing passengers which belt will deliver their luggage. There is little else in the hall apart from toilets and lost baggage desks but most passengers will pass through quite quickly unless their baggage has been mislaid. In this case they report the problem and hope it turns up later. Compensation is payable if baggage is lost.

CASE STUDY
Missing baggage

Ann Lertora was taking a holiday. She travelled with British West Indian Airways (BWIA) from New York to Tobago via Trinidad, the sister island of Tobago. When she checked in at JFK (Kennedy airport) her bag was labelled to Tobago, she was handed the receipts and she was told her bag would go right through to be collected on disembarkation in Tobago.

On arrival in Tobago there was no bag and handlers told her she should have collected it in Trinidad and rechecked it for Tobago. Ann reported her lost bag and completed a form.

A clerk telephoned Trinidad baggage department but there was no reply. As the clerk was evidently busy, Ann suggested that she try and 'phone herself from their office. The staff were very friendly and welcomed her into the office. They were very busy and so left her alone in their office several times when she answered the 'phone in case it was someone about her luggage. She asked the clerk if it was worth sending a fax. The clerk pointed to a fax machine covered in unread faxes and said 'no one will go near the fax machine'. After three hours Ann gave up trying to contact Trinidad baggage handling or BWIA and went to her hotel. For the next three days Ann, or a staff member from the hotel, tried to get in touch with Trinidad and failed. At Tobago airport each day they told Ann her bag 'might arrive today'.

The bag finally arrived two days before the end of the holiday. Ann took a taxi to the airport to collect it. She was told she was entitled to compensation but after an hour of waiting for staff to deal with her she once again gave up and returned to the hotel.

1. **Find out Ann's entitlement to compensation under the Montreal Convention.**
2. **Suggest improvements to customer service at BWIA and at Trinidad and Tobago airports' baggage-handling departments.**
3. **Ensure you know the location of New York, Trinidad and Tobago.**

Customs

In the UK there are three customs channels. These are:

* Red – for those with goods to declare
* Blue – for those entering from another EU country with nothing to declare

* Green – those entering from a non-EU country with nothing to declare.

CASE STUDY

Using the allowances table on page 229 determine which channel each of these passengers should use:

* Mr Rogers arrives in the UK from Rome, he has purchased 600 cigars and four litres of Italian wine.

* The Owens arrive in Manchester from Orlando, Florida. They have 400 cigarettes, two litres of gin and £667 of gifts between them.

* Mrs Edwards arrives from Cyprus into London. She has bought 50 cigars, one litre of wine and 50mls of perfume.

Mrs Nowaja arrives from Nairobi into Heathrow. She has an ornamental elephant with tusks. The customs officer confiscates it. Why?

Arrivals

A meeting place is always provided at arrivals so that relatives and friends can easily find people. Taxi drivers make signs with the names of the people they are waiting for. Flight arrivals information is given on screens throughout the airport so it is easy to see if a flight has landed. Airport Internet sites in the UK give live arrivals information so if you are going to meet someone you can check if their flight is delayed before you leave home.

Passengers who are transferring to another flight at an airport will wait in a transit lounge until their new flight is ready to board. Often baggage is checked right through and is supposed to arrive with the passenger at the end destination. Unfortunately, this is where much baggage gets lost when the transit process does not run smoothly. It is probably safer to collect baggage from the first flight and recheck it for the next leg.

A group of schoolchildren aged 13 and 14 years old are taking a trip from your regional airport to Paris. Although, they will be accompanied by teaching staff, the group leader wants to make sure they are aware of the procedures they will go through at the airport to reach their flight. Aware of your knowledge of these procedures she has asked you to provide information for the children.

Prepare a step-by-step instruction sheet for the children, describing the procedures they will go though at the airport. Include illustrations if you wish.

This task may provide evidence for P4.

A very detailed instruction sheet may provide evidence for M2.

In-flight customer service and on-board facilities

In-flight customer service

The level of service offered on board a flight varies according to the type of airline, the type of aircraft and factors such as length of flight, time of day and costs of providing services. In this section we will take a closer look at what passengers can expect on board a flight.

Traditional scheduled airlines

Traditional or full service scheduled airlines usually offer different classes of service. A small aircraft such as a Boeing 737 operating intercity in Europe may have an economy service and business-class service. The aircraft is not sufficiently large to offer business and first class. Even on a short flight, passengers are offered a meal appropriate for the time of day and a free bar in business class. In economy, passengers will be offered drinks but may have to pay for them on some airlines. British Airways, however, still includes food and drink in its economy service. In business class, the food will be better and served on crockery instead of plastic and there will be more leg room. Providing this level of service can be difficult for cabin crew on a short flight. A

flight from London to Amsterdam, for example, is only 40 minutes and yet the cabin crew may have to attend to over 140 passengers.

The diagram shows the configuration of a British Airways 737. Club Europe is the name given to business-class travel.

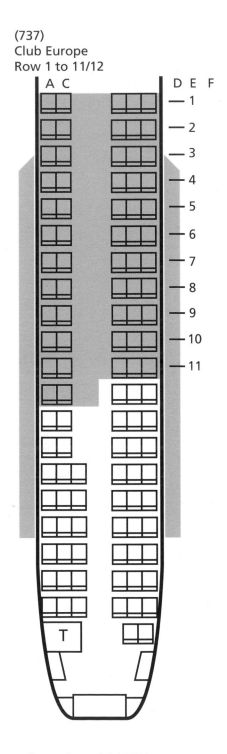

Seating configuration of BA 737

Long-haul flights have to provide catering over a longer period and these flights are on larger aircraft so there is capacity for more than two classes of traveller. Virgin Atlantic offer:

* Economy
* Premium Economy
* Upper Class.

On a typical flight to New York from London the service in economy would be as follows:

Departure at 2pm – passengers board and find pillows and toiletry bags on seats. These include a notepad and pen, tissues, eye shades and toothbrush.

Shortly after departure free drinks are served. After this lunch is served with a choice of two dishes. Throughout the flight passengers can request drinks and orange juice and water are brought round. Ice cream is also served and afternoon tea is provided about an hour before arrival.

Variations of this type of service are provided according to time of day and length of flight. Similar service can be expected from other airlines on long haul but Virgin Atlantic has an award-winning entertainment system with individual seat back screens where passengers can choose which movie or television programme to watch or even play computer games.

Premium economy is the next class of service and is similar to economy but with more leg room.

Upper-class passengers travel in luxury with seats that convert to beds. A bar area is provided and there is a massage and beauty area so that passengers can have treatments if they wish.

The extract below from the Virgin Atlantic website shows what to expect when travelling in upper class.

* **Sleep** – and stretch. At the touch of a button the seat flips over to become the biggest fully flat bed in business. Every seat has aisle access so there's no stepping over your neighbour.
* **Work** – every suite is fitted with laptop power access and a large table with plenty of room to spread out or have an informal meeting.

* **Play** – with a multi-directional 10.4" TV screen, you're in your own private cinema. With a huge choice of films, TV programmes and games.
* **Dine** – order what you want when you want from our Freedom menu, or why not invite a friend to join you for a drink, or a snack.
* **Relax** – put your feet up. Your soft leather seat reclines even for take-off and your ottoman also acts as a seat for a guest or for beauty therapy treatments.

Charter airlines

Charter flights used to try and emulate the service levels offered by traditional scheduled airlines but in economy class only. However, in recent years the charter airlines have changed the services they offer. Many now offer a premium service particularly on long-haul flights, in response to customer demand. You would not expect this service to offer the luxury of Emirates or Virgin Atlantic but passengers do get more leg room and slightly better food than previously.

On short-haul flights the trend has been to decrease the services offered and charge passengers for extras. For example, passengers can have a meal but will pre-order it and pay £10. Emergency exit seats with more leg room may carry an extra charge. Passengers who want to make sure they can sit together will pay extra to pre-allocate their seats. All these charges bring extra revenue to the charter airline or holiday company renting the aircraft.

Excel Airways is a good example of a charter airline as it operates both long-haul and short-haul flights. The long-haul service operates to some of the Caribbean islands, for example Tobago and Grenada.

Excel Airways operate with three classes on the long-haul routes. These are Economy, Premium Economy and First. The chart below gives details of some of the services on board Excel flights. Note that the entertainment is shown on one screen at the front of the cabin and there is no choice.

Service	Short Haul (All flights under 6 hours)	Economy (Barbados)	Premium (Barbados)	Excel One (Barbados)
Seat Pitch	29–30"	32–33"	34"	45"
Hold Baggage Allowance (please note that no one item may weigh more than 32kgs)	20kgs	30kgs	30kgs	40kgs
Hand Baggage Allowance	5kgs	5kgs	5kgs	5kgs
Excess Baggage Charge Per Kilo	£5**	£8	£8	£8
Minors Must be accompanied under the age	12	15	15	15
Pre-bookable seating	£10	£15	£15	FOC
Extra Leg Room Seats	£30	£60	N/A	N/A
Leather Seats	x	x	x	x
Duty fee service	x	x	x	x
Inflight meal		x	x	x
Choice of 2 entrees	x	x	x	
Choice of 3, three course meals				x
Continental breakfast / Afternoon Tea		x	x	x
Warmed Rolls / Pastries			x	x
Complimentary wine with meal		x	x	x
Champagne, bucks fizz or water before take			x	x
Cheese and Dessert Tray				x
Tea and Coffee	x	x	x	x
Juice and water throughout flight		x	x	x
Kids Packs		x	x	x
In flight entertainment	x	x	x	x
Individual and held player with library of				x
Complimentary Headsets		x	x	x
Blankets		x	x	x
Pillows		x	x	x
After Dinner Chocolates		x	x	x
Port / Liqueurs				x
Newspaper	x***	x***	x	
Choice of Newspapers				x
Complimentary Magazines			x	x
Priority Disembarkation			x^	x
Separate Check in			x	x

x = is available
* Manchester Lounge to be confirmed
**£6 Egypt and Gambia

***On inbound sector only
FOC = This service is offered free of charge
^After Excelone passengers

Low-cost airlines

The whole premise of low-cost airlines is to cut costs as much as possible so that low prices can be charged. If costs are cut then services are either cut or paid for as extras. Sometimes flights are free apart from taxes to promote custom and the airline makes its profits from all its add-on sales. Low-cost airlines sell food and drinks on board. They charge a lot for excess baggage. In addition, their baggage allowances are lower (Ryanair has 15kg). In common with other airlines they sell gifts and perfumes on board. They also make revenue through commission on selling insurance, hotel accommodation and car hire through their websites.

These are the services that passengers on low cost airlines can expect to be **excluded** from their fare:

* allocated seats
* food and drink
* headrest covers
* blankets
* entertainment.

Passenger concerns and staying healthy

Most people suffer no ill effects from air travel but there are health and safety issues of which passengers and crew should be aware. The Civil Aviation Authority has an Aviation Health Unit. Its responsibilities are to:

* provide informed advice about aviation health issues
* collate existing research on aviation health
* identify the need for future research
* manage and support future research activities.

Passenger complaints to the unit are concerned with:

* cabin air
* medical kits – or lack of
* DVT
* allergies
* cleanliness of aircraft.

Although these are passenger concerns they are not all proven issues, for example, whether recycled air is more likely to transmit infection.

DVT

A serious concern is deep vein thrombosis (DVT) or economy-class syndrome as it is known. The condition is potentially life threatening and is thought to be caused by long hours of sitting in one cramped place.

Airlines are well aware of the DVT problem and offer advice on exercising in-flight to passengers.

The Excel Airways magazine *Altitude, Winter 2004* offers the following advice on aeroplane aerobics:

BEFORE YOU START

Remember, it's important to get some exercise to prevent stiffness and encourage blood circulation, even on a short flight.

Respect the space and safety of other passengers when exercising.

Take care to breathe normally and keep your back straight.

Don't overstretch yourself – there's no need to impress your fellow passengers!

Ankle circles

Raise your feet a few inches off of the floor and slowly rotate each foot in a clockwise direction 10 times. Now repeat the exercise rotating the feet counter-clockwise.

Ankle circles

Arm curls

Stretch both arms out in front of you with palms face upwards. Bend your elbows and slowly touch your shoulders with your hands. Gently release your arms back into the outstretched position. Repeat 5 times.

Knee lifts

Raise your leg with your knee bent and lift your feet a few inches off of the floor. Repeat 10 times with each leg.

Knee lifts

Feet exercise 1

Start with your feet flat on the floor. Keeping your heels on the floor, point your feet upwards (as far as you can) then slowly lower back to the floor. Now, keeping the balls of your feet on the floor raise your heels upwards (as far as you can), then slowly lower back to the floor.

Feet exercise 2

Whenever possible during the flight, stand up and slowly raise both heels off the floor so you're on tiptoe, then lower your heels slowly back ot your normal standing position.

Shoulder rolls

Sit up straight and stretch your spine. Then make a rolling movement with your shoulders, keeping your neck and arms as steady as possible. Repeat this exercise 10 times.

Jet lag

Another concern, although less serious, is jet lag.

> **Key concept**
>
> **Jet lag** is the disruption of the body's circulation rhythms by travelling through time zones. The most common symptoms are extreme fatigue, irritability and sleep disruption. It can take a few days to recover from jet lag.

There are means of minimising jet lag. Passengers should get a good night's sleep before they travel and then try to adapt their body rhythm to the time zone of the country to which they are travelling. This is done by taking meals and sleeping at times appropriate to the new time zone.

Infectious diseases

The air on aircraft is recycled – the concern for passengers is the belief that airborne infections are easily transmitted between passengers. This could mean catching a cold, flu, measles, mumps or even tuberculosis. However, more research is required to see whether infections are transmitted on aircraft.

Hypoxia

This is the term used for oxygen deficiency. It occurs when there is a decrease in partial pressure of inspired oxygen. This happens in an aircraft when it flies at high altitudes such as 10,000 feet and above. The effects are usually mild but include lesser powers of judgement and self-criticism. People who drink a lot are more likely to suffer the effects of hypoxia and this in turn can lead to air rage.

Air rage

> **Key concept**
>
> **Air rage** can be described as disruptive behaviour by passengers on an airline. This could cover many situations but generally air rage is behaviour which jeopardises the safety of the aircraft or the passengers.

Air rage is due to a number of factors including:

* alcohol
* anxiety
* large numbers of people in a small space
* boredom
* no-smoking environment
* flight delays.

Unfortunately incidences of air rage seem to be on the rise and cabin crew have to be trained to deal with them. This involves recognising the signs and knowing what to do. Most incidents occur in economy class and involve males in their 20s and 30s who have been drinking.

Crews are taught to pacify angry passengers where possible and keep them under control by talking. It is vital to try and defuse an angry situation. Physical restraint is the last resort but aircraft do carry handcuffs and sometimes straitjackets. It must be stressed that the use of these devices is very rare.

Alcohol on board

Passengers are warned not to drink too much on board as the effects are aggravated at higher altitudes so drunkenness and dehydration occur more quickly. You will remember that such drunkenness is covered by the Air Navigation Order of 1995. Many successful prosecutions have been made. Ironically, airlines continue to serve alcohol throughout flights, and it is often free.

Heart attacks and medical emergencies

Cabin crew are trained in basic first aid but are unlikely to be able to deal with extreme medical emergencies. Some aircraft are fitted with defibrillators in case of heart attacks on board but if there is a likely fatality, usually pilots divert aircraft to the nearest airport. Emergency medical kits are usually carried on aircraft but the contents vary. There is only a requirement to have them if there are more than 250 passengers on board or the aircraft cannot reach an airport within 60 minutes.

Safety information

When all passengers are on board and seated the crew present them with a safety demonstration. This usually takes place as the plane is taxiing before the crew have to take their seats for take-off. The safety demonstration varies according to the airline and type of aircraft but always covers:

* seat belts
* emergency exits
* emergency floor lighting
* oxygen masks
* life jackets
* safety information cards.

Cabin crew are given a script to read – a tape is often played with the same information in different languages. It is important that all passengers can understand the information. A typical safety briefing is given here.

Ladies and Gentlemen

Please pay attention to our safety demonstration. This is important even if you are a frequent flyer.

Your seat belt fastens and adjusts like this (demonstrate) and unfastens like this.

Infant seat belts are provided. Whenever the 'Fasten Seat Belt' sign is illuminated you must go back to your seat and fasten your seat belt securely. For your own comfort and safety we recommend that you keep your seat belt loosely fastened and visible at all times so that you are not disturbed during flight.

On this Boeing 737-400 there are emergency exits on both sides of the aircraft and these are being pointed out to you now. There are two at the rear of the cabin (point) two over wing exits on each side in the centre (point) and two at the front of the cabin (point).

Please take a moment to locate your nearest exit bearing in mind it may be behind you.

To help you find your way to the exits, additional lights will be provided in the aisle at floor level (point).

In the unlikely event of having to use the escape slide leave all hand baggage behind and remove high heeled shoes as they may impede your exit.

If the cabin air supply fails, oxygen will be provided. Masks like this (show) will be released from the panel above your head. Stay in your seat and pull the mask towards you. Place the mask over your nose and mouth like this and breathe normally. Do make sure your own mask is fitted before helping anyone else.

Your life jacket is underneath your seat. In the event of landing on water, remove the life jacket from its container and pull it over your head. Pass the tapes around your waist and tie them in a double bow (demonstrate). To inflate pull the red toggle. The air can be topped up using this mouthpiece. There is a whistle for attracting attention. Do not inflate your life jacket until you are outside the aircraft.

Please study the safety card provided in your seat pocket. It also has details of the brace position which you must adopt in an emergency landing. Please ensure that mobile phones and any other electronic equipment is switched off.

Please make sure that your seat is in the upright position, your table is folded away, the armrest is down and your seat belt is fastened. Thank you for listening and we hope you enjoy your flight.

It's not as easy as it looks! Ask your tutor to provide the props and give the safety demonstration to your colleagues. Ask them to criticise (constructively) your performance

The safety card referred to in our demonstration is provided in each seat pocket so that passengers can refer to the card and remind themselves of safety features. The information on the card differs for each aircraft. Our example shows part of the safety on board requirements for an Airbus A340-300.

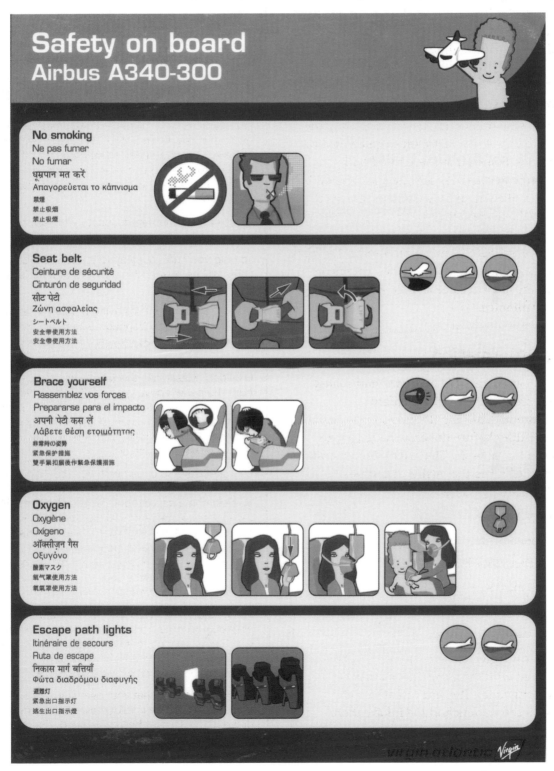

The crew must also inform passengers about smoking restrictions. Smoking is banned on aircraft and smoke detectors are fitted in the toilets in case anyone tries to smoke. Cabin crew have to tell passengers to keep emergency exits clear of baggage and to be careful when taking baggage out of overhead lockers. Passengers must switch off mobiles throughout flights and refrain from using other electronic equipment during take-off and landing. This is a lot of information for cabin crew to give and they also have to monitor passengers to make sure they comply with instructions.

Facilities for special needs passengers

There are very few facilities for special needs passengers actually on board aircraft. Remember CODPIE? These are passengers who should not be placed next to emergency exits. Cabin crew will check they have not been allocated these seats. Some airlines may provide the following:

* disabled toilet facilities

* crew who speak more than one language

* braille safety instructions

* safety videos with subtitles

* induction loops

* special meals

* extra oxygen.

Facilities for children

Infant seat belts are provided for children of up to 2 years old. After this age they must occupy their own seat.

Airlines want to make provision for families and so welcome children by providing activity packs and children's channels on entertainment systems. Children's meals are available and toilets have nappy-changing facilities.

Some airlines accept unaccompanied minors as passengers but each airline has a different policy on this. At best, children as young as five are accepted for travel and a member of crew is designated to supervise them. There is a charge

for the service. Many airlines do not accept unaccompanied minors as the cost is too great.

Knowledge check

1 What is the role of a travel consolidator?

2 Why are airlines keen to encourage online booking?

3 What are the benefits to customers of airline alliances?

4 Why is it useful to take an E111 on holiday with you in Europe?

5 What is the difference in security measures between landside and airside at an airport?

6 What are the benefits of shops at the airport to the airport owner?

7 What are the services offered by a ground handling agent?

8 Describe the procedure at the check-in desk.

9 What does a despatcher do?

10 How do low-cost airlines make money apart from the sale of airline seats?

11 Who does the Aviation Health Unit report to?

12 Explain what measures can be taken to prevent DVT.

13 How might you avoid jet lag?

14 Which Act covers drunkenness on board an aircraft?

UNIT 25 ASSESSMENT ASSIGNMENT

Lamborough City Council is considering investing in the development of Lamborough airport. The site and the small airport on it are owned by the City Council but the area is currently only used by light aircraft and one tour operator who use the airport for charter departures to holiday destinations. There would be extensive costs involved in development but the airport could be a source of considerable income to the Council if the development were successful. Before deciding on the extent of investment the Council wishes to take expert advice. You have been called in on secondment from your work in airport management to carry out research and produce a report which will help the City Council determine what development and facilities are needed at the airport.

Part 1:

1 The Council want to know if it would be worthwhile allowing a travel agent to operate from the airport. Describe the options available to customers when arranging a booking and booking a journey and make a recommendation to the Council. Describe the type of customer likely to use each option and why.

This task provides evidence for P1 and P2.

Part 2:

2 You must advise the Council on what facilities and personnel to introduce to the airport. You need to make a visit to another airport which is thriving and find out about the infrastructure and facilities.

You should report on:

- the infrastructure
- the facilities provided
- the roles and responsibilities of customer-facing personnel (both airline and airport)
- procedures for processing passengers for a flight.

This task provides evidence for P3 and P4.

3 Show how the various departments work together and ensure the safe and swift processing of passengers. Explain the necessary procedures in depth.

This task provides evidence for M1 and M2.

4 Evaluate recent improvements or changes made at the airports in terms of the benefits they bring to the procedures essential for processing passengers both before and after the flight.

This task provides evidence for D1.

Part 3

5 The City Council has received several requests from airlines who wish to operate from the airport. The Council is concerned that they only allow reputable airlines with a high level of service to use the airport. To give the Council an idea of service levels, you should research an example of each of the following categories of airline:

- traditional scheduled
- charter
- low cost

and describe the in-flight customer service and on-board facilities.

This task provides evidence for P5

Work that compares and contrasts the service and facilities will provide evidence for M3.

Work that evaluates the service and facilities and makes recommendations for improvement will provide evidence for D2.

Index

Page numbers in italics refer to illustrations or charts, those in bold type refer to definitions or key concepts.